Murder Machine

"The inside story of a single Brooklyn gang that ꟷꟷ ꟷ Americans than the Iraqi army. You'll be ducking for cover on every page."

—Mike McAlary, columnist, *New York Post*

"In a masterpiece of crime reporting, the authors re-create the DeMeo underworld in gripping detail. A MASTERPIECE OF TRUE CRIME REPORTING."

—*Publisher's Weekly*

"A modern-day 'Murder Incorporated'… A vicious Gambino crime family crew so brutal that even John Gotti feared them. A vivid, chilling tale of mob treachery and depravity that should dispel any remaining romantic myths about Mafia life. HIGHLY RECOM-MENDED."

—*Library Journal*

"First-rate story of a Mafia murder crew so deadly that even John Gotti turned aside a contract on its leader. Vivid, hair-raising, day-to-day-in-the-life-of narrative: the BEST MOB BOOK IN RECENT MEMORY"

—*Kirkus Reviews*

"THE MOST AMAZING WISEGUY STORY YET. It's the saga of a crew of killers run amok, a cross between The Godfather and The Texas Chainsaw Massacre."

—Gail Collins, columnist, *New York Newsday*

Mob Star: The Story of John Gotti

"What a fascinating portrait they've drawn of this man Gotti: Handsome, ambitious, quick-witted, and enormously successful in his own way. But at heart (he is) a beast that will tear your throat out just for the fun of it."

—Mike Royko, Pulitzer Prize winning columnist and author of *Boss*

"Tireless reporting and tight sentences that make you run to the next page."

—Jimmy Breslin, Pulitzer Prize-winning columnist and author of *The Gang That Couldn't Shoot Straight*

"A fascinating look at John Gotti, the ultimate wiseguy."

—Nick Pileggi, author of *Wiseguy* and *Casino*

The Complete Idiot's Guide® to the Mafia

"Mobspeak is put in laymen's terms. Capeci lays down the codes and rules and describes the crime families. He details the chain of command. He tells about those who inspired "The Sopranos" and examines killings, convictions and the board of directors, plus other questions most people are too scared to ask."

—*New York Daily News*

"You don't have to have a high mob I.Q. to enjoy (this book)."

—*Newark Star-Ledger*

"(In this book) Capeci gives us the results of the research that has been the spine of his journalistic life. Nobody knows more about the subject."

—Pete Hamill, best-selling author and columnist

JERRY CAPECI'S
gang land

PREVIOUS PAGE: Policemen carry the body of reputed Mafia leader Carmine "Lilo" Galante from the Joe & Mary Italian-American restaurant in Brooklyn, N.Y., Thursday, July 12, 1979. Galante was shot and killed while lunching in the restaurant's backyard. *(AP Photo)*

JERRY CAPECI'S
gang land

Jerry Capeci

ALPHA

A member of Penguin Group (USA) Inc.

For Hap Hairston, editor extraordinaire and good friend; always
there for me—and "Gang Land"—until the end.

International Standard Book Number: 1-59257-133-6
Library of Congress Catalog Card Number: 2003110660

05   04   03   8   7   6   5   4   3   2   1

Interpretation of the printing code: The rightmost number of the first series of numbers is the year of the book's printing; the rightmost number of the second series of numbers is the number of the book's printing. For example, a printing code of 03-1 shows that the first printing occurred in 2003.

Printed in the United States of America

Contents

Part 1 – 1989

January 8, 1989	At Holiday Bash, Many Married to the Mob	3
February 5, 1989	You Saw the Movie, Now Read the Letter	5
February 14, 1989	Flip-Flop by Witness: I Lied for Gotti	8
April 4, 1989	More Wiseguy Wisdom Courted	10
April 25, 1989	Bad Timing Gets Charlie Canned	12
May 2, 1989	Louie the Pigeon's Ruffled Sparklers	14
June 13, 1989	Gotti Convicts Get a Second Bail Break	17
June 20, 1989	Chin's in for the Fix—Again	19
July 4, 1989	If He Met Cohn, Rudy Ain't Talking	21
July 11, 1989	The System's Not Playing Fair, Says Persico	23
August 1, 1989	For This Con, Numbers Don't Add Up	25
August 8, 1989	My Defendant! My Money!	27
September 19, 1989	Two Killers Facing Coke Charges	29
October 3, 1989	The Case of the Chivalrous Mobster	31

Part 2 – The Early 1990s

February 27, 1990	A Mere $4 Mil Sparks Suspicion	35
April 24, 1990	Mob Men Take Heat So Women Won't	37
May 1, 1990	Angry Goes the (Alleged) Don	39
June 12, 1990	Widow of Accused Mobster Sues Government	42
July 17, 1990	FBI Claims New Goods on Gotti	44
April 3, 1991	Clam Up, Gotti Warns	47
May 28, 1991	Pen(itentiary) Pal Does Write Thing	50
June 4, 1991	May Not Be True, but It's a Good Tale	53
June 18, 1991	Boss Debunks Ex-FBI Writers	56
August 27, 1991	One for Hall Of Frame, Eh, Dap?	59
September 3, 1991	Colombos Set to Play Family Feud	62
October 8, 1991	Gang's All Here (or Dead or Rotting)	65
October 22, 1991	Windows Trial Pane and Gain	68

November 26, 1991   Judge Has Ax to Grind 71
December 24, 1991   Christmas Alone for Luchese Boss 73
January 7, 1992   Family Feud Shifts to Overdrive.............................75
January 21, 1992   Even Mob Thinks He's Got It Coming 77
January 28, 1992   Sam Bull: Rat in Shining Armor? 79
February 4, 1992   Doing In Dapper Don from the Grave 81
March 3, 1992   It's a Day of See or Be Seen 83
March 10, 1992   Give Sammy a Grammy for Song........................85
March 17, 1992   Don't Know Beans about Frank 87
March 24, 1992   Gotta Give the Don His Due on Gripe 89
March 31, 1992   Finally, Judge Leo Roars Loud 91
June 24, 1992   Last Hurrah: Still All in the Family 93
July 14, 1992   Stir-Ring Trouble from Jail: Don's Still the Boss....95
July 28, 1992   Wife Who Sits & Waits—in Jail.............................97
September 1, 1992   Is It the Shoes? Only He Knows...........................100

Part 3 – The Mid-1990s

January 5, 1993   Theories Abound in Scarpa Slay Try 105
January 12, 1993   Stickup Plan Got Stuck: Couple's Spree Short,
    Not Smart 108
January 19, 1993   In His (God)father's Footsteps 111
February 2, 1993   Lucheses Keep It All in the Family.....................113
February 16, 1993   Mob Firebug Gets Warm Bed—in Jail.................116
March 9, 1993   Son Also Wises: Feds Target 'Acting Don'
    Junior Gotti 118
April 13, 1993   Colombo Consigliere Singing for Fed Captors 120
April 27, 1993   Time's Running Out for Persicos 122
June 9, 1993   Judge Got Bum Rap For Biased Remark 125
July 4, 1993   Lefty Guns & FBI Pal Back on Street 127
July 13, 1993   Ah, When Mobsters Were Mobsters 129
August 24, 1993   Justice Imperiled When Judges Lie 132
September 7, 1993   He Ducks Feds & Rivals—Usually 134
September 21, 1993   Gotti's Stamp on N.Y.: Gambinos Peddle
    Stolen Postal Goods 136

CONTENTS

October 19, 1993	Forget It, This Book's a Fantasyland	139
November 9, 1993	Really Long Wait for Sign from God	142
February 1, 1994	State Takes Fourth Shot at Cop-Slay Suspects	144
February 8, 1994	Barber Of B'klyn Sings Aria to Feds	146
March 15, 1994	Loan Shark Flaps His Jaws	149
April 26, 1994	A Closet Full of Turncoats	151
June 14, 1994	No Tipping the Capo to Legendary Mobster	153
August 2, 1994	O.J. Shamus Digs for Gotti	155
August 23, 1994	Playing Feds & Friends Like Fiddle	157
August 30, 1994	Gotti's Lawyers Survive Hot Spell	159
September 13, 1994	It's Deal Time for Gravano	162
September 20, 1994	Rays of Light Shed on Pizza-Drug Link	164
September 27, 1994	His New Family Praises the Champion Turncoat	166
October 4, 1994	It's No Bull to Us, Say Mob Guys	168
October 12, 1994	The Man Gotti Never Got	170
November 22, 1994	Both Sides of the Wire	173
December 6, 1994	Hearts, Flowers, Bullets	175
January 31, 1995	Wiseguy Looks for 2M Leg Up	177
February 28, 1995	Keeping Up a Gotti Tradition	179
March 14, 1995	Trash Talk from Turncoat Will Dump on Garbage Deal	181
January 10, 1995	Serpico Gets the Last Laugh	183
March 21, 1995	Mob Suspect's Wake-Up Call	185
April 4, 1995	Fish Mart Rap's a Fluke, He Says	187
September 16, 1996	Feast Washout for Tony Waterguns	189
September 30, 1996	Garbage Boss Gets No Respect	191
November 4, 1996	Greater Blouse a Three-Family Affair	193
November 11, 1996	Watt's the Story on Joe	195
November 18, 1996	Home Is Where the Heart Is	197
November 25, 1996	Did You Hear the One about the Wiseguy Who …	199

Part 4 – The Late 1990s

January 20, 1997	Gaspipe's Follies	205
March 24, 1997	Junior Wants His Civil Rights	207
April 7, 1997	Fat Pete Sits One Out	209
September 15, 1997	Gaspipe's Worst Enemy—Gaspipe	211
November 10, 1997	Death by Reputation	213
December 15, 1997	Sammy Wants the Home Court Advantage	216
January 12, 1998	Bum's Rush for Mob Capo	218
February 9, 1998	Junior Pays for Dad's Deeds	220
March 9, 1998	Sonny's Home Again—for Now	223
May 4, 1998	Luchese Class of '91	225
December 21, 1998	The Prosecutor	228
January 18, 1999	As the Mob Turns	232
May 3, 1999	Colombo Boys Win the War	235
May 17, 1999	Life Without Honor	239
June 7, 1999	One from the Weasel's Book	242
June 24, 1999	Gangster Goes Down the Sewer	246

Part 5 – The New Millennium

January 6, 2000	Respect—Real or Imagined	251
January 13, 2000	Bosko's Back	254
January 27, 2000	Junkyard Dog	257
February 3, 2000	Cheap Talk	260
February 17, 2000	Getting In the Last Licks	262
May 11, 2000	The Neck Plans Ahead	266
December 7, 2000	Win Some, Lose Some	269
March 22, 2001	Wiseguy Talk Ain't What It Seems	272
March 29, 2001	Soup, Chickens, Seinfeld & Longhorns	276
April 26, 2001	Mirror, Mirror …	279
May 31, 2001	Operation Payback	282
June 14, 2001	An Unspeakable Crime	285
February 14, 2002	Warden Has Time on Her Side	288
March 28, 2002	Sammy the Jerk	290
April 25, 2002	Mafia Sperm Wars	294

June 13, 2002	John Gotti: October 27, 1940—June 10, 2002	297
July 11, 2002	In Death, the Dapper Don Was Dissed	299
July 18, 2002	Mob Wife Makes a Split Decision	302
January 9, 2003	Feds: Yes, We Have Some Bonannos	305
January 23, 2003	Feds Nail Joe Waverly for 1987 Murders	308
January 30, 2003	Waterfront Wiseguy Turns on the Mob	311
February 13, 2003	Law & Order, Brooklyn Style	314
March 3, 2003	The Bonanno Boat Springs a Big Leak	317
April 10, 2003	Chin Fesses Up; His Lawyer Doesn't	319
	Index	320

Foreword

It's about time someone collected Jerry Capeci's "Gang Land" columns into a book. The man's been writing history for several years now, shining his light on a landscape of interest to crooks, cops, gangsters, agents, prosecutors, lawyers, judges, buffs, journalists, and no doubt a few scholars. Jerry and his light have staying power.

Meanwhile, many of the incorrigibles he's told us about are history. Unlike those "gonefellas," to borrow from a famous headline over a *New York Daily News* story about mafia boss John Gotti finally getting sent downriver by a jury, Jerry and his column are still open for business, on and offline, some 15 years after the doors opened. The names and the stories change, but Jerry endures.

At the *Daily News*, I camped next to Jerry for several years. Now that I think about it, we wrote that story with the "gonefellas" headline. Our desks were in a four-desk arrangement that we called the "pod." At different times over the years, the pod's other two desks were occupied by big talents—Gail Collins, Mike McAlary, Ying Chan, and Tom Robbins.

Of those people, I was the newest to New York. I learned a lot from all of them, but I learned the most about New York—and about being a reporter in it—from Jerry. He was New York in a way the rest of us could never be. He was Brooklyn born and bred, and had worked his way up from the "shack"— the press room at police headquarters where newspapers send young reporters to learn how things work.

Jerry learned well. He became a law enforcement expert. He learned how to dig out information. He developed an army of confidential sources. I began becoming the beneficiary of this when I arrived from Chicago at the *Daily News* in 1986, not long after the *News* coaxed Jerry over from the *New York Post*. The *News* was redesigning its newsroom and after it was over, I ended up next to Jerry in the pod. Unlike Jerry, I had never spent a day in a police shack. I was always a general assignment reporter. I liked the variety, but the cost was that I never became an expert at anything.

One day the *News* assigned me to do a feature story on the hubbub at Gotti's first federal trial; he had just arrived sensationally on the scene as the main suspect in the beautifully choreographed assassination of the man he was said to have replaced as Gambino family boss. The trial had to do with other crimes, but it was the media's first chance to see him up close. I constructed a little story based on Gotti's courtroom act (co-defendants stood when he entered the room) and interviews with little old ladies craning at the courtroom door to get a peak. An ambitious literary agent saw the piece, called me up and the next thing you know I had a contract to write a book about Gotti.

I was about the least qualified reporter in New York for the job. It took me a few seconds to realize I needed someone who knew the territory, and so the Jerry-Gene partnership was born. We wrote that book, *Mob Star: The Story of John Gotti*, and were deep into our second, *Murder Machine*, before I really got to know him. But during those two years, I learned what a reporter's reporter he was. Stuff we needed, he just got. Not just the easy stuff, like public records, but the private records that for various legal reasons don't get into trial transcripts. Jerry got these extracurricular files, reports, and memos—material that made it possible for us, without the cooperation of Gotti and other gangsters, to recreate scenes and conversations from their lives, develop their characters, tell their stories.

It was not until we lost our day jobs that I began to get to know Jerry well. In the fall of 1990, the *News* provoked a strike by trying to shove new contract terms down the throats of its union truck drivers. I'm sure that it never crossed Jerry's mind to do anything but to join in solidarity with these workers and go on strike too. I followed him, but he had a lot more to lose. His column was going great, he had a mortgage and three kids on their way to college. But Jerry, as I was getting to know, lived his life by some core beliefs. One was, you have to stand up to bullies.

Jerry became one of the strike's leaders, as both strategist and spokesman. As the strike dragged on and moved into 1991, he and some others cooked up an idea sure to get our cause some notice. We would invade the *News'* Brooklyn office, barricade ourselves inside and wait for the cops to come evict us while all our friends in other media recorded the proceedings. It went off perfectly. Using keys the *News* forgot we had, Jerry led nine more of us into the Brooklyn office early one morning and announced our takeover. In a few hours, we had a couple hundred supporters outside. We said everything we wanted to say about the strike before surrendering and marching out in handcuffs to a police van waiting to take us to the pokey and a new identity—the "Tabloid Ten."

In a few more months, the *News* caved in, sold out and we got our jobs back. I remember well the morning we walked back in. My growing admiration for my partner deepened further when I looked across the newsroom and saw Jerry, the toughest guy I know, the man who covered gangsters, stood up to bullies and yelled across negotiating tables at management flunkies, begin to cry as he watched his co-workers sit down at their old desks, the ones the scabs had occupied for half a year.

Working day and night, Jerry and I finished *Murder Machine* in time to get ready for another big story—the fourth trial of John Gotti in five years. By hook and by crook, it turned out, Gotti had beaten that federal case that led to *Mob Star: The Story of John Gotti* and also had beaten two state cases to become about as big as a story gets in New York (before 9/11, I should add). Jerry and I were assigned to cover the fourth trial as a team. Though we now had two books under our belts, it was the first time we had actually gone out and covered a story together.

It was the most fun I ever had as a reporter. There was one stretch of 11 days I think where Jerry and I had "the wood"—the lead front-page story—every day. We had Gotti's desperate mouth to thank for some of those woods, but many were the result of Jerry's resourcefulness and connections. I understood now that I was partners with a master reporter, and I came to almost expect the exceptional from him.

A couple stories got us in hot water with the judge in the case; he called a hearing and likened us to safecrackers or something like that—naturally we were ecstatic. Finally, we had something in common with Gotti. By now, Jerry was not only the star columnist, but also an internationally known expert on organized crime, and reporters from near and far drew insight and soundbites from him. On some days, such as when Gotti was finally found guilty, it was hard getting our work done, but we did.

That trial led to another book, *Gotti: Rise and Fall*, which became a movie, and magazine assignments and more talk shows that we can remember. In a few more years, at almost the same time, though we didn't plan it that way, Jerry and I moved onto lives beyond the newspaper business. It was time to go. But he kept writing his column, which led to another book for him and now this one. As I said, the man has staying power.

I write this as I sit in a room of a renovated 300-year-old hunting lodge beside a grand castle in Salzburg, Austria. I am here with academics from Asia and the United States, and we have been talking about values that people share across cultures. And now on CNN, a news flash says the top two newsroom bosses at *The New York Times* have just walked the plank to take responsibility for a young reporter who lost sight of his journalistic values.

This bulletin is a kicker from heaven because it leads me to ask, what values do we want in a reporter? How about honesty, independence, and fairness? And what makes a good reporter? How about intelligence, tenacity, and strength? It's all here for you to see in these collected columns. I hope you enjoy them as much as I did when I was back in the pod, learning about New York and how to be a reporter in it.

Gene Mustain
Salzburg
June 6, 2003

Introduction

In October 1976, I was a reporter for the *New York Post* working the 6 A.M. to 1 P.M. shift at Brooklyn Police Headquarters when I got an assignment that transformed me into a so-called "mob expert"—the funeral of Mafia boss Carlo Gambino.

When I got to the Roman Catholic Church in the Gravesend section of Brooklyn—wearing the only dark suit I owned—I saw guys with big necks stopping reporters from entering the church. So with my notebook inside my jacket pocket, I circled around and entered the side door, walked behind the altar, took my notebook out and told the priest who was preparing for the services that I was a reporter and wanted to get the correct spelling of his name.

I wrote it down, thanked him, put my notebook in my pocket and after he accompanied me out from behind the altar, I walked down a side aisle and sat down in the first row of open seats that I came to as other mourners were entering the pew from the center aisle.

I gave a respectful nod to the good fellow sitting beside me—he reciprocated—and we turned our attention to the altar, just like everyone else in the church.

Fifty minutes later, I filed out with the other mourners. When I hit the top step, I took out my notebook and began feverishly writing down everything I could recall of the priest's words and other details from the service when I heard a television reporter call out my name.

"You got inside. I want to interview you for the six o'clock news," she said.

Presto. As if by wizardry, I was transformed from a veteran police reporter to a Mafia expert—not because I knew anything about the mob but because I used the side door when the main entrance was closed to me.

In getting information for my "Gang Land" column over the years, I have tried to employ the same principle I used to cover Carlo Gambino's funeral–taking whatever avenues available to me.

Among other things, I have used official and unofficial court records, FBI documents, and police reports. I have spoken to a variety of sources of information, including cops, agents, prosecutors, defense lawyers, wiseguys, their relatives, and their victims, to name some of the most obvious.

First and foremost I have tried to paint as accurate a picture as I could for my readers, using common sense and the special insights about the landscape that I picked up along the way to put the activities of the wiseguys and their pursuers into proper perspective.

My work may not have always been right on target, but when it wasn't, it didn't miss by much. In any event, it has always been based on what I have seen, or heard, from as many sources that I could muster. As I learned a long time ago—and as you will see in the columns in this book—you can't make this stuff up.

Acknowledgments

There's no way I can possibly acknowledge all the people in the journalism business who helped me and the "Gang Land" column over the past 15 years, but at the *New York Daily News*, I start with Gil Spencer and Jim Willse, the paper's top editors in 1988, and thank them for taking a chance on an idea that wasn't theirs, and running with it.

For bringing "Gang Land" back into a daily newspaper last year, I thank Seth Lipsky, president & editor of *The New York Sun*, and Stuart Marques, the paper's news editor.

At the *News*, there were quite a few line editors who helped put the column into readable English during its seven year run, including Arthur Browne, Bill Boyle, and Jay Maeder.

For alerting me about an item or two, or feeding me an anecdote along the way, "Gang Land" tips its cap to *Daily News* reporters Ying Chan, Mike Claffey, Robert Gearty, Bill Kleinnecht, David Martin, Mike MacAlary, John Marzulli, Michele McPhee, Patrice O'Shaughnessy, Helen Peterson, Willie Rashbaum, Ruben Rosario, Barbara Ross, and Greg Smith.

Others in the journalism trade who lent a hand when they could, include: Mike Albans, George Anastasia, Jo Barefoot, Devlin Barrett, Bill Bastone, Pete Bowles, Chris Cornell, Irene Cornell, Edward Fay, Pablo Guzman, Patty Hartado, Claudia Kist, Jill Krause, Terri Lichtstein, Mike Lipack, Phil Messing, John Miller, Dom Marrano, Juliet Papa, Ruth Pollack, John Roca, Kati Cornell Smith and Angela Troisi.

Two former *Daily News* colleagues who were there at the outset, Gail Collins and Gene Mustain, deserve a special mention. Gail, a former columnist who now runs the "Editorial Page" at *The New York Times*, first suggested the idea, encouraged me, helped get me started and then left for bigger and better things. Gene, a former reporter who teaches journalism at Hong Kong University, came up with the name for the column–you may have noticed in the foreword that he has a way with words–and has always been there with an idea, a concept, a word, or phrase, or paragraph, and much more, especially on deadline.

Former *Daily News* reporter Tom Robbins, now toiling at the *Village Voice*, also gets a special thank you. Tom, who supplied "Gang Land" many tips, anecdotes, and documents over the years, is an indefatigable all-purpose "Gang Land" guru whose insight and overall value to the column is impossible to describe.

And then there's Hap. Hap Hairston was one of the column's editors at the *Daily News*, and with all due respect to the others, he was the best. Hap was irreverent and irascible but when it came to his craft, there was no one better. Like he did with all reporters and columnists, he would sit me next to him, and note with a touch of arrogance, that at that moment, on deadline, when it mattered most, "I'm your best friend."

With "Gang Land," Hap stopped saying that a long time ago. It was always understood.

In 1996, after the *News* decided seven years was enough, Hap, who had suffered a heart attack and was back at work, told me to stop feeling sorry for myself and keep the column going online. "I'll edit it," he smiled. "It'll drive them crazy."

The rest, as the saying goes, is history. Hap guided the column year after year, week after week, one line at a time, even after we both left the *News*. Hap never fully recovered from his heart ailments; during one hospital convalescence, he took his laptop with him to edit that week's column.

After battling a myriad of health problems, Hap died in his sleep in December 2002, at age 53. Sleep well Hap, sleep well.

In the Alpha family, much thanks to Acquisitions Editor Gary Goldstein for bugging me and Alpha Books about doing a best of "Gang Land" book, and to Production Editor Billy Fields for his patience, professionalism, and willingness to go all out to get this book published.

A special thank you to the *New York Daily News*, which granted permission to reprint the "Gang Land" columns that were first published in the *New York Daily News* from January 8, 1989 through April 5, 1995.

PART 1
1989

On January 8, 1989, as John Gotti strutted through the streets of Little Italy daring the feds to make a case against him, and as wiseguys from all five families battled each other and the law, the *New York Daily News* reacted with a new weekly feature—the nation's only column devoted exclusively to organized crime.

Reporter Jerry Capeci, the paper said, would write a weekly column called "Gang Land" about "the world of organized crime in New York." "Gang Land" would feature stories about "life and death, loyalty and betrayal, greed and honor."

The column occasionally broke news, but more often it gave insight and context to the day's major stories about mob hits and other mayhem involving the Dapper Don, his Daffy Don rival Vincent "Chin" Gigante, and a host of others, including many with colorful nicknames like Jimmy the Gent, the Fixer, and Louie the Pigeon.

During that first year, the reporter and the newspaper fine-tuned the column's focus and purpose. "Gang Land," which first ran on Sunday but soon found a permanent home on Tuesday, began a highly successful seven-year run in the *News* as a must-read for wiseguys, wannabes, and the law enforcement officials who pursued them.

Nicholas Pileggi, author of *Wiseguy* and *Casino*, explained its appeal this way to the *Los Angeles Times*: "In New York, mobsters can't communicate with each other on the phone, and they can't send each other faxes, so they're reduced to reading the newspapers to find out what's going on. Every Tuesday, when Capeci's column appears, you can see Lincoln Town Cars with smoky windows pull up to newsstands. You can just bet that a 300-pound guy with a pinkie ring lumbers out and says: 'Gimme da Nooz.' "

Former federal mob prosecutor Edward McDonald put it this way to *Times* reporter Josh Getlin: "Jerry stands head and shoulders above the other reporters, and there are a lot of hardworking journalists covering this issue. The reason is that he works harder and has sources that nobody else has. He's plugged into that world better than anyone else in this town."

In the same article, author Jack Newfield had this explanation: "Jerry's great gift is that he gets under everybody's skin. He works both sides of the street, and it shows."

At Holiday Bash, Many Merried to the Mob

Some of the most gala parties of this past holiday season went virtually unnoticed—except by law enforcement authorities.

The best and the biggest was the be-there-or-else Christmas bash thrown by John Gotti for about 1,000 mobsters, associates, wives, children, and other guests.

Like most business organizations, the city's mafia families celebrated the season of good feelings with such events.

And just like the parties of legitimate concerns—coincidentally, the Brooklyn U.S. Attorney's party was the same night as Gotti's—mafia soirees often reflect an organization's success and the taste of its leaders.

Take Gotti's.

As the bosses of four New York families spent the holidays in federal prisons, things couldn't have been better for the swashbuckling don, who took over the country's largest crime family three years ago, beat a racketeering charge, and has been riding high ever since.

After nondescript affairs the last two years at the refurbished, but cozy, Ravenite Social Club on Mulberry Street in Little Italy, Gotti went in style this Christmas.

From about 7 P.M. to 2 A.M. on December 20, his guests danced to continuous music from two bands and consumed an estimated $200,000 worth of food and drink at the spacious El Caribe Beach Club.

"For the most part," said one source, "wives, children, and other guests came in the early part of the evening and the wiseguys stayed on into the early morning."

5-Foot Teddy Bears

Many of the revelers received 5-foot teddy bears and other stuffed animals as favors from the host, who arrived with a flourish about halfway through the affair.

Gotti was driven to the Mill Basin, Brooklyn, club in a white limo, attended by three capos who escorted him in a second car.

Underboss Frank "Frankie Loc" Locascio, 56, of the Bronx, and consigliere Salvatore "Sammy Bull" Gravano, 43, of Staten Island, came with their own crews.

Detectives from the Organized Crime Control Bureau, who videotaped the comings and goings, saw mobsters from the Colombo and Bonanno families, including Bonanno acting boss Anthony Spero, 59, of Brooklyn.

Neither Spero, nor Genovese crime boss Vincent "Chin" Gigante, 59, hosted Christmas parties, at least any the cops could find.

It's unlikely that Gigante, whose rackets closely rival Gotti's, would allow an ostentatious affair. Gigante, who occasionally walks through the streets in his bathrobe, reputedly feigning insanity, has a low-key, cautious style.

But cops found parties thrown by the Luchese and Colombo clans.

The Lucheses had an affair in Brooklyn on December 16 attended by about 200, although acting boss Victor Amuso, 54, of Queens, was not spotted.

The party was at the Glen Terrace, where late Luchese capo Paul Vario used to meet former Brooklyn Democratic boss Meade Esposito during the 1970s, according to Henry Hill, central figure of Nick Pileggi's book *Wiseguy*.

The Colombo family, long based in Brooklyn, moved its party to Queens—to the Trophy Club, a Middle Village storefront that is the domain of acting boss Benedetto "Benny" Aloi, 53, of Floral Park.

You Saw the Movie, Now Read the Letter

Let's dip into the mailbag for a good-natured complaint we got last week from an apparently faithful reader in Marion, Illinois.

The letter came from the federal penitentiary there and was handwritten by the one-time leader of the Colombo crime family, a man who once sat on the Mafia's ruling commission. It seems he picked up an error in our report about the Christmas parties hosted by John Gotti and others.

"Hello Jerry," the letter opened.

"Hey, I thought we were alright. So why are you making me older than I really am? You made me 57 years old. I am only 55 and will be 56 on August 8. Don't rush these years past me. I'll need my youth to be able to finish this 100 years I have to do. And if you keep treating me bad and making these mistakes about me I'll have to start reading Pete Hamill's column. And you won't be the famous Jerry Capeci in my book anymore.

"Stay well, Carmine 'Junior' Persico."

What's the real story behind the way Gotti was busted two weeks ago for conspiring in the 1986 shooting of a carpenters' union official?

Gotti's lawyer, Bruce Cutler, claimed that his man was picked up by 100 cops and subjected to a night in jail. Cutler said lawmen should have made nice and invited the polite Gambino don to surrender.

So why didn't they do that? Well, they wanted to add insult to injury and nail Gotti for an illegal gun that they hoped to find in his car.

It was about 5:35 P.M. on January 23, and 23 detectives, investigators, and FBI agents were near the Ravenite Social Club on Mulberry Street.

The thinking was that Gotti may have been getting ready to drive to a wake—although it's hard to imagine the fastidious don wearing a yellow mock turtleneck to such an occasion.

Detectives with the Manhattan district attorney's office were dressed for success: in uniform. "We didn't want another Detective (Anthony) Venditti disaster," said one police official, referring to the

1986 cop killing believed to have been done by mobsters who mistook Venditti for a rival hood.

Gotti stepped out of the Ravenite and walked north toward Prince Street, attended by the usual bodyguards, Jack Giordano and Ignatio Alogna.

The plan called for Gotti to be arrested when he got into his car. That would give cops a chance to search the vehicle, and charge him and his strong-men with weapons possession—should a gun just happen to be found in the glove compartment.

But Gotti, the former truck hijacker from Queens turned Little Italy regular, must have sensed something was up. He and Giordano crossed the street, circled the block, and returned to Prince Street while Alogna dropped back and returned to the Ravenite.

Up the block Gotti went, with plain-clothes cops trailing behind and detec-tives stationed around the neighborhood craning for a sighting.

If he got into a car, the cops figured, they could still block the street and arrest him. But then Alogna was seen driving down Broadway, a wider street that is harder to block.

As Gotti neared the Prince Street Subway kiosk at the corner of Broadway, Alogna was driving around the block. "If Iggy picks him up and there's a chase, all hell will break loose," thought the man in charge.

Uniformed detectives Frank Bayrodt and Joseph Buffalino slapped the cuffs on Gotti as plainclothed Organized Crime Task Force investigator Joseph Coffey and Detective Sgt. James O'Brien brought up the rear.

"In the beginning the plan was sound, but Gotti just outsmarted them," said one law enforcement official not involved in the arrest.

———

Persico and imprisoned Mafia bosses Fat Tony Salerno and Tony "Ducks" Corallo got bad news from the federal appeals court in Manhattan last week when it affirmed their convictions in the historic Commission case.

But they got a dissenting opinion about whether prosecutors had proved that the commission had sanctioned the 1978 killing of Mafia boss Carmine Galante.

"The government's proof rests, in my view, on an analogy to the movie *The Godfather*. However, a movie script does not constitute the kind of proof required to sentence men to prison for 100 years," wrote Judge Myron Bright, a visiting judge from Illinois.

———

Federal Judge Raymond Dearie has heard many people say "you got the wrong man" in his 16 years as a judge, prosecu-tor, and defense lawyer.

Last week, it was finally true.

Kenneth Manning, 27, found himself in Dearie's Brooklyn courtroom standing next to Delroy "Uzi" Edwards, the accused leader of a violent Jamaican drug ring who earned his street name by carrying a submachine gun under his coat.

"Your honor, I'm not supposed to be here, I have nothing to do with this case," said the bewildered Manning.

After some checking, and double-checking, a smiling Manning was taken back to Rikers Island to finish up a six-month rap for a drug sale.

What about the right Manning? He's 30, nicknamed Bud, and he's at the Brooklyn House of Detention. According to the Department of Correction his first name is Anthony; according to the U. S. attorney's office, it's Kenneth. Whichever, he's due to be arraigned this week.

Flip-Flop by Witness: I Lied for Gotti

Matt Traynor now says he lied when he told the story of the prosecutor and her panties to help John Gotti beat the rap at his sensational racketeering trial. He also says Gotti's lawyer, Bruce Cutler, had him do it.

Traynor, a troubled bank robber from Ozone Park, is slated to plead guilty today to committing perjury at Gotti's 1986 trial, creating a circus with stories of sex and drugs involving prosecutor Diane Giacalone and drug agent Edward Magnuson.

Traynor was initially supposed to be Giacalone's first witness against Gotti, but she dropped him after catching Traynor in a lie. He then went to work for the defense, testifying that Giacalone and Magnuson had induced him to falsely implicate the Gotti gang in crimes.

"She gave me everything," Traynor testified. "Even her panties out of her bottom drawer, to facilitate myself when I wanted to (have sex). She said: 'Make do with these.'"

Recently, however, a new version of events emerged in a Nassau County court hearing at which prosecutor William Dempsey moved to void a plea bargain with Traynor in yet another case.

Before the Gotti trial, Nassau prosecutors agreed to let Traynor plead to a 1984 bank robbery and take a 5-to-10-year sentence in return for cooperating with the prosecution. Based on his testimony at the Gotti trial, they moved to revoke the deal.

The star witnesses at the hearing were Brooklyn Assistant U.S. Attorney Charles Rose and Lt. Remo Franchesini, of the Queens District Attorney's office. Both testified about jailhouse interviews with Traynor after Gotti walked.

Franchesini said Traynor told him that the story of the panties "was Cutler's brainstorm." And Franchesini and Rose both testified Traynor told them Cutler came up with the drug idea.

According to a transcript of his talk with Rose, Traynor said: "(Cutler) said to mention that Magnuson had given me Valiums because this is what John Gotti wants. (John) didn't like the way Magnuson treated him when he put the cuffs on him."

Cutler responded furiously.

"Traynor has flip-flopped more times than a pancake in a fast-food house," he said. "Nobody put any words in Traynor's mouth other than the government. Everyone knows he is a head case. The government will tell you themselves. The government will never stop trying to undermine that acquittal."

Still, at the end of the hearing last week, Traynor agreed to new deals. First, he's scheduled to plead to the bank robbery and accept a 7-to-14-year term. Then, time permitting, he's scheduled to show up in federal court, plead to perjury, and accept up to five years.

Then again, you never know with Matt Traynor.

Talking about the Gotti gang, some guys just *love* to rub it in.

Take John Carneglia, an old pal who beat the same rap as Gotti.

> "Traynor has flip-flopped more times than a pancake in a fast-food house."
> —Bruce Cutler

Carneglia's brother, Charles, got out of that case by skipping town and coming back three years later when prosecutors wished the whole thing would go away. They dropped the charges.

So when John Carneglia recently found himself next to prosecutor Robert LaRusso and FBI agent William Noon in Judge Joseph McLaughlin's Brooklyn courtroom, he couldn't help himself.

Carneglia, Gene Gotti, and Angelo Ruggiero are awaiting trial in a 1983 heroin case that has already resulted in two mistrials.

"Hey, how about giving me a deal like that? I go away for a couple of years, and I'll start a new life," Carneglia began.

No response.

"Yeah," joked Carneglia, pouring on the salt. "Maybe I'll go to Montana or Chicago. And when I come back you dismiss the charges."

Again, no response—at least not one that was audible or visible.

More Wiseguy
Wisdom Courted

Henry Hill, the central figure in Nick Pileggi's *Wiseguy*, will be making an encore appearance on the witness stand in Brooklyn Federal Court next month— just as Warner Brothers begins shooting the movie version of his life.

Hill will be testifying at a hearing for Jimmy "the Gent" Burke, the suspected mastermind of the spectacular Lufthansa Airlines robbery who was convicted on racketeering charges in 1981 for fixing Boston College basketball games.

Hill was a star witness against Burke, and Burke's lawyer is now seeking to have the conviction overturned on the grounds that a cooperation agreement between Hill and Brooklyn Organized Crime Strike Force Chief Edward McDonald was a sham.

The agreement has a standard tell-the-truth-or-else clause that calls for the witness to be prosecuted for all the underlying crimes in the agreement if it's ever proven he lied on the witness stand.

Burke's lawyer, Jay Goldberg, claims McDonald used that provision to "devastate" the defense by telling the jury "Hill would have to be crazy to lie." He also

contends that, in fact, Hill did lie on the stand about his own drug use.

"In the Eastern District (Brooklyn), in particular, when it comes to the Strike Force, the government never intended, then or now, to prosecute anyone who testifies favorably for the government even if the person lies," said Goldberg.

"Judges know this, lawyers know this, but disgracefully, the jurors are not told this and the result is that during deliberations jurors are led to believe that the witness has a motive to testify truthfully, when he doesn't," said Goldberg.

At a hearing, McDonald told Judge Jack Weinstein he *did* intend to prosecute Hill if he violated the agreement and maintained that he had no evidence that Hill had lied on the stand.

Burke recently completed his racketeering sentence and began a 20-years-to-life sentence for a 1979 murder.

Weinstein has indicated he is unlikely to overturn the conviction, but did order Hill to testify May 3.

The movie version of Hill's life, as directed by Martin Scorsese of *The Last Temptation of Christ* and *Raging Bull* fame, is currently in preproduction and expected to begin filming here next month. Robert De Niro is expected to play Burke.

It's not clear yet who'll play McDonald in the movie, but one prerequisite is that he know basketball and have at least a fair jumpshot. His defense should be suspect, though.

McDonald, coincidentally, is a Boston College graduate and even played a little freshman basketball for BC. When McDonald was investigating the point-shaving conspiracy at his alma mater, the FBI was having a tough time locating Ernie Cobb, a BC starter implicated in the scandal and later acquitted at trial.

One day, McDonald found himself in a pickup game at BC's gym. A younger and much quicker guard consistently beat him to the hoop as McDonald's team was ripped up.

When McDonald asked, he learned his nemesis was Ernie Cobb, the guy who beat the strike force in a different court a few years later.

While on the subject of college basketball: *Time* magazine reported last week that University of Nevada at Las Vegas players Moses Scurry and Dick Butler had lunch with Richard "the Fixer" Perry in 1988 at Caesar's Palace.

Perry was convicted in 1974 of fixing Superfecta harness races at Yonkers and Roosevelt Raceways. He also pleaded guilty to conspiracy charges in the BC point-shaving case in a deal that spared him a prison sentence.

Perry was said by Hill to have been the gambling expert relied on by Burke and the late Luchese capo Paul Vario. Scurry told *Time* that he knew Perry and had accepted small amounts of "tip money" from him on a few occasions.

Bad Timing Gets
Charlie Canned

For the first time in more than 25 years, reputed Bonanno capo Charles "Little Charlie" Musollo spent a night in jail last week when his son couldn't get to court in time to post his home as collateral for $250,000 bail.

Musillo, 63, of Staten Island, was indicted in Florida on racketeering, drug, and gambling charges for allegedly supervising a multimillion-dollar gambling and cocaine operation.

Musillo came into the courtroom of U.S. Magistrate Carol Amon smiling and laughing, but left scowling and handcuffed a few minutes later when Organized Crime Strike Force prosecutor Patrick Cotter demanded the letter of the law.

Musillo, whose last prison days were in 1962 for a federal drug-trafficking conviction, was released on bail the following afternoon when his son arrived from New Jersey with the deed to his home.

The three Gene Gotti heroin trials have given new meaning to "second seat," a term usually used to describe a prosecutor who backs up the lead government attorney.

The "second seat" that's now drawing attention is in the jury box.

In the first trial, Juror No. 2 was dismissed when he admitted he was not a citizen.

In the second trial, Juror No. 2 was arrested when U.S. marshals found coke on him during deliberations.

In the third—and ongoing trial—Juror No. 2 was replaced for not disclosing that his cousin is a prosecutor.

"Can we leave that seat blank?" asked Assistant U.S. Attorney John Gleeson last week when the coincidence was noted by lead prosecutor Robert LaRusso.

The current No. 2? She's anonymous.

FBI agent William Noon, the case agent for the Gotti trials, has been the butt of many jokes by defense lawyers Ronald Fischetti and Gerald Shargel.

Jurors have chuckled over Noon's working on the Gotti drug investigation for seven years, more than half his 12 years as an agent. They've also laughed about how, after the tapes were locked up for five years in FBI cabinets or safes, agents threw them in the back of an electronics expert's station wagon and didn't see them for months.

Yesterday, during questioning about the cabinets in his supervisor's office, Noon said he didn't inspect the furniture. Aren't FBI agents trained observers? asked Shargel.

"Not with regard to my supervisor's furniture," said Noon.

———

A former Mexican cop accused of being part of a multimillion dollar heroin ring claims he was investigating a "supposedly high-level drug dealer from the U.S." when he was arrested last October.

In court papers, Margarito Villagrana said he came to New York to chase down a man he thought was a major drug dealer, but wound up getting busted himself—and then discovered that his quarry was an informant for the Drug Enforcement Administration.

Villagrana's claims will be a key part of his defense, as well the defense of Pedro Guillen, who was arrested with him on October 22.

At the time of the bust, Villagrana states in his papers, he was former Mexican federal cop and was awaiting appointment with the police of the Mexican state of Guerrero.

"Although Villagrana had not yet been appointed to a position with the Guerrero police," said his lawyer, Frank Oritz, "he nevertheless related to the chief executive officer" that he was going to "follow up the investigation on his own by attending the meeting in New York."

Villagrana also claims he got started on his probe because Guillen, who *was* a Mexican cop, introduced him to Giuseppe Angelo Sylvestri and told him that "Angelo" was "offering to buy drugs … for importation to the U.S."

Guillen's lawyer, Susan Kellman, said her client, too, was investigating drug dealing by Sylvestri, who turned out to be working with the DEA.

The defense maneuverings are the latest developments in a case described several months ago by "Gang Land" in a column that pointed out that, although the DEA announced the arrests with great fanfare, no heroin was seized, the DEA was not sure the heroin existed and at least one of the men was a former cop.

New York DEA chief Robert Stutman responded angrily in a letter published in the *Daily News*. Yesterday he said: "It would be inappropriate for me to comment since the matter is in the courts. It sounds like a typical defense motion that we seen dozens of times a week."

Louie the Pigeon's Ruffled Sparklers

The Genovese crime family is ready to explode over what police did to Louie the Pigeon last week.

More accurately, the family is fired up over what cops did with 150 tons of fireworks—worth a cool $5 million— seized from an upstate warehouse after they busted Louis "Louie the Pigeon" Cinquegrana for selling $10,000 worth of fireworks, a misdemeanor charge carrying 90 days in jail.

Police rented 25 trucks; loaded up 10,000 30-pound cartons of Roman candles, rockets, aerial displays, and other fireworks; and shipped them to the department's bomb detonation site at Rodmans Neck in the Bronx. There, they were to be blown up because they constituted a "dangerous condition."

"I really blew up," said Cinquegrana's lawyer, Robert Blossner, who argued that police created the "dangerous situation" and got a court order blocking the police plan.

State law provides for destruction of fireworks sold for distribution in New York City. At a hearing, Manhattan Assistant District Attorney Robert Viteretti said that $10,000 worth of fire-works came from the warehouse and was intended for distribution here. Therefore, he argued, the entire $5 million inventory was intended for distribution here, and should be destroyed.

Judge Patricia Williams could decide the case today.

———

The feds busted reputed Mafia capo Thomas Gambino for the first time last week, but the way he avoided photographers you'd think the 59-year-old son of family founder Carlo Gambino has been preparing for it for a long time.

Gambino was arrested by FBI agents on obstruction of justice charges at 8 A.M. Wednesday. Two photographers and a reporter were ready to catch him when he left the Brooklyn Federal Courthouse.

Shortly before noon, Gambino and a bodyguard came out, their right arms up shielding themselves from the cameras— or so it seemed.

The photographers snapped away but the Gambino who walked out was younger brother Joseph Gambino, who looks like Thomas and was dressed in a blue suit, like the one Thomas wore in court.

As the decoys got in a car and the photographers turned back toward the sidewalk, Thomas Gambino, now wearing a white raincoat, walked past them and into the car, which pulled away smartly. Thomas Gambino had strolled out of the courthouse 20 seconds behind his brother, arm in arm with lawyer Michael Rosen. He's due back in court June 26.

Gambino, nephew of Mafia boss Paul Castellano, is a millionaire businessman who owns several Garment District trucking companies. And law enforcement officials believe he was being groomed to take over the crime family when his uncle was assassinated on December 16, 1985.

When Castellano was killed, Gambino went from claimant to the throne to one of 23 or so capos under John Gotti. He displayed his allegiance to Gotti in April 1986 by attending the wake of Gotti underboss Frank DeCicco, who was blown up as vengeance for Castellano's death.

Gambino had actually made his peace with Gotti months earlier, and Gotti was keenly aware of Gambino's area of expertise. On February 2, 1986, six weeks after Castellano's killing, Gotti was overheard on a state Organized Crime Task Force bug talking about a crew member who was "going into the garment center" and obviously had not touched base with Gambino.

"Why didn't he just call Tommy Gambino?" asked Gotti. "He would be the right guy to tell. The guy's got 482 trucks down there. Wouldn't he be the right guy to tell?"

He certainly would be, according to the task force, the FBI, and the Brooklyn Organized Crime Strike Force, which are jointly probing Gotti, the Garment District, and the family hierarchy.

Brooklyn Federal Judge John Bartels may have dozed during the prosecutor's opening remarks in the Gene Gotti heroin-trafficking trial, but the 91-year-old judge spends more waking hours on the bench than most trial judges.

In this day of complex and crowded caseloads, nearly all judges, federal and state, conduct trials four days a week and reserve the fifth day for sentencings, motions, and all other business. Not Bartels.

Last Friday morning, under gentle prodding from lawyers, Bartels, who cracked that the defense lawyers would "not go back to the office anyhow," reluctantly agreed to recess the trial at 4 P.M. instead of the normal 5:15.

But then cross-examination of a former cop and allegations that someone had looked at him nastily while he was testifying kept the lawyers arguing until 6 P.M.

Gotti Convicts Get a Second Bail Break

New York FBI organized crime agents and supervisors are furious at Brooklyn U.S. Attorney Andrew Maloney for over-ruling two prosecutors and putting off a hearing to revoke bail for convicted mobsters Gene Gotti and John Carneglia.

What really galled the FBI was that trial judge John Bartels, who had let the men remain free on bail when they were convicted of heroin trafficking, had apparently changed his mind and decided to jail them, quickly.

Last week, Bartels moved the session up from June 20 to today. Assistant U.S. Attorneys Robert LaRusso and Ephraim Savitt said fine; the defense objected, Bartels said today.

Gotti's lawyer, Ronald Fischetti, appealed to Maloney, who told his prosecutors to put it off; Bartels said June 26.

FBI agent Jules Bonavolonta, chief of the FBI's organized crime units, said he "was incensed" by Maloney's decision at first, but reluctantly went along with it after he called Maloney to complain.

"Some agents are still upset—they should be, these are serious felons—but Maloney explained that Fischetti had a serious problem of a sensitive nature and Maloney would put on the record that the FBI was opposed to the delay," said Bonavolonta.

The timing of the flap—a day before Maloney had FBI agents serve reputed Mafia boss John Gotti with a civil complaint alleging that the Gambino mob controls garbage collection on Long Island—didn't help Maloney with the FBI.

"It makes no sense," said one agent. "We tell John Gotti to stop picking up the garbage, and we tell his brother and another guy to take a few more weeks off, when we've been trying to put them in jail for seven years."

Maloney declined to discuss the matter.

Retired Gambino family consigliere Joseph N. Gallo was not quite so lucky the other day when his bail was revoked and—at age 77—he went to prison for the first time to begin a 10-year sentence.

Gallo was convicted of racketeering charges in 1986 and ordered to begin serving his term after the U.S. Supreme Court affirmed his conviction.

Citing poor health, his lawyers sought to further delay his surrender, but Organized Crime Strike Force prosecutor Douglas Grover objected, and Judge Jack Weinstein ordered Gallo to prison.

Gallo, whose mandatory release date is January 28, 1996, will be eligible for parole on September 28, 1992.

———

Another close friend of John Gotti's, reputed mobster Michael "Mickey Boy" Paradiso, did much better last week, in a bizarre case in which he was charged in the killing of a small-time hoodlum who informed on his brother, Philip.

In 1986, while Paradiso was on trial for drug trafficking, brother Philip was working for the FBI. Philip tape-recorded Michael admitting that he killed Frank Morici in 1978 because Morici had informed on Philip.

"This morning they showed me a piece of paper," Mickey Boy told Philip on November 7, 1986. "There's 10 names there. I killed every one of them, starting with Frank Morici for you."

Assistant Brooklyn District Attorney Eric Kraus played the tape for the jury, and called an informer who testified that Mickey Boy did the shooting.

Lawyer James DiPietro told the jury the informer was the real killer and Paradiso was a "tough guy from a rough neighborhood" who was merely showing off and boasting to his little brother when he said he killed Morici and nine others.

After five hours of deliberations, the jury acquitted Paradiso, who still has eight years ahead of him for a conviction on the 1986 federal drug charges, but not the 25 years to life that a murder rap could have brought.

———

Speaking of Gotti's friends, would you believe Larry Davis? *(Editor's note: Davis, a drug dealer, had been found not guilty by a Bronx jury of the attempted murders of nine police officers in a blazing shootout.)* We don't either, but that's what the acquitted cop shooter said when the feds sent him back to state prison to serve his 5-to-15-year sentence for weapons charges.

On January 26, according to a Correction Department document, Davis told two correction officers "that while he was at the MCC (Metropolitan Correctional Center), he was visited by John Gotti's wife and daughter and that he has John Gotti's home telephone number."

Chin's in for the Fix—Again

Reputed Genovese crime boss Vincent "Chin" Gigante, who occasionally walks around his Sullivan Street haunts in a bathrobe and slippers, must be worried that the feds are closing in, again.

FBI agents who've been chasing him around for more than five years have long maintained that Gigante, 60, goes into his crazy act whenever he's concerned that he may be close to indictment.

For the 25th time in the last 20 years, Gigante has been institutionalized for schizophrenia, according to the Rev. Louis Gigante, the South Bronx priest who insists that his brother has nothing to do with organized crime.

"He was hallucinating to the extent that we couldn't hold him," Gigante told *Daily News* reporter Bob Gearty.

Rev. Gigante, who started proceedings earlier this year to have the Chin declared incompetent, declined to name the hospital, but said his brother was committed by his 87-year-old mother and another brother.

"Gang Land's" not looking to start any more trouble for Gigante, but we hear that the IRS has started poking around, too.

There's nothing more frustrating than tales of criminal investigations that don't go anywhere because of turf battles between competing law enforcement agencies. The latest saga:

John LaPerla and Anthony Valenti—two federal investigators who actually do cooperate with each other—have been looking into the tangled financial dealings of businessman Irwin Schiff ever since the mob-connected wheeler-dealer was slain in a Manhattan restaurant in 1987.

LaPerla's a U.S. postal investigator; former IRS agent Valenti is a criminal investigator for Brooklyn U.S. Attorney Andrew Maloney—but they've worked pretty well together since they teamed up.

So far, the investigators have built cases against 17 public officials, bank executives, and businessmen who've been hit with charges of fraud, tax evasion, money laundering, bribery, and check kiting.

You'd think that by now LaPerla and Valenti would have gotten their hands on every document with Schiff's name on it, especially reports of Schiff interviews by other federal gumshoes, such as FBI agents.

Among other things, Schiff told the FBI that late Queens Borough President

Donald Manes had gotten a $1 million bribe and was to receive a second $1 million in return for a Queens cable TV contract, and that convicted former Brooklyn Democratic boss Meade Esposito was a conduit for the payoffs.

These findings were turned over to defense lawyers representing New Jersey mobsters, but the FBI never gave the information to Valenti, LaPerla, or federal prosecutors in Brooklyn.

"That's typical FBI bull," said one investigator. "They're great for taking information but they never share it."

FBI spokeswoman Lorraine Johnson did not respond yesterday to several requests for an explanation.

————

Delroy "Uzi" Edwards and Samuel "Baby Sam" Edmonson would as soon shoot it out as look at each other when they were running rival crack gangs in Brooklyn.

They haven't mellowed since they were each jailed on murder and drug raps last year, according to last month's

Department of Correction reports about the Rikers Island Central Punitive Segregation Unit, where they were both housed.

On May 24, Baby Sam, who was known for his proficiency with a 9-mm. handgun, allegedly slashed Edwards in the face with a razor blade as they came together in a cell block.

Two days later, Uzi, whose weapon of choice is obvious, slashed the face of one of Baby Sam's associates with a cardboard-box cutter while both were enjoying their daily one-hour recreation periods.

The next day, Baby Sam was attacked by two inmates apparently sympathetic to Uzi and he was hospitalized with stab wounds of the ear, elbow, back, and temple.

"They are sufficiently separated now," said Ruby Ryles, deputy commissioner for public affairs. Edwards, who began trial yesterday on federal drug and racketeering charges, has been transferred to federal custody.

If He Met Cohn,
Rudy Ain't Talking

Mayoral hopeful Rudolph Giuliani has spoken out on many issues relating to crime and politics lately, but he has been ducking "Gang Land" about a meeting sources said he had with the late Roy Cohn when Giuliani was U.S. Attorney.

Sources said Cohn, a power broker who hobnobbed with judges and politicians while representing top mobsters like Fat Tony Salerno and John Gotti, met with then-Manhattan U.S. Attorney Giuliani.

"Gang Land" tried to ask Giuliani about a Cohn meeting when we learned that a mob turncoat said he had given Cohn $175,000 to buy a two-year reduction in the federal sentence of a brother of reputed Mafia boss Vincent "Chin" Gigante.

As the *Daily News* reported Sunday, informer Vincent "Fish" Cafaro said he delivered the money to Cohn after the sentence of Mario Gigante was cut to six years in 1985. Cafaro said he didn't know what Cohn did with the money.

Cohn, who had not represented Gigante at the trial, filed a motion to reduce the sentence in September 1984. It was granted, without explanation, on January 15, 1985, according to court records.

Giuliani, who began as U.S. attorney in June 1983, the same month Mario Gigante was sentenced, declined numerous requests to be interviewed about the case.

Robert Bucknam, a former federal prosecutor now working in Giuliani's mayoral campaign, said Giuliani opposed the reduction and did not meet with Cohn from September 1984 through January 15, 1985, while Cohn's motion was pending.

Bucknam declined to answer all other questions, including whether Giuliani had met with Cohn before September 1984.

Don't invite to the same recreation period: Louis "Bobby" Manna and Gene Gotti.

Manna, a convicted Genovese family consigliere, was found guilty last week of plotting to kill Gene and brother John Gotti, the reputed Gambino boss, in a turf fight over control of New Jersey rackets.

Gene Gotti, a reputed Gambino capo who was recently convicted of heroin trafficking, had his bail revoked last week for continued antisocial activity.

Both have been billeted in the Metropolitan Correctional Center awaiting sentencing. Does this mean tension in the cellblock? While MCC officials weren't available to talk about the matter yesterday, they seem to have the situation well in hand.

Manna is housed on the 11th floor, Gotti on the ninth, and their visiting days and hours are different.

Police brass expect no explosions or light shows to emanate from 101st Avenue in Ozone Park today at the annual John Gotti Fourth of July Barbecue.

For nearly 20 years, Gotti has hosted an annual barbecue and fireworks extravaganza outside the Bergin Hunt and Fish Club, the social club that reportedly has long served as the base of his alleged criminal operations.

Chief of Department Robert Johnston Jr., who felt police were embarrassed by the well-publicized and unrestrained fireworks demonstration outside the social club last year, vowed, "It won't happen again."

Queens cops didn't spend the year plotting search-and-destroy missions, but they did make "mental notes" about Johnston's stated wishes and have let word out that cops won't stand still for a repeat of last year's blast.

Speaking of fireworks, reputed mob associate Louis "Louie the Pigeon" Cinquegrana, who was busted last April on charges of selling $10,000 worth of the stuff to an undercover cop, went to trial last week.

Cinquegrana's arrest has hit the Genovese crime family where it hurts most, in the pocketbook. The most harm it can do to Cinquegrana is 90 days, if he is found guilty of the misdemeanor charges.

When he was arrested, cops seized 150 tons of Roman candles and rockets, etc., stored at Cinquegrana's warehouse on the theory that the entire load was intended for sale in New York City, that it was dangerous, and should be destroyed.

Bomb squad cops, who've had a record 400 tons of confiscated fireworks to destroy this year, have just about completed burning off Louie the Pigeon's load, estimated at $5 million.

The System's Not Playing Fair, Says Persico

Mafia boss Carmine "Junior" Persico joked about his 100-year racketeering sentence a few months ago when he wrote to "Gang Land," but he's taken a different tack in recent correspondence to Federal Judge John Keenan.

Persico, 55, claims Keenan, federal prosecutors, and his own attorney teamed up to deny him a fair trial in an effort to protect defense lawyer Stanley Meyer.

His problems arose, said Persico, because a key witness against him, Fred DeChristopher, claimed Meyer had delivered evidence to Persico while he was a fugitive.

Prosecutors suggested that Meyer's name be excised from DeChristopher's testimony because he represented another figure in the case, and Persico said his lawyer, Frank Lopez, agreed "to protect his associate, friend, and former law partner.

"Lopez and Meyer reacted to the situation much like ostriches who, when danger approaches, hide their heads in the sand," said Persico, and it prejudiced him in two important ways.

One, Meyer was not called as a witness to rebut the allegation, which Meyer now swears was false; and two, the jury had to believe Lopez was the unnamed lawyer involved in the shady activity.

"Carmine Persico got an entirely fair trial," said Aaron Mareu, associate Manhattan U.S. attorney, who tried the case and said his office expects to "prevail on the merits."

Manhattan prosecutors never hit Meyer with criminal charges stemming from DeChristopher's allegation, but the lawyer has had his fill of grief from Brooklyn Assistant U.S. Attorney Ruth Nordenbrook.

For more than a year, Nordenbrook has been investigating tax-fraud charges stemming from allegations provided by another of Meyer's former law partners, Martin Light, who cooperated with the feds after he was convicted of drug charges in 1984.

Meyer was cited for criminal contempt for failing to turn over documents to the grand jury that later were found during a court-authorized search of his Manhattan law office, sources said.

All proceedings have been sealed, but "Gang Land" hears that Judge Jack Weinstein tentatively has scheduled a nonjury trial of the charges, which carry penalties of up to six months, for next week.

Nordenbrook, Meyer, and his lawyer, Gustave Newman, refused to discuss the case which sources say may yet be resolved before trial.

A few months after Persico was jailed for racketeering, a Brooklyn federal jury acquitted reputed Mafia boss John Gotti of the same charge in what many people said was an outrageous verdict.

A victorious lawyer in the case, George Santangelo, who also races and breeds horses, thought so, too, because he named a favorite mare's foal Outrageous Verdict.

At Belmont a few weeks back, Outrageous Verdict won for the second time in his brief career at 11-to-1 odds.

Last Friday, Outrageous Verdict moved up into an allowance race, and the 3-year-old gelding was sent off as the 5-to-2 second choice of the track crowd. Two beneficiaries of the outrageous verdict by the Brooklyn jury, Gene Gotti and John

Carneglia, were unable to see the horse win, going away by nine lengths and returning $7.40 at the track and $7 at OTB.

By then they were in jail beginning the 50-year sentences they received that morning for heroin trafficking, a sentence defense lawyers called pretty outrageous.

"Gang Land" picked up a few more details last week about a meeting Rudolph Giuliani had with the late Roy Cohn while Giuliani was Manhattan U.S. attorney.

The issue arose when we learned that a mob turncoat said he gave Cohn $175,000 to buy two years off an eight-year sentence that mob capo Mario Gigante got in 1983 for loan-sharking. The informer said he gave the cash to Cohn in 1985, after the sentence was cut to six years.

The question was: Did Cohn meet Giuliani to discuss Gigante's case?

Sources now say no. They say that Cohn met Giuliani to discuss Mafia boss Paul Castellano. They also say Cohn made only an ineffective, halfhearted pitch on behalf of Castellano, who was then the target of a major prosecution by Giuliani's office.

Giuliani, a Mayoral hopeful, still refuses to discuss the matter.

For This Con, Numbers Don't Add Up

Bearing in mind that prolific killers like James Cardinali, Vito Arena, Mickey Featherstone, and Jimmy "the Weasel" Fratianno are all free men for telling tales about old friends, consider the following scenario:

A prisoner has served more that 11 years for narcotics violations. While in prison, he works undercover for 15 months, and then spends the next seven years testifying, helping to convict 44 murderers and drug dealers.

He gives information both about a terrorist involved in robberies and prison escapes, and about a former inmate arrested with documents describing the planned murder of public officials, including President Ronald Reagan.

He also testifies before congressional and presidential commissions on the narcotics industry, gives life-saving tips to undercover narcs, and alerts officials to how prisoners deal drugs through jailhouse phones.

And to make the situation really improbable, assume our man is a former junkie who turned his life around, graduated from college *cum laude* and won first prize in a national poetry-writing contest for federal prisoners.

If such a prisoner did exist, by now he'd be released into the federal witness program.

Not if his name is Leroy "Nicky" Barnes.

Barnes, now 56, achieved national infamy when, on June 5, 1977, he appeared on the cover of *The New York Times* magazine under the headline, "Mr. Untouchable."

"This is Nicky Barnes," said the text on the cover. "The police say he may be Harlem's biggest drug dealer. But can they prove it?"

According to courthouse legend, President Jimmy Carter saw Barnes's picture and ordered an all-out effort to convict him. Then-U.S. Attorney Robert Fiske tried the case, Barnes was convicted, and, in January 1978, he began his sentence—life without parole.

In July 1981, Barnes, upset that a major drug dealer was sleeping with his woman, began cooperating, although he knew that only a presidential pardon or commutation could get him out of jail.

"His cooperation was extraordinary," recalled U.S. Attorney Benito Romano.

Now, there is no question Barnes did terrible damage as a heroin dealer. And he has admitted ordering the executions of four people while a member of "The Council," a group of Harlem heroin merchants who formed a Mafia-type commission to regulate drug dealing.

Still, Romano and his predecessor as U.S. attorney, Rudolph Giuliani, have urged the Justice Department to recommend a pardon or sentence commutation for Barnes.

To this date, the department has not acted. If it doesn't, Barnes will remain in jail. And there lies an interesting question of justice.

Cardinali, Arena, and Fratianno have each admitted murdering at least four men as contract killers for the mob. Featherstone did the same for the Westies. All four have testified, but together their record on convictions comes nowhere near Barnes's. All have gotten out in less than half the time Barnes has spent in prison.

"For reasons of equity, and fairness, when you put (Barnes's) case alongside all the others, he deserves his freedom," said Edward McDonald, former head of the Brooklyn Organized Crime Strike Force.

Why, then, is Barnes still behind bars?

"It's still too hot a political potato for people to digest," said McDonald. "He was the biggest drug dealer in America. And he flaunted it. He pranced around in fancy clothes and fancy cars, a woman on each arm, giving out turkeys at Thanksgiving. He was the John Gotti of the mid-1970s."

In the end, though, McDonald believes Barnes's release "would be good for law enforcement. It would encourage more people (in jail) to cooperate. His case discourages people from cooperating now. 'Look at him. He's still in. Why should I cooperate?' is what they say now."

Romano feels the same, but with the pardon request pending, he won't discuss the overall merits of freeing Barnes.

Barnes, who has ignored requests for comment, has maintained in testimony that he has turned himself around.

"I embrace traditional values now, education ... maybe starting a family somewhere along the line," he has testified. "I mean positive, good, constructive values, the values that should be held in all communities.

"I am not trying to say that I am a number one American. I am just a guy that came from the street and made a sharp turn, that's all."

My Defendant! My Money!

Rarely do defendants beat the system and the judge out of money—all on the same day.

But that's what happened in Brooklyn last month when Justice Leonard Yoswein gave Wanda Patterson $2 subway fare and told her to come back the next day when she ended up in court—down on her luck and under arrest on a bench warrant.

Unfortunately for Yoswein, Patterson hasn't yet found her way back to court, where she is, once again, a fugitive in three indictments charging her with selling crack.

Drug defendants have fled before, and they will again, but rarely do they make a getaway with money provided by a judge on the same day they're found and arrested by an overworked and under-staffed police warrants squad.

Yoswein is no naive newcomer to the bench, either. For eight years, he has been the chief judge of about 50 judges who sit in Brooklyn Supreme Court.

Yoswein wouldn't talk about it, but it's likely that July 6 will go down as one of his more embarrassing days. Yoswein was filling in for the assigned judge, and Patterson, who was coughing, was brought before him.

In a whisper, Patterson said she missed her court date a month earlier because she was in the hospital.

Yoswein read the court file—apparently misreading part of it, because he stated incorrectly that Patterson had no prior bench warrants—and released her, order-ing Patterson to appear the next day before Justice Michael Pesce.

The prosecutor who happened to be in court when Patterson was brought in was unfamiliar with the case. He did not double-check Yoswein's reading of the file, and did not object to the release.

Apparently moved by Patterson's tale of woe, the judge got off the bench, took $2 out of his pocket and told a court offi-cer to give it to Patterson, who took the money and ran.

———

Last week, on the day the *Daily News* reported that accused crack kingpin Howard "Pappy" Mason had put out a contract on Charles Rose, the chief fed-eral narcotics prosecutor in Brooklyn, Rose took a team of prosecutors and trav-eled to Mason's home turf in Queens for a showdown.

There, with solid support from prosecutors Bob LaRusso and Tom Roche, Rose pitched the Brooklyn U.S. Attorney's office to a 4–3 win over Manhattan counterparts in their annual softball game at Shea Stadium.

Prosecutor Leslie Caldwell, who teamed up with Rose to convict Pappy's mom on drug charges, did not make the game, which evened the series at 2–2.

Sources said Caldwell was in the office putting the finishing touches on a superseding indictment, due next week, charging Pappy with ordering the murder of police Officer Edward Byrne.

———

Manhattan federal prosecutors didn't do well on the diamond last week, but one, Peter Lieb, did very well in court in his third try against reputed Gambino capo Joseph "Joe Butch" Corrao, whose earlier trials ended in hung juries.

Corrao was found guilty of obstruction of justice and conspiracy for alerting another mobster about a sealed indictment that Corrao learned about from a woman who worked at the Foley Square courthouse. He faces 10 years in prison and $500,000 in fines at sentencing next month.

Corrao, who briefly served as underboss to reputed Mafia boss John Gotti in 1986 and beat a Brooklyn racketeering indictment in 1987, owns several Italian restaurants and much real estate in Little Italy.

Gotti picked one of Corrao's restaurants, the Café Biondo, to spend his last free moments in May 1986 when Gotti's bail was revoked before the start of his racketeering trial. Gotti was acquitted the following March.

Lawyer Gerald Shargel, who argued that Corrao had merely passed along gossip, said the case was "a RICO (racketeering) nightmare, in reverse. He was acquitted of racketeering, then gets convicted of a lesser charge, after three tries. Give the government enough chances and sooner or later they'll convict anyone."

Two Killers Facing Coke Charges

Joseph Testa and Anthony Senter got life plus 20 years sentences last week for, among other things, dismembering people in bathrooms. Now the feds want to give them more time for doing coke in courthouse johns.

Testa and Senter belonged to a Mafia crew that used the bathroom of its clubhouse to slice victims into disposable parts—crimes "so horrendous and inhuman" that Manhattan Federal Judge Vincent Broderick said he wanted them in prison "as long as could be possible."

The U.S. Attorney's office apparently wishes the same. It intends to press charges that the two men snorted cocaine in Foley Square rest rooms during recesses in their 17-month trial. Conviction may mean two more years in prison.

In October 1988, during the eighth month of the trial, the men were nabbed on drug possession charges when feds reportedly found coke on them and in Senter's car, near the courthouse. The charges were sealed until last week.

"Gang Land" hears the feds were tipped off about the men's alleged drug use by James Cardinali, a five-time killer and former coke fiend, who happened to be housed in a section of the Metropolitan Correctional Center reserved for informers.

Sources said Cardinali had figured the men were doing drugs when he spotted them several times from a window as they went to a car, took something out of the trunk, and sat in the car for a few minutes.

———

Although the federal government says Giuseppe "Joe" Gambino is a heroin and cocaine trafficker, an informer who helped the FBI infiltrate and bug his Brooklyn headquarters says he never saw Gambino take part in any deals.

William Kane, who carried a briefcase with an eavesdropping device, drove a car that was bugged and helped plant another bug in Caffe Giardino in Bensonhurst, says he was "afraid" even to mention drugs in Gambino's presence.

Sources said Kane had bought heroin from others but never saw nor heard anyone implicate Gambino in discussions about heroin or cocaine.

On September 26, 1987, while working undercover at the club, Kane found 2 pounds of white powder in a plastic bag in Gambino's basement desk and took a small sample that proved to be cocaine, according to court records.

Despite that, Kane, 45, testified last month under questioning by lawyer David Breitbart in a Philadelphia case that "Joe V never did narcotics" and Kane "would be afraid to mention narcotics in his presence."

According to court documents, Kane became friendly with Gambino in the early 1980s after he installed a cigarette machine in Gambino's Cherry Hill, N.J., restaurant. By 1984 they were partners in a vending machine business that distributed poker machines in Bensonhurst clubs and candy stores.

Kane lived in South Jersey but was "always around" 18th Avenue and Caffe Giardino to maintain and service machines. Only Gambino, co-defendant Lorenzo Mannino, and Kane had keys to Gambino's desk.

Kane may not think Gambino is a drug dealer, but the feds obviously do. Last week they added more charges, including four murders, to his drug and racketeering indictment.

Assistant U.S. Attorney Frances Fragos declined to discuss Kane's expected testimony, although she has stated in court papers he is a cooperating witness.

Last week, lawyer Bruce Cutler and appellate specialist Judd Burstein cited confusion between them and their client and Kane's Philadelphia testimony to beat back an effort by the prosecution to revoke Gambino's $3 million bail.

Fragos and co-prosecutor Andrew McCarthy had charged that Gambino violated his bail provisions by obstructing justice—threatening a witness in order to change his testimony—and by being seen with reputed mob associates on 18th Avenue.

Prosecutors refused to reveal the obstruction evidence and defense lawyers said it was *their* confusion that confused Gambino about where he could and could not go. Judge Whitman Knapp congratulated the lawyers for creating enough confusion and refused to revoke Gambino's bail.

Trial is set for April.

OCTOBER 3, 1989

The Case of the Chivalrous Mobster

High-ranking mobsters in four New York City Mafia families are in serious trouble because mob associate Barclay "Bobby" Farenga is a chivalrous gentleman at heart.

Farenga—a drug dealer, admitted killer, and Genovese crime family associate—triggered what federal officials say is the most significant organized crime investigation in years when he was busted on cocaine charges in November 1987.

As the *Daily News* disclosed Sunday, Farenga, 42, and his business partner, Peter Savino, are now key witnesses in a federal grand jury probe of more than $40 million in contracts for the installation of replacement windows in the city's 238 Housing Authority projects.

Among other things, Farenga claims to have bribed union and city Housing Authority officials for years.

He also brags that he has a soft spot for the women in his life—that he began cooperating to get drug charges dismissed against three women arrested with him: a girlfriend, her sister, and their mom.

Last week, Farenga discussed his decision to cooperate when he testified at the trial of mob associate Nicholas Guido, who was charged with the 1986 shooting of reputed Luchese mob underboss Anthony "Gaspipe" Casso.

Farenga admitted under cross-examination that he cared about the sentence he eventually gets for drug and labor racketeering charges, but insisted to defense lawyer Jay Horlick that wasn't his main reason for testifying.

"The main thing," said Farenga, "is the women are already released and that was the main part of it."

After the charges were dropped against Farenga's girlfriend, she began seeing Guido, but Farenga claimed he was not testifying against Guido out of jealousy.

The jury must have believed some of Farenga's testimony because it convicted Guido of assault charges, although it did acquit on the more serious attempted murder charges.

Dying a slow death, the Brooklyn Organized Crime Strike Force carried on last week, with only eight of its normal complement of 15 prosecutors.

The greatly reduced force continued with the Window probe, took several important guilty pleas and worked over the weekend to keep two mobsters in jail.

Because of a decision by Attorney Gen. Dick Thornburgh, the Strike Force is due to be merged with the U.S. Attorney's office later this month.

The guilty pleas were entered by two mob-connected officials of Local 66 of the Laborers' International Union, who admitted to labor racketeering charges stemming from the Luchese family's control of the union for more than 30 years.

Business manager Michael LaBarbara and his assistant, James Abbatiello, entered their pleas before Uniondale Federal Judge Jacob Mishler, who set sentencing for December 15.

The case against co-defendant Peter Vario, a reputed Luchese mobster and the union's vice president, has been put off indefinitely while Vario recuperates in a Long Island hospital from severe depression brought on two months ago when his only daughter was killed in a car crash.

LaBarbara, 52, of Holtsville, faces up to 30 years and $1.5 million in fines; Abbatiello, 59, of Westbury, faces 12 years and $750,000 in fines.

Under the plea bargain agreed to by prosecutors Bruce Maffeo and Arthur Semetis, LaBarbara and Abbatiello will quit their union posts for at least 13 years. Both remain free until sentencing.

Over the weekend, Strike Force prosecutors Patrick Cotter and Kimberly McFadden successfully argued that reputed Colombo capo Frankie "the Bug" Sciortino and an associate, Frank Cammarano, were dangers to the community and should be denied bail.

Cammarano was charged with extorting $200,000 from three Kennedy Airport freight-forwarding companies from August 1983 to May 1985; Sciortino was charged with threatening a potential witness with violence if he testified against him.

Both are still in jail—Cammarano on $50,000 bail set yesterday and Sciortino detained without bail pending further proceedings today.

PART 2
The Early 1990s

In the early 1990s, "Gang Land" moved into high gear. The Law was stepping up its assault on John Gotti and wiseguys from all five families, and the Colombo family was engaged in a bloody war that left 12 dead and many more injured before the shooting stopped.

"Gang Land" was there as the Dapper Don became the Teflon Don when he beat his third straight case in four years. "Gang Land" was there for his classic courtroom confrontation with Sammy Bull Gravano, and the jury's resounding guilty verdict that condemned Gotti to die in prison.

Two months before the shooting started, "Gang Land" forecast the Colombo war between rebel forces aligned with acting boss Victor "Little Vic" Orena and loyalists of jailed-for-life official boss Carmine "Junior" Persico.

A few years later it became clear that the Persico faction had prevailed, but during the early 1990s while the issue was still in doubt, Persico took time out to write and complain about a couple of things "Gang Land" reported—and didn't report—about him.

FEBRUARY 27, 1990

A Mere $4 Mil Sparks Suspicion

Salvatore Reale, a former John Gotti pal booted out of town by a federal judge two years ago, was stopped along the Texas-Mexico border riding in a car on a drug smugglers highway with nearly $4 million in the trunk.

The swashbuckling, free-spending former private eye, who played host at a 14-hour lunch for police brass and Queens District Attorney John Santucci in 1983, was not charged with any crime, but lost his money—at least temporarily.

Drug Enforcement Administration officials in El Paso are examining the cash cache—$3.8 million in U.S. currency and 140,000 Swiss francs (about $95,000)—while they investigate the case.

Whatever the outcome, the episode could cost Reale his freedom if Brooklyn Federal Judge Jack Weinstein, who gave Reale probation on an airport extortion rap, doesn't buy his story that the cash is gambling winnings he's saved over 15 to 20 years. A nest egg, if you would.

In addition to kicking Reale out of the Big Apple for five years, Weinstein ordered him to avoid drugs, alcohol, gambling, and all illegal activity, or face the full 15 years of the suspended sentence.

The judge said he had "no doubt" Reale deserved a "substantial" prison term but feared Reale, who claimed psychiatric problems, might commit suicide or be killed by others in prison.

On February 6, Reale was a passenger in a 1988 Lincoln that was stopped on Interstate 10 at a border patrol checkpoint 3 miles west of Sierra Blanca, Texas, a town of 700 a few miles from the Mexican border and about 80 miles south of El Paso. The car is owned by former Police Lt. Michael Doyle, who attended the marathon Santucci lunch at the Altadonna restaurant, and later was Reale's private-eye partner.

"We get a lot of drugs and cash seizures around here, but usually not that much at one time," said Sierra Blanca Chief Deputy Sheriff Bub Lewis.

The money was discovered in two suitcases after Reale aroused the suspicions of a U.S. Border Patrol crew and its sniffer dog when he stopped at the checkpoint about 11:30 P.M.

"He seemed a little edgy and avoiding eye contact with the agents," said one federal official.

"The dog picked up on something in the trunk, maybe a drug residue, and they found the cash in the trunk," said Lewis.

Reale, who told border officials he was en route from his Scottsdale, Arizona, home to Miami, was being driven by a convicted felon from Queens—which doesn't set too well with Ralph Kistner, chief federal probation officer in Brooklyn.

"He told us he was driving to Florida with his wife," said Kistner. "Why was he with this guy, and what was he doing in a car registered by someone in New York?" He said investigators were also looking into "the possibility of tax fraud" and hoped to "present the facts to the court later this week."

No matter how Reale fares with the feds in El Paso and Brooklyn, he's on the outs these days with reputed Mafia boss Gotti. In an easy-to-hear taped conversation played at Gotti's recent trial, the Dapper Don complained that when "Reale talks to a guy, the guy wants to shoot him in the ... head. You know how that ... bum is, he never forgot, he's a half a cop."

When Reale was indicted on the airport extortion scheme, the feds described him as "Gotti's man at Kennedy Airport."

These days, the other guy acquitted in the Gotti trial, Anthony "Tony Lee" Guerrieri, holds the title, and he's awaiting trial in Brooklyn Federal Court.

Guerrieri, a former business partner of Reale's, is charged with extorting $450,000 from Stair Cargo, a Kennedy Airport trucker. Guerrieri, a company official and two officials of Teamsters Local 295, are charged with demanding and receiving the payoff in return for labor peace.

Guerrieri's not antisocial, but he skipped the Ravenite Social Club celebration that followed his and Gotti's acquittal on assault charges. If he's spotted at Gotti's Mulberry Street headquarters, Brooklyn Federal Judge Joseph McLaughlin can revoke his bail.

Joseph Sclafani, the mob associate with Costabile "Gus" Farace when he was slain, pleaded guilty last week to federal harboring charges but still refuses to admit he had a gun that night.

Sclafani, who was seriously wounded in the gunfire that killed Farace as they sat in a car in Brooklyn, faces five years on the federal rap but faces up to 15 years on the state gun charges filed by District Attorney Charles Hynes.

Hynes would not discuss the case, but sources say homicide prosecutor Sari Kolatch is refusing to reduce the charges unless Sclafani cooperates in the murder probe of Farace, who is suspected of killing DEA agent Everett Hatcher.

Mob Men Take Heat So Women Won't

A reputed Bonanno capo and his son-in-law stood up for female members of their families and pleaded guilty to federal tax charges so that the capo's wife and daughter and the son-in-law's mother could escape prosecution.

Reputed capo Anthony Graziano and John "Porky" Zancocchio, a reputed Bonanno mobster, appeared in Brooklyn Federal Court and owned up to hiding assets in the names of others, including their relatives, and evading about $100,000 in taxes.

Graziano, 49, is a close associate of imprisoned Bonanno crime boss Joseph Massino, and has several arrests on his record. The tax charge is his first felony conviction in 30 years.

Zancocchio, 32, reportedly heads a $280 million-a-year bookmaking ring that took bets from high rollers like former baseball player Pete Rose, himself an admitted tax cheat who was thrown out of Major League Baseball for life for gambling.

In return for pleas—Graziano for tax evasion and Zancocchio for failing to file, a misdemeanor—prosecutors dropped pending mail fraud charges against Graziano's daughter, Lana.

Assistant U.S. Attorney Ruth Nordenbrook and Staten Island Assistant District Attorney Elizabeth Foley also promised not to charge Graziano's wife, Veronica, and Zancocchio's mother, Rose, with aiding and abetting the men to hide hundreds of thousands of dollars in assets.

Graziano's wife and daughter had cars, houses, and other property in their names, and Mrs. Zancocchio allowed the men to put a pizza parlor, Mama Rosa's Restaurant, in her name, according to court papers.

When a five-year rackets probe by Foley—complete with wiretaps— uncovered little racketeering but lots of tax dodges, Nordenbrook hit Lana Zancocchio with mail fraud and promised similar charges against the other women if Graziano and Zancocchio did not plead guilty.

Plea negotiations took more than five months, according to Graziano's lawyer, Jeffrey Hoffman, who took the blame for prolonging the guilty plea until last week.

"I tried to convince Mr. Graziano not to plead guilty because I knew we would win at trial. But he refused to put his wife and daughter through a trial and eventually pleaded guilty to spare them."

As part of the deal, Graziano associate Vincent Rossi also pleaded guilty to tax-fraud charges. Graziano faces five years and $250,000 in fines when he is sentenced in June; Rossi faces three years and $250,000 in fines; and Zancocchio one year and $100,000 in fines.

Mob marriages often have unusual provisions, whether written or not, but partnerships between crime families can get sticky, especially when three mob families are involved.

Take a pact among the Genovese, Luchese, and Gambino crime families to share labor racketeering spoils from the Long Island construction industry that was memorialized in a 1983 conversation between Luchese crime family underboss Salvatore Santoro and mobster Peter Vario.

When Vario said then-Gambino boss Paul Castellano was entitled to only $600 of $21,000 in construction payoffs because $19,000 of it was from an "old" deal between the Luchese and Genovese mobs, and only $2,000 was to be split three ways, Santoro was beside himself.

"This is petty on your part," said Santoro.

To Santoro, the thought of telling Castellano he was entitled to only $600 of $21,000 in payoffs was enough to make Santoro stutter.

"Now I got to tell him, 'Wait, you're not entitled to this because this is old money.' I know he's going to say, 'What do you mean old money? You got a partner or not?' That's the way he's going to talk to me. And I'm going to bring you to listen to him."

Unfortunately for the record, the solution to Santoro and Vario's problem with Castellano was never picked up on any bug or wiretap. Unfortunately for Vario, enough of the conversation was recorded to convince a jury that he was guilty of racketeering.

Vario faces up to 20 years and $250,000 when he is sentenced in June.

Angry Goes the (Alleged) Don

When you're the reputed head of the nation's largest crime family, life is not all sweetness and light.

With his third consecutive acquittal and his son's marriage, John Gotti is riding high, but he still has to contend with day-to-day annoyances, some more serious than others.

Sources say Gotti is none too happy with the press extravaganza that surrounded his son's wedding; is steamed that the son of a trusted soldier was allegedly involved in the killing of a fugitive hit man; and is furious that Salvatore Reale, his one-time man at Kennedy Airport, may have skimmed millions from him.

In Reale's case, Gotti is not alone in his anger.

A Brooklyn federal judge and the FBI have been upset, too, since border patrol agents searched the trunk of a car three months ago and found $3.8 million belonging to Reale.

The judge, Jack Weinstein, refused to grant Reale bail last month. He reiterated his unhappiness Friday when he told Reale he "was serious" about sending him to prison if Reale pleaded guilty to violating probation.

Reale, who said he wanted to plead guilty at the start, called "time out" to confer five times outside the courtroom with his attorney before he finally went through with the guilty plea.

The FBI, which had no role in Reale's current problems, and some federal prosecutors are upset that Weinstein disclosed that he gave Reale a suspended sentence for an extortion rap because he previously had cooperated with the government.

"If the judge was angry at Reale for violating his probation, he had every right to send him away for the full 10 years, but not to reveal his informer's status," said one Justice Department official.

Reale, who is in segregated confinement for his own protection, faces up to 10 years when he is sentenced later this week.

Described by the feds as "Gotti's man at Kennedy Airport" when he was charged with extorting $50,000 from an air freight carrier, Reale fell out of favor with the Dapper Don years ago. But this latest episode has Gotti and other reputed mob associates of Reale really steaming, sources say.

The reason: The entire cache of $3.8 million was in old bills, circa 1981 and earlier, and the feeling among wiseguys is that Reale must have skimmed a lot of that cash from them.

The second source of Gotti's anger is that young mob associate Joseph Sclafani was involved in the execution of Costabile "Gus" Farace, the suspected killer of federal drug agent Everett Hatcher.

"Gang Land" hears that Gotti has voiced his displeasure that Sclafani, 24, son of reputed Gotti soldier Augustus "Little Gus" Sclafani, was on the scene when Farace was gunned down last November.

After the killing of Hatcher, the FBI and Drug Enforcement Administration harassed mobsters all over the metropolitan area and beyond in an effort to capture the bearded, muscular killer. And sources say that Sclafani was part of a team that lured Farace to Bensonhurst, Brooklyn, and killed him when he refused to turn himself in.

Sclafani, who drove Farace to Brooklyn, allegedly knew about the hit and was supposed to join in the shooting of Farace when a van of hit men arrived. Wounded in the attack, Sclafani was charged with weapons possession, and pleaded guilty the other day.

Under gentle, leading questioning by Brooklyn Supreme Court Justice Frank Egitto, Sclafani claimed that he was not part of a hit team. He claimed in court that Farace gave him the gun in the car, that he intended to return it, and that when he fired the gun, he was actually firing at the men shooting from the van.

That explanation upset Assistant District Attorney Sari Kolatch, who objected that Judge Egitto was "feeding" Sclafani a scenario and that Sclafani was simply agreeing with him.

"He's not stupid," she said.

"I really think what your Honor is trying to do is to cover the record when you give him the minimum" sentence under the law, 1.5 to 4.5 years, said Kolatch, who had submitted a letter from District Attorney Charles Hynes recommending the maximum 5-to-15-year sentence because Sclafani refused to cooperate.

Egitto said he was not "an arm of the DA's office," had not made up his mind, and would be fair to both prosecution and defendant. He said he would sentence Sclafani later this month after reading the probation report and weighing all the facts of the case.

Finally, Gotti attorney Bruce Cutler said the reputed don was upset that reporters and photographers hounded Gotti and his family at their Howard Beach, Queens, home during the recent wedding preparations of John A. "Junior" Gotti.

That may be so, but Gotti got the last laugh.

From a rotating security camera that scanned the front and side entranceways of his house, Gotti got more pictures of

photographers and reporters than they
got of him and his son. And no one got
pictures of the bride on her wedding day.

Widow of Accused Mobster Sues Government

The government accused her husband of killing many people. Now, Rose Gaggi is making a pretty strong case in federal court that government negligence killed him when he was in Manhattan's Metropolitan Correctional Center.

She claims that while her husband, Anthony "Nino" Gaggi, was having a heart attack, prison guards forced him to walk up and down a flight of steps and change into a regulation prison jumpsuit before he could be treated.

The government concedes the basic facts in the widow's lawsuit, but denies that negligence contributed to Gaggi's death.

Gaggi, a 62-year-old Gambino capo who suffered from hypertension and angina, had a lower bunk, was taking medication, and was on a special diet because of his heart disease. He died of a heart attack at 2 A.M. on April 17, 1988, as he was being prepared for an electrocardiogram at the prison hospital, according to court records.

At the time, he was on trial for racketeering, charged with supervising a mob crew that the FBI says killed 75 people, many whose bodies were dismembered, carted to a dump and never recovered. At trial, six co-defendants were convicted of racketeering, involving 11 murders.

According to the suit, Gaggi suffered "physical distress and trauma" the morning before he died but was not allowed to see a doctor all day. About 11:30 that night, cellmate and co-defendant Ronald Ustica, other prisoners, and a prison employee alerted the guards that Gaggi was having chest pains. Four guards visited the cell before a physician's assistant examined him.

When the assistant determined that Gaggi needed treatment, the guards led him, "bent over with pain," down a flight of steps to an elevator bank. But one of the guards, Levirteen May, "ordered Mr. Gaggi to climb the flight of stairs he had just descended, return to his cell, and change into a prison jumpsuit," the suit said.

In court papers, Assistant U.S. Attorney Richard Goldstein did not dispute any facts citied by Gaggi's widow, but denied that negligence by the government or the guards led to his death.

Two guards, including May, have since resigned. An investigation by prison officials found no wrongdoing by any guards, said a spokesman, who added that regulation jumpsuits are required when inmates leave their cells.

Gaggi's widow, who is seeking $6 million in damages, declined to speak to "Gang Land." Her lawyer, Thomas Battistoni, said the government has "stonewalled us at every turn" since the lawsuit was filed last year.

The first status conference on the case is set for later this month in Brooklyn Federal Court.

If there was any doubt that former Colombo capo Michael Franzese was telling the feds everything he knew, it ended last week when he gave up a janitor.

Ornge T. Tutt has been charged with leaking information to Franzese five years ago that a Brooklyn federal grand jury was investigating him and was about to indict him on racketeering charges.

Tutt, whose "girlfriend-fiance" at the time was on the grand jury that indicted Franzese, allegedly earned about $1,000 for the details he supplied about the probe and witnesses who testified before the panel.

Franzese couldn't block the indictment, but he intimidated witnesses and used Tutt's information to "insulate" some of his assets, according to a two-count indictment against Tutt.

Franzese associate Frank "Frankie Camp" Campione and John "Johnny AMC" Vanasco, who employed Tutt as a porter at a automobile dealership on Long Island, were charged with conspiracy to obstruct justice in a separate case.

Five years ago, when Jamaican posse leader Delroy "Uzi" Edwards wanted to buy a new house to cook cocaine into crack, he took $150,000 in small bills and walked around the corner from his Brooklyn headquarters and hired Oswald Silvera, a Harvard Law School graduate who had put out his shingle.

Last week, Silvera pleaded guilty to cooking up a phony $125,000 mortgage from a company he controlled to conceal the assets from the IRS. Silvera faces five years when he is sentenced. Edwards, convicted of racketeering and six murders, is serving seven consecutive life sentences plus 15 years.

JULY 17, 1990

FBI Claims New
Goods on Gotti

The FBI has amassed a "mother lode" of tape-recorded evidence against John Gotti that virtually guarantees a rematch between the reputed Mafia boss and federal prosecutors in Brooklyn.

The FBI has obtained "mountains of evidence" against Gotti and the hierarchy of the Gambino crime family, including taped conversations linking Gotti to the 1985 slaying of former Gambino boss Paul Castellano, the *Daily News* has learned.

A timetable for the expected racketeering indictment is not yet set, but two antagonists at Gotti's 1986–1987 racketeering trial in Brooklyn Federal Court, Assistant U.S. Attorney John Gleeson and defense lawyer Bruce Cutler, will be there, sources close to the investigation said.

Gotti's first racketeering trial ended in acquittal and catapulted him to national notoriety as the Dapper Don and reputed head of the Gambino family. In that case he was charged with crimes including gambling, loan-sharking, and murder.

The sources said the FBI now has substantial new evidence, including taped conversations of Gotti and his men during an investigation spanning more than two years. The new tapes were picked up on an FBI bug, but the sources declined to elaborate about the conversations or where the electronic device was located.

Hearing Problem

"Initially, there was a problem with audibility, but that was solved," said one source.

The bug picked up key discussions around the beginning of this year as Gotti prepared for his state trial on assault charges stemming from the shooting of carpenters union official John O'Connor.

"It's the mother lode," said another source.

"This mother lode of new evidence," Cutler said with a laugh, "is the same quote-unquote mother lode as in the last three cases, I'm sure. When they want us in court all they have to do is give me a phone call and Mr. Gotti and I will be there to meet the fourth frame-up job."

Gotti has been under investigation by the Manhattan District Attorney and the

U.S. Attorney in Manhattan since December 16, 1985, when Castellano was gunned down in front of a midtown Manhattan steak house while he was on trial.

Assistant Manhattan U.S. Attorney Walter Mack, who was prosecuting Castellano for racketeering at the time, and Assistant Manhattan District Attorney Patrick Dugan began a joint probe into the execution-style slayings of Castellano and key aide Thomas Bilotti.

"Murder for Hire"

Murder is normally a state crime, but Mack teamed up with Dugan hoping to prosecute Gotti under the "murder for hire" federal statutes if they could prove Gotti ordered the killing to take over the crime family.

At the time, Gotti was about to go to trial for federal racketeering. On March 13, 1987, when he beat that case, the FBI and the Organized Crime Strike Force in Brooklyn immediately began another racketeering investigation of Gotti.

Early last year, as the Brooklyn racketeering investigation and Manhattan murder probe floundered, the Manhattan District Attorney's office charged Gotti with assault for allegedly ordering the 1986 shooting of O'Connor.

While that case was pending, Manhattan prosecutors obtained more evidence linking Gotti to the Castellano killing and began to think seriously about

charging Gotti with the murder, the sources said. But federal prosecutors in Brooklyn, armed with evidence obtained from the FBI bug, argued that they should prosecute Gotti and make Castellano's murder part of their case.

FBI Confident

After Gotti's acquittal in the O'Connor shooting, FBI organized crime supervisor Jules Bonavolonta reminded reporters that the FBI had never brought charges against Gotti and was hot on his trail. "He knows we haven't brought a case against him, and he also knows that when we do, he's finished," said Bonavolonta.

In recent months, with Mack and his boss, U.S. Attorney Otto Obermaier, lobbying for Manhattan, and Gleeson and his boss, U.S. Attorney Andrew Maloney, pushing just as hard, it looked to many insiders that the long-standing competition between the Southern and Eastern districts had developed into a feud.

Sources on both sides said the feuding ended when the U.S. Supreme Court indicated in an unrelated case that a "murder for hire" prosecution would preclude separate double jeopardy provisions of the Constitution.

Mack, Gleeson, and Bonavolonta all refused to comment yesterday.

Cutler bristles about the persistent efforts of the FBI and federal prosecutors to convict his main client. "The whole U.S. government and all its prosecutors are fighting with each other to see who can try to put one man in jail. It's a disgrace."

APRIL 3, 1991

Clam Up, Gotti Warns

Fearing that one of his lawyers was leaking information to "Gang Land," John Gotti ordered him to shut up or suffer the consequences—such as a trip down an elevator shaft, according to secret FBI tapes.

The tapes caught the front-page-loving Gambino boss in a decidedly surly mood toward his lawyers and the press, and they were recorded about the time that Gotti's chief attorney called "Gang Land" with a midnight message.

"John read your column today and he was upset about it," lawyer Bruce Cutler said in that call. "He told me to give you a message. This is not a threat now, just like a joke. He'd like to kick you in the ass ...."

Tapes Recorded in '89

The Gotti tapes were recorded in late November 1989 by a bug the FBI placed at the don's Little Italy headquarters, the Ravenite Social Club. They are among scores—still under seal—in which Gotti and his confederates were allegedly caught planning murders and other nasty things.

The tapes are expected to be key evidence at Gotti's upcoming racketeering trial. Numerous news organizations, including the *Daily News*, have asked for them to be unsealed. The conversations described here are the last to surface from the secret trove.

The lawyer who was the immediate target of Gotti's wrath was Gerald Shargel, who worked with Cutler to win Gotti's acquittal on assault charges last year, and whom Gotti suspected of leaking to "Gang Land."

Holding court in the Ravenite on November 28, 1989, an infuriated Gotti complained that many of Shargel's clients were treated well by "Gang Land" while "everybody else is bad."

Speaking of Shargel, he said: "One day, I'm gonna show him a better way than the elevator out of his office—this (expletives deleted)."

"You know why he's doing this?" asked Gotti in an apparent reference to a story about how the federal government was having a tough time convicting Joseph "Joe Butch" Corrao, a reputed Gotti capo and Shargel client. The article described Shargel as a "top criminal lawyer."

"He's not doing this because he likes Joe Butch, he's doing this to have his name in the paper, 'Jerry Shargel, top criminal lawyer,'" said Gotti.

Two days later, Gotti's former lawyer, Michael Coiro, came to the Ravenite after his own conviction on obstruction of justice charges. Gotti told Coiro he'd instructed Shargel on the virtues of *omerta*—particularly when it comes to dealing with this columnist.

"Gave Him a Blast"

"Jerry came down, I gave him a little blast last night," said Gotti. "Yeah, he admits he told him things in the past, this Capeci, but he said he was being helpful. We'll give him the benefit of the doubt."

"Jerry said, 'Listen, John. You know I got one love—you.' Good. That's all well and good. 'But let me tell you something,' I told him, 'I ain't got one love.' I told him, 'You know how I feel, Jerry. I wanna know the truth about everybody. It'll help everybody.'"

That night, Cutler called "Gang Land" at home around midnight to complain that Gotti thought that day's column had devoted too much space to a judge's ruling that prosecutors could use a 1985 set of tapes at Gotti's assault trial.

Along with the kick-you-in-the-ass message, Cutler said that Gotti "thinks you're not giving him a fair shake, prejudicing the jury against him even before the trial starts."

"Come on," "Gang Land" retorted. "It was a pretrial decision, it was buried in the middle of my column, and the *Post* had it, too."

"Yeah, but you're like E.F. Hutton," said Cutler. "When you talk, people listen."

Yesterday, Shargel declined all comment, and Cutler said: "The only reason I ever call you is to complain about the untruths that are contained in your slanted pieces."

Cutler also said that, in reporting on this latest batch of Gotti tapes, "Gang Land," once again, had taken Gotti remarks "totally and completely out of context and put a government spin on them."

He declined, however, to correct the context or explain the remarks in any way.

Still Being Held

While he awaits the start of his racketeering trial, Gotti is being held in the Metropolitan Correctional Center. Meanwhile, prosecutors have described Cutler and Shargel as "high-priced errand boys" for the mob. They argue that the two lawyers should be disqualified from representing Gotti and his co-defendants at trial because the tapes indicate they are "house counsel" to the crime family.

Denying impropriety, Cutler and Shargel are fighting to stay on board.

Brooklyn U.S. Attorney Andrew Maloney, who hasn't tried a case in a decade, is planning to be part of the prosecution team when the case finally goes to trial, probably in the fall, according to sources in Maloney's office.

Maloney, who has never tried a racketeering case, hasn't yet decided whether to serve as lead counsel or merely assist prosecutors John Gleeson, Laura Ward, and Patrick Cotter, sources said.

The appearance of *the* U.S. attorney at the trial could play right into the hands of defense strategy that paints Gotti as the victim of a vendetta by prosecutors who've lost to Gotti three straight times, courthouse observers yesterday told Ruben Rosario, our man at Brooklyn Federal Court.

Pen(itentiary) Pal
Does Write Thing

Mafia boss Carmine "Junior" Persico, who managed to joke about his 100-year prison sentence in a letter to "Gang Land" two years ago, is a little testy these days, judging from his latest correspondence.

Persico took issue with a special Sunday *Daily News* section that chronicled our mob coverage over the years and credited him with the sensational 1957 assassination of Murder Inc. boss Albert Anastasia in a hotel barbershop.

"You inaccurately associated my name with the Anastasia assassination," wrote Persico, who then showed off some of the legal expertise he picked up by representing himself in the historic Commission case.

(His legal work at trial, it must be noted, was no worse than that of lawyers hired by other mob bosses, who were all convicted and sentenced to the same 100 years.)

Persico said that the details of Anastasia's death came from statements of an informer contained in an FBI "302" form; that the word "assassinated" never appeared there; and therefore, he said,

"Gang Land" was guilty of "misquoting the 302."

Like any good lawyer worth his fee, however, Persico omitted a few things. He left out that the informer was a relative who hid him for months and that the informer described Persico thumping his chest and saying, "The FBI knows who really hurt Anastasia, but that fag Crazy Joe Gallo took the credit."

In the same letter, however, the Mafia boss had a much better gripe. He pointed out that recent testimony in the so-called Windows case has put the lie to a 1986 sentencing memo in which federal prosecutors accused him "of participating in the murders" of brothers Ralph and Thomas Spero in 1980.

"If you are following the testimony of the case under way in Brooklyn," noted Persico, "you see that government informer Pete Savino … has confessed on the stand to these murders."

"I see no mention (of this) in your column," wrote Persico, who concluded by asking "Gang Land" to right the three wrongs that he noted.

After due consideration, "Gang Land" gives one of its most dedicated readers and frequent pen pals a "yea" on the Spero brothers complaint, but a "nay" on the Anastasia gripe.

Two out of three ain't bad.

Mob associate Savino has at least one more week of direct testimony at the Brooklyn Federal Court racketeering trial of nine reputed mobsters and associates accused of monopolizing the city's replacement-window business.

In the first three weeks of trial, however, it's become very clear that Savino didn't like defendant Joseph "Joe Cakes" Marion when he was recording conversations.

Savino, in his many hours of taped conversations, bad-mouthed window installer Marion as a "greedy" no-good thief who constantly stole from fugitive Luchese mob boss Vittorio "Vic" Amuso and corrupt ironworkers union officials.

"I'm the guy that got all the evidence against him," Savino told defendant Caesar Gurino in one discussion. "He stole over $250,000 from Vic," he said, adding that Amuso made Marion "take a second mortgage on his house" to pay him back.

Savino noted that Amuso got $100,000 back from the second mortgage and another $100,000 from a windows deal. But he said Marion still owed Amuso $50,000, and was "lucky (Amuso) didn't kill him."

Another time, while Savino was meeting with union official John "Sonny Blue" Morissey to give him a $9,000 kickback, the men discussed a coded nickname they used to refer to Amuso—"Jesse."

"The guy who should have been named Jesse is Fat Joe Marion, because Joe Marion is Jesse James," said Savino, adding, "Vic is too honorable for that name."

Said Marion's lawyer, Harry Batchelder: "It's all part of a Savino scam, and I think I can prove it."

Philadelphia mobsters, under Angelo Bruno and Nicodemo "Little Nicky" Scarfo, were second to none when it came to violence.

Brains, however, were not always a strong point, according to former Philadelphia underboss Philip "Crazy Phil" Leonetti, who took the witness stand at the Windows trial before Savino.

Take, for example, the retribution murder of a "wild kid" named Anthony Barrone, who had killed an associate who worked the door at a mob nightclub.

Barrone was shot to death inside a bar by a South Philadelphia father-and-son team. According to Leonetti, they enlisted another gangster to help carry Barrone's body into the trunk of a car for a ride to a mob graveyard in New Jersey.

At the Walt Whitman Bridge, the three gangsters wheeled into the exact-change lane, only to realize too late that none had any change. So, as angry drivers honked their horns, one mobster jumped out and ran to the next booth for change of a dollar.

May Not Be True, but It's a Good Tale

Dressed all in black, two FBI agents, one armed with an automatic and the other with a dart gun to ward off "restless Dobermans," had 25 seconds to break in and deactivate the sophisticated alarm in the Godfather's house.

At 1:31 A.M. on March 18, 1983, agents Joseph O'Brien and Andris Kurins prevailed—they planted a bug in Paul "Big Paul" Castellano's home on Staten Island, they recall with dramatic detail in their new, supposedly nonfiction book, *Boss of Bosses*.

"We went in. We planted the mike," they write in the introduction. As an old editor once said, "Great story, if true."

The truth is, the agents were not involved in the job, and many other agents and others in law enforcement who worked on the case say the first-time authors also made up conversations—including some they imply came straight from the bug in the slain mob chieftain's home.

What's more, in revealing some conversations that were not made up, the agents may have violated laws prohibiting federal agents from revealing privileged information, according to several law enforcement officials with knowledge of the case.

The officials say the agents violated the spirit and letter of the court order that permitted the FBI to bug Castellano's house, and breached the FBI's professional ethics standards.

"We're supposed to uncover criminal activity, not find out gossip and pillow talk," said one agent, referring to Castellano's romantic involvement with his maid. "And when we do, we're certainly not supposed to spread it."

Indeed, according to their book, when Castellano complained to the agents that the bug told them "all sorts of things about me that no one really has the right to know," O'Brien assured him: "There's this thing called minimization. We try not to listen to personal stuff."

"It's the Madonna of mob books—pure trash," said Edward McDonald, the former Organized Crime Strike Force chief who supervised the Castellano probe. "They're printing things that Kitty Kelley wouldn't write about. The idea of FBI agents listening to conversations they shouldn't have been listening to in the first place, and then selling them in a book—it stinks."

Mark Pomerantz, a former law professor at Columbia University and currently a partner at Roger & Wells, told "Gang Land" the agents could be charged with contempt of court for revealing taped conversations from the court-authorized bug.

If Castellano were alive, added Pomerantz, he could sue the agents for improper disclosure of information they learned officially. "Writing a book is not on the list of reasons the material could be disclosed," said Pomerantz.

"It's ironic," added McDonald, "that throughout the book they portray themselves as men of honor dealing with a man they had come to respect who happened to be on the other side of an honorable war. It seems these men of honor weren't able to win the war, so what they weren't able to do to him in life, they're going to do to him in death—*and* they're making money to boot."

McDonald's last point, the agents' earning money from official privileged information, is just one aspect of an internal investigation being pursued by the FBI, according to the sources.

New York FBI Chief James Fox refused to discuss the inquiry but left no doubt he and his bosses are unhappy about the book, although not because the agents puffed up their own importance in the case and allegedly made up quotes.

"This sort of publication, for money if they get it, is a horrible precedent," said Fox. "We have over a thousand agents, and probably two to three hundred have fantastic stories, ones that could knock your socks off."

"Gang Land" wonders if by taking an extreme view of literary license, O'Brien and Kurins have exposed themselves, and other FBI agents, to some nasty cross-examination about their motives and truthfulness when they testify in court. ("Were you thinking about justice, or writing your book, Mr. FBI Agent?")

It's one thing for hoods like Henry Hill to make up stories. It's quite another for the good guys to do it.

O'Brien refused all comment; Kurins did not respond to a phone message. The book's publisher, Simon & Schuster, did not respond to requests for comment.

———

We don't mean to nitpick, but in the same book, a caption writer misidentified Lanza's restaurant, a legendary First Avenue Italian eatery that's been around since the turn of the century, as Larry's Restaurant. What's embarrassing is that the name of the restaurant, in a perfectly legible neon-light sign, is as clear in the picture as the "Lanza's" written in this paragraph.

Philip Leonetti, the former Philadelphia mob underboss, is not crazy, was never called "Crazy Phil" by his mob cohorts, and will forever be known in "Gang Land" simply by his given name, Philip. Leonetti, who'll point the finger at John Gotti for ordering the 1985 killing of

Castellano, got the name from a radio announcer. When Leonetti told his uncle, Mafia boss Nicodemo "Little Nicky" Scarfo he wanted to sue the announcer, Scarfo told him: "What are you, crazy? People would kill for a nickname like that."

Boss Debunks Ex-FBI Writers

The two former FBI agents peddling sensational tales about Paul Castellano narrowly escaped a grilling that would have exposed their flights of fiction nationally, live on the *Larry King* cable television show.

Hawking their book, *Boss of Bosses*, in which they detail how they supposedly bugged the late don's Staten Island home, Joseph O'Brien and Andris Kurins took a turn at the microphone on King's CNN call-in show Friday night.

What they didn't know is that their audience included plenty of hostile FBI agents, including New York FBI boss James Fox, who says there "are some major inaccuracies in their description of the break-in."

Chief among them is that O'Brien and Kurins were not the agents who broke into the house and planted the listening device in Castellano's kitchen—one of the key premises of the book.

"I wanted to call and ask them about their roles in the bugging, but I missed the phone number at the beginning of the show," Fox told "Gang Land" yesterday.

The very thought of such a call is wonderful because it could have finally debunked the dramatic duo's account of how in a lightning strike they broke into Castellano's home and deactivated a sophisticated alarm system.

Dressed all in black and armed with a small automatic and a dart gun, the former agents describe themselves in the book as making their way to the kitchen area, dismantling a European lamp, planting a bug, putting the lamp back together and making their escape—all within 12½ minutes.

In truth, as "Gang Land" reported two weeks ago, the agents were nowhere near the scene, and may not even have been on Staten Island.

"It's a big lie," said one FBI supervisor of the agents' claim to have bugged Castellano's house.

"They made it up out of whole cloth," said a second high-ranking FBI agent.

The two agents—who purport to be on the trail of pulling in a million dollars from the book—resigned from the FBI under pressure last week in exchange for being able to keep their royalties, however large or small they prove to be.

King discussed that issue with the pair on his show, then took a call from a viewer who had the same question the FBI's Fox had in mind:

"Did you actually go into his house, or is that just something you wrote in the book?"

Responded O'Brien: "I understand that a reporter by the name of Jerry Capeci claims in an article that Andy and I did not break into Castellano's house and bug it. Jerry Capeci is a gossip columnist."

Now, it's not that I mind being placed in the august company of Richard Johnson and Liz Smith, but that doesn't seem like much of an answer. To his credit, King pressed O'Brien.

"You did break into the house and bug it? How'd you get in?"

O'Brien huffed, and Kurins puffed, and they both punted, saying they couldn't give away "bureau techniques" or "methods of operations."

"But the book describes the technique, doesn't it?" asked King.

"That's right, so people can read the book and see the whole thing," said O'Brien.

Terrific.

The book's publisher, Simon & Schuster, has not responded to numerous requests for comment.

In a statement given to "Gang Land" by his lawyer, O'Brien said: "By and large, the book is totally true and factual. Naturally, in some part of the book, we had to take some literary license. The deviations we made—we had to make, we were required to make—are insignificant and don't detract from the story at all."

The key words there are "by and large" and "literary license."

———

Things have gone from bad to worse for Gerald Guterman, the former real estate tycoon who was indicted on tax fraud charges on the testimony of yuppie mobster-turned-informer Michael Franzese.

Last year, Guterman was charged with buying labor peace and mob protection from Franzese when Guterman was renovating some 2,500 apartments and converting them into condos and co-ops.

Now, Raphael "Red" Celli, Guterman's former construction manager, has pleaded guilty to misdemeanor tax charges before Judge Reena Raggi and agreed to testify against Guterman.

And, according to court papers filed by Assistant U.S. Attorney Michael Considine, the feds learned that Guterman filed a "significantly altered" copy of his company's 1987 tax return in a Denver bankruptcy fraud proceeding involving him and his estranged wife.

Sources aid the allegedly "fraudulent" filing will now be added as a new charge carrying an additional five years in prison.

Guterman's lawyer, Gerald Shargel, declined comment.

———

William "the Wild Guy" Grasso, slain underboss of New England's Patriarca crime family, really earned his nickname.

Last week, federal informant Jack Johns testified in Hartford that once, when Johns neglected to cut Grasso in on a deal, Grasso told him. "You ever take a score again without telling me, I got a hole I'm gonna throw you in."

Johns added that Grasso promised to bury him with one arm sticking out of the ground so he could walk by and kick it every day.

Nasty.

AUGUST 27, 1991

One for Hall Of Frame, Eh, Dap?

John Gotti thought he was being a wiseguy when he and his top aides stopped talking business at the Ravenite Social Club in Little Italy because they *knew* the place was bugged.

In an exercise of caution, the Dapper Don moved high-level discussions to a hallway behind the Ravenite and an apartment above the club.

Turns out that Gotti & Co. had neutralized the bug in the Ravenite, but the bugs in the hallway and the apartment picked up virtually every incriminating word by Gotti, reputed underboss Frank "Frankie Loc" Locascio, and consigliere Salvatore "Sammy Bull" Gravano.

Now they're all in jail without bail, awaiting trial on racketeering and murder charges.

On the tapes, the three men are heard discussing killings and ways to beat the judicial system in such clear fashion that a relatively liberal judge has remanded them as dangers to the community who are likely to obstruct justice if out on the streets.

To start at the beginning, Michael Cirelli, a Gambino associate for many years, was the caretaker of the Ravenite Social Club. Until his death on January 16, 1988, he lived above the club, in apartment 10, at 247 Mulberry Street.

In 1979, Cirelli, armed with a baseball bat, chased detectives from the Manhattan District Attorney's office out of the building when they tried to bug the joint. They had apparently given the building's guard dog some doped-up meatballs.

Right after Cirelli died, FBI agents bugged the Ravenite.

A few months later, they bugged Gotti's Ozone Park headquarters, the Bergin Hunt and Fish Club, where Gotti and Gravano talked business on Fridays and Saturdays. In July 1988, that eavesdropping device was discovered, and Gotti and company "ceased talking inside the club," according to court papers filed in Brooklyn.

No one ever found the Ravenite bug, but six days after finding the Bergin bug

Gotti and company took "affirmative steps" and rendered useless the bugs they *knew* were there by installing a "noise-generating system," according to court papers.

On September 12, 1988, the FBI gave up listening.

Informants told the feds that Gotti was using a hallway behind the club and Cirelli's old apartment for high-level conversations with Gravano and Locascio. The FBI got new court orders, and the worm turned.

"The irony is," said one source, "that they went from an area where they were jamming conversations of 30 to 40 guys all talking at once about a million different things to a soundproof room where they talked about whacking guys."

———

"Nothing personal."

That was the message the reputed mobster Joseph Bilotti got when his younger brother Thomas was one of two men Gotti allegedly executed as he took over the Gambino crime family, sources tell "Gang Land."

Gravano and former Gotti underboss Frank DeCicco personally delivered the message, along with a $50,000 loan-sharking bankroll and an ultimatum to take the money, push it out on the street, or die, the sources said.

After a tense meeting with DeCicco and Gravano at a diner, Bilotti agreed to take the money—and live, the sources said.

Last week, Bilotti, 58, was indicted on federal loan-sharking conspiracy charges dating back to March 1986, three short months after his brother and Paul Castellano were killed in front of Sparks Steak House in midtown.

In the four-count indictment, Bilotti is charged with using threats to collect debts from Ernest Benfante, of Staten Island.

It's unclear whether Bilotti was overheard on any Ravenite bugs (there was also one on the sidewalk, outside the club), but at his arraignment last week, Bilotti learned that Benfante had worn a wire during the investigation.

Assistant U.S. Attorney Laura Ward, also one of three prosecutors in the Gotti case, declined to comment about the case or what our sources said about the Gotti offer that Bilotti couldn't refuse.

"It's a shock to me," said Bilotti's attorney, David Ironman. "My knowledge of Joseph Bilotti is that he's a hardworking guy whose last name has thrust him into an unfortunate situation."

Ironman, who noted that his client has no prior convictions, said he would be better able to discuss the case next week—after he receives copies of the Benfante tapes.

———

In his racketeering indictment, Gotti is charged with five murders, including those of Castellano and Thomas Bilotti.

In court papers, however, he is accused by FBI informants of ordering many more, including those of two mob-associated businessmen involved in the private carting industry who were slain in front of their homes.

Edward Garofalo, slain last August, was ordered killed by Gotti at the behest of Gravano; Fred Weiss was killed in September 1989 because he was "believed to be weak and susceptible to cooperating with the government."

SEPTEMBER 3, 1991

Colombos Set to Play Family Feud

Families are supposed to stick together, but mobsters in the Colombo family are sticking it to each other and "Gang Land" sources on both sides of the law say that bodies could start dropping any day.

Judging from the first official encounter, however, mobsters aligned with a faction that still considers imprisoned Carmine "Junior" Persico its boss look like Keystone Kops.

And those carrying the mantel of Victor "Little Vic" Orena act like they're working for Inspector Clouseau.

On June 20, four Persico loyalists, including *consigliere* Carmine Sessa, were staked out at Orena's Long Island home on assignment to kill him, but panicked when Orena arrived home earlier than they expected and spotted them, according to court papers.

"They weren't ready, at that point, to shoot him," said Assistant U.S. Attorney Laura Ward during a detention hearing before U.S. Magistrate John Caden last week for Robert Zambardi, another anti-Orena member of the alleged hit squad

that couldn't shoot. Zambardi is charged with loan-sharking.

Orena was more than a little upset when he saw the Persico troops almost at the ready, so he put out contracts against Sessa and Zambardi, who were warned by the FBI about the retaliatory contracts—like they couldn't figure that out.

Since then, however, Orena allies haven't been able to find them, and both sides in the family dispute are watching their backs, fronts, and sides.

Sources say the family feud stems from Persico's desire to turn the crime family over to his son, Alphonse, a reputed capo not scheduled to be released from federal prison until July 1993, and Orena's desire to keep it himself.

Each side of the 10-capo, 100-or-so mobster family feud has members looking to start the shooting, sources say. So far, however, family elder Vincent Aloi, a former acting boss himself, has maintained an uneasy peace through sit-downs with both factions.

"It's the feds and their so-called informants (there are five cited in the court papers) who are stirring up trouble among the old friends, who aren't violent at all," said Zambardi's lawyer, Frank Lopez, who has also represented Persico.

So far, there's been no bloodshed, but both sides fire real bullets, and the situation is serious.

Three years ago, for example, when former acting boss James Angellino tried his own power play, he was quickly dispatched by mobsters then loyal to both Orena and Persico.

———

Magistrate Caden, who decided the allegations about Zambardi's foray at Orena's house were "closer to innuendo than proof," had a much different attitude at another detention hearing for reputed Luchese boss Vittorio "Vic" Amuso.

Amuso, who was nabbed near Scranton, Pennsylvania, after 14 months on the run, would not flee now, argued defense lawyer Martin Geduldig, because this time his friends and relatives were going to put up cash and their homes as collateral.

He would not betray "those he loves and cares for," said Geduldig.

"If the past is any guide to the future," countered Assistant U.S. Attorney Neil Ross, "he would abandon his family again."

The alleged crime boss, who didn't bat an eye when Ross accused him of ordering killings or when Caden detained him without bail, glared, looking like he

wanted to jump down the prosecutor's throat when he questioned Amuso's love of his family.

———

Because he failed to signal when he made a left turn, Frank Lastorino, reputedly a Luchese mobster with close ties to acting boss Alphonse "Little Al" D'Arco, is in danger of suffering his first conviction—a gun rap—at age 50.

To add insult to injury, Brooklyn cops impounded his 1990 Lincoln and accused him of being a coke user after they pulled him over and arrested him at E. 55th Street and Flatlands Avenue last February.

Officers Donald Alesi and Steve Zimmerman say that when Lastorino got out, he left his door open and they saw a small black pouch with the handle of a .22-caliber Beretta sticking out of it on the front seat.

When they drove him to the 63rd Precinct, they found a folded-up dollar bill with a half-gram of coke under the backseat of the police car and added misdemeanor drug charge, but ran with the gun rap, which carries a maximum seven years in prison.

During a pretrial hearing, lawyer Benjamin Brafman contended that the cops unlocked the glove compartment to find the gun, and argued it should be suppressed from evidence at trial.

With nothing to contradict the two cops' testimony, however, Brooklyn

Supreme Court Justice George Wade will be hard-pressed to rule for Lastorino, and Lastorino will be pressed hard to cop a plea—a guilty plea.

OCTOBER 8, 1991

Gang's All Here (or Dead or Rotting)

It was that kind of reunion that can only happen in gangland.

Almost everyone was there—except for those who were dead or in jail.

Participants in the federal racketeering trial of a killer mob crew said to have murdered 200 people came together on an auspicious occasion—the appeal of the convictions of members of Roy DeMeo's gang found guilty of 11 murders.

DeMeo's main men, Joseph Testa and Anthony Senter, each got life plus 20 years in prison after a 17-month trial in the bloodiest and most gruesome story ever told in a federal court.

Many killings took place in a Brooklyn apartment that served as a slaughterhouse where victims were dismembered, wrapped in plastic bags, and placed in cardboard boxes that were tied up neatly and taken to a nearby dump.

"When the person would walk in somebody would shoot him in the head with a silencer; somebody would wrap a towel around to stop the blood and somebody would stab him in the heart to stop the blood from pumping," testified key witness Dominick Montiglio.

"They would drag him into the bathroom, put him in the shower, bleed him, pull him out, put him on a pool liner in the living room, take him apart, and package him," said Montiglio, who tied Mafia boss Paul Castellano to the crew.

"This trial was so long and so complex it was impossible for the jury to reliably decide the case," argued Herald Fahringer, Testa's lawyer.

That argument and similar ones by Senter's attorney, Benjamin Brafman, were given little merit by the three Second Circuit U.S. Court of Appeals judges.

"There was much vacation time," said Judge Milton Pollack, noting that after each break in the trial, "jurors would come back refreshed and pay closer attention to the evidence because they weren't tired anymore."

Former prosecutor Walter Mack and five investigators, FBI agents, and detectives who spent 10 years and two trials probing and proving the case smiled and nodded their approval at the judges' disdain for the defense.

On the other side of the spectator section, however, there were only glares of disapproval toward the appeals judges from Testa's wife, JoAnne; his brother Patrick; and nephew Frederick Johnson.

Joseph Testa and Senter, who were indicted with Castellano and 21 others in 1984, were acquitted of trafficking in stolen cars in the trial Castellano was part of when he was killed. Before trial, Patty Testa, who was not charged with any murders, pleaded guilty to conspiring to sell stolen cars.

DeMeo, a Gambino mobster under Castellano, was killed on orders from the boss in 1983 in an unsuccessful effort to short-circuit the probe.

Jacqueline Todaro, whose father, Fred, was killed by the crew, told "Gang Land" she was glad the men who did it, including her cousin Douglas Rega, were in prison, "but there can never be enough satisfaction; I lost my father."

Another Testa brother indicted in the stolen-car conspiracy case, Dennis, stayed away from the appeals court, with good reason.

Dennis Testa, who is charged with murder, has been a fugitive since 1984. He is also wanted on charges of hiding fugitive Luchese boss Vittorio "Vic"

Amuso, who was arrested along with Fred Johnson last July near Scranton, Pennsylvania.

Testa, who allegedly used the alias Joseph Ricci to help Johnson hide Amuso, quietly walked away from the mall where FBI agents nabbed Amuso and Johnson. Johnson is free on bail in the harboring case.

Thanks to the many readers who took time to call or write to inform us that we screwed up two weeks ago when we identified a picture of reputed Bonanno *consigliere* Anthony Spero as Luchese capo Frank Lastorino.

"Gang Land" pleads guilty with an explanation (some editor did it), but takes full responsibility for misidentifying the Brooklyn street corner where Spero coops his prize-winning pigeons. It's Bath Avenue and Bay 14th Street, not Bay 16th.

Lastorino and other Lucheses are worried about acting boss Alphonse "Little Al" D'Arco's defection to the feds, but a few connoisseurs of Sicilian cooking have another concern—the closing of Little Al's SoHo restaurant.

"I'm very disappointed," said one regular patron, an executive secretary who sought out "Gang Land" when she learned from a *Daily News* front-page story last week that La Donna Rosa had closed the previous Thursday.

"The seafood was always fresh, the pasta dishes were delicious, I was planning to take my family there this week," she said.

"Real good food, strictly Sicilian cooking," agreed Dominick Ferrantino, next door at Ferrantino Oil. "You really couldn't beat it, they gave you a veal steak this thick," he said, his thumb and forefinger 2 inches apart.

Daily News restaurant critic Arthur Schwartz, who panned La Donna Rosa in Sunday's *News*, must have been there on a different day, quite some time ago.

Windows Trial Pane and Gain

The problem with a split jury verdict is figuring out who won and who lost.

Today, "Gang Land" tries to sort out the winners and losers in the Windows case, the labor-racketeering trial that last week ended in complete acquittals for five defendants and partial acquittals for the others.

The biggest loser may be reputed Luchese family boss Vittorio "Vic" Amuso, who hid out in Scranton, Pennsylvania, for 14 months and got arrested much too late to be acquitted along with his mobster pals.

Amuso sits at the Metropolitan Correctional Center, waiting for Windows II and his chance for acquittal on racketeering charges stemming from the mob's involvement in the replacement-window industry.

Peter Gotti, Caesar Gurino, Joseph "Joe Cakes" Marion, Thomas McGowan, and reputed Genovese capo Joseph Zito all win. But Zito wins biggest because of the free publicity he got for his popular Little Italy restaurant, Ruggero.

Venero "Benny Eggs" Mangano, Benedetto "Benny" Aloi, and Dennis DeLucia lose. They were convicted of extortion. Reputed Luchese underboss Anthony "Gaspipe" Casso, who is hiding out in Scranton or points north or west, is also a loser.

Peter Savino, the Genovese associate-turned-informer, wins a new identity in the Witness Protection Program and a sweetheart deal that washes away six murders, but he loses a lucrative window business and a $500,000 home. This one's a wash.

Reputed Genovese boss Vincent "Chin" Gigante loses. He had a chance for exoneration but settled for a court finding that he was too crazy to stand trial.

Luchese capo Peter "Big Pete" Chiodo, who survived a 12-shot mob rubout attempt and joined Savino as a witness, wins. Even if they get very angry, feds don't shoot witnesses who give false or incoherent testimony.

Genovese capo Dominick "Baldy Dom" Canterino and reputed Colombo associate Vincent "Three Fingers" Ricciardo lose. They suffered heart attacks, were severed from the trial, and lost all chance for acquittal.

Residents of city projects win. By all accounts, the replacement windows installed during the last 10 years by the suspect companies cited at the trial worked well, keeping cold out, heat in, and fuel-oil costs down.

The FBI, Brooklyn U.S. Attorney Andrew Maloney, and trial prosecutors Gregory O'Connell, Charles Rose, and Neil Ross all lose for obvious reasons.

Organized Crime Strike Force prosecutor Mario DiNatale, who worked on the case but resigned when the strike force was merged into the U.S. Attorney's office, wins simply because he had no part in the trial.

Completely victorious lawyers Bruce Cutler, Benjamin Brafman, Harry Batchelder, Alan Futerfas, and Peter Driscoll are winners. Mostly victorious attorneys Frederick Haftez, Jeffrey Hoffman, and Michael Washor are losers.

Judge Raymond Dearie and federal and state judges in the New York metropolitan area are big winners because Cutler left town yesterday for a two-month federal racketeering trial in Chicago.

The hot dog man in the park across from the Brooklyn federal courthouse got a reprieve when the judge refused early on to order a mistrial. During the six-month trial, the defendants ate more hot dogs than Yankee fans consumed last season. He also wins because Windows II is around the corner.

John Gotti wins because older brother Peter's acquittal enhances the Dapper Don's Teflon image. The downside comes in January, when Peter is sure to be a daily spectator—and nudge—when the reputed Gambino crime family chief goes to trial on racketeering and murder charges.

Whenever "Gang Land" stopped in at the Windows trial, Joseph "Butter" DeCicco, an uncle of slain Gotti underboss Frank DeCicco, was always optimistic about the outcome for close friends Peter Gotti and Caesar Gurino.

DeCicco, a perpetually smiling, happy-go-lucky type, would say, "The case is falling apart" or "You missed some great testimony yesterday."

It's always easy to maintain that attitude when you're not a defendant. But 13 years ago, when DeCicco was in the dock, in the same courtroom, he had the same way about him and got a big win.

Back then, DeCicco was charged with conspiring, along with another reputed gangster and two podiatrists, to pay a $100,000 bribe to a state official to keep podiatry services under the state's Medicaid reimbursement program.

One day, when a prosecutor admired DeCicco's tie, DeCicco removed it and gave it to him. When the prosecutor tried to reciprocate with his tie, DeCicco refused, saying, "I didn't say I liked your tie."

His defense was simple: He collected the cash but never bribed anyone. He always intended to keep the money, and he did. He ripped off the "greedy podiatrists" and may have been guilty of grand larceny, but not bribery.

The jury acquitted him on its first vote.

"It's my lucky courtroom," DeCicco said Friday, an hour before the verdict was announced.

Judge Has Ax to Grind

Call him the grudge judge.

The public—the reading, listening, and viewing public—is paying for a 50-year-old beef that Brooklyn Federal Judge I. Leo Glasser has held against the press since he worked briefly, for a newspaper.

This revelation comes not from informed "Gang Land" sources but from Glasser himself, who is presiding over the pending murder and racketeering case, U.S. vs. John Gotti and Frank "Frankie Loc" Locascio.

Last week, at a scheduled pretrial proceeding in the case, Glasser blasted the press, saying he sometimes reads newspaper stories about his cases and wonders "whether I was even present at the proceedings being reported on."

During the Gotti proceeding, according to the official transcript, Glasser said his bad feelings about the press arose in 1941, when his city editor at the old *Journal American* tried to embarrass Millicent Hearst, the publisher's wife, by proving that milk given away for her pet project, Free Milk Fund for Babies, "had germs in it."

After the paper stole bottles of milk off front stoops, analyzed them, and learned the milk was germ-free, said Glasser,

"The city editor's reply was, 'God damn it. I want germs in the milk.'"

That may be true, but none of it gave the judge the right to move the proceeding from his courtroom to his chambers and exclude the nine newspaper, television, and radio reporters assigned to cover the proceeding.

In case after case, the 2d Circuit Court of Appeals and the U.S. Supreme Court of Appeals have ruled that, absent extreme circumstances, court proceedings—including pretrial ones—should be open to the public.

A few years back, when Manhattan Federal Judge Shirley Wohl Kram announced that she was moving a pretrial proceeding of two drug defendants into her chambers, a *Daily News* reporter asked her to reconsider. Kram said no, but invited the reporter into chambers to cover the proceeding.

Several times during the recent Windows labor-racketeering trial in Brooklyn, when Judge Raymond Dearie questioned jurors in his chambers, he allowed one or two pool reporters to attend.

Kram and Dearie were not being nice to reporters, they were upholding the law and protecting the rights of the public—the newspaper readers, radio listeners, and television viewers—to know what's going on.

When Glasser was handed a note, requesting, at a minimum, that he allow a pool reporter to attend the conference, he refused, telling the assembled lawyers and prosecutors: "I don't think it is a media event."

It certainly wasn't. It was a pretrial proceeding in one of the most important New York stories of the decade, the fourth indictment in five years against John Gotti, a reputed boss of the largest Mafia family in the country who had beaten prosecutors the first three times.

Already, the U.S. Attorney's office has received scores of calls from reporters all over the world who plan to cover the trial. Whether Glasser likes it or not, they will come.

Instead of trying to obstruct press coverage of the case, Glasser should plan to move the case from his courtroom, which holds about 100 spectators, to a large, ceremonial one that can accommodate about 400.

Another culprit in this sorry situation is the so-called people's lawyer, U.S. Attorney Andrew Maloney.

Despite Justice Department guidelines dictating that the "government has a general overriding affirmative duty to oppose closure" of court proceedings, Maloney stood mute when Glasser locked out the press.

Called by "Gang Land" yesterday, Maloney said he wasn't sure about the guidelines and declined comment.

The guidelines, which apply to all federal proceedings, read, in part:

"The government should take a position on any motion to close a judicial proceeding, and should ordinarily oppose closure; it should move for or consent to closed proceedings only when closure is plainly essential to the interests of justice."

———

FBI, DEA, and NYPD officials were unanimous in their fury about the Sunday night ABC special that made Assistant U.S. Attorney Charles Rose the hero in the hunt for Gus Farace, the drug dealer suspected of killing Drug Enforcement Administration agent Everett Hatcher in 1989.

"It came across as a one-man Charlie Rose show," said New York FBI boss James Fox, "when, in reality, it was a joint effort of the NYPD, DEA, and FBI. Agents are furious how the TV version was distorted."

"Jim Fox is absolutely correct," agreed Rose. "It was total team effort. Hollywood is Hollywood, though. I guess in condensing nine months into two hours they missed a lot."

DECEMBER 24, 1991

Christmas Alone for Luchese Boss

Due to circumstances beyond his control—a warrant for his arrest—Vittorio Amuso spent last Christmas in a cold and lonely motel room near Scran-ton, Pennsylvania, far from his loved ones.

This Christmas doesn't seem any brighter for the reputed boss of the Luchese crime family, who is stuck in an even smaller, colder room in the Metropolitan Correctional Center, so he wrote a letter to Santa Claus.

But Santa, who wore black robes instead of a red-and-white suit, said Amuso had been naughty instead of nice and refused his plea for two weeks at home with his wife and family.

Even with Amuso's wife, brothers, and friends in court to show support, Brooklyn Federal Judge Raymond Dearie last week rejected his request for a Christmas furlough and heeded arguments of federal prosecutors to keep him in jail.

Having pledged $4 million in homes and businesses to guarantee Amuso would return to his cell after 14 days of freedom, family and friends were brought to court by lawyer Gerald Shargel for much more than moral support.

Amuso, who suffers from bursitis, was not present to see the group. Last time he was in court, said Shargel, Amuso was manhandled, and his "shoulder swelled up to several times the normal size."

"Mr. Amuso does not seek to travel to (his) lawyer's offices, nor does he ask permission to go shopping or travel to his relatives. Mr. Amuso merely wishes to spend the holidays with his family," said Shargel.

Prosecutors Charles Rose and Gregory O'Connell countered that Amuso was a fair-weather friend who ordered several killings while he was a fugitive and that a Christmas present from the judge could mean death for others.

Amuso's request was a "subterfuge" so he could flee again, charged the prosecutors, adding, "but for his apprehension at the hands of the FBI, Amuso would be missing his second Christmas with his family"—who at least can visit him now.

There will not be any mob retaliation against the suspected killers of Genovese soldier Gaetano Amato, because he should have known better than hang out in a war zone.

That's what his reputed capo, Salvatore "Sally Dogs" Lombardi decreed recently, according to law enforcement officials on the case. The 78-year-old was gunned down in the crossfire of the Colombo mob war.

"Amato's been around a long time and has only himself to blame for being in the wrong place at the wrong time," was the essence of Lombardi's official ruling, said one source.

Amato was killed early this month as he walked out of a Gravesend, Brooklyn, social club with Joseph Tolino, the intended target of Colombo gunmen loyal to imprisoned boss Carmine "Junior" Persico.

Ruling that Amato virtually committed suicide was easy for several reasons, noted one cynical source.

"Amato was old and was not a big money earner," the source said. "If he had been a skipper (capo) or a big money guy, there very well could have been a different ruling."

Mobsters Henry "Hank the Bank" Smurra and Rosario "Black Sam" Nastasa, both Persico allies, were early casualties of the Colombo war, executed by mobsters loyal to Victor "Little Vic" Orena.

When they were gunned down—Smurra in his car and Nastasa in his social club—their mob associates may not have been sure by reading newspapers that omitted street names, as the following anecdote illustrates.

Several years ago, before Hank the Bank became a "made member" of the crime family, he was approached by a detective as he walked along a Bay Ridge, Brooklyn, street with another mob associate.

"What were you doing getting into a car with Rosario Nastasa the other day?" asked the detective.

"We don't know any Rosario Nastasa, and if we did, we wouldn't tell you anyway," said Hank.

When the detective, who was certain they knew him, showed them a picture of Nastasa, Hank the Bank and his associate laughed and said in unison: "Rosario Nastasa? That's Black Sam."

Family Feud Shifts to Overdrive

Michael Persico, whose imprisoned father, Carmine, is waging war over his family's rights to head the Colombo crime family, has got the feds as well as his father's mob enemies gunning for him.

Carmine Persico wants the reins of power to go to older son Alphonse when he gets out of prison next year, but Michael's problems are more immediate.

The feds are investigating allegations that the younger Persico used a Brooklyn car service as a base for a loan-sharking operation that used bills for taxi fares to hide high-interest payments from loan customers.

As ammunition, sources said, Assistant U.S. Attorney George Stanboulidis and the FBI are using an accountant who allegedly ripped off millions of dollars from friends and relatives investing money through him.

Last year, FBI agents raided the Bay Ridge office of Romantique Limousine Inc. on 11th Avenue and carted away books and records that were subpoenaed by a federal grand jury in Brooklyn, sources said.

The feds are also investigating allegations that Persico faction loyalists had used the car service as a money-laundering clearinghouse and to shuttle drug customers to and from a local night-club, sources said.

Romantique uses a Lincoln and a Jaguar, among other vehicles, according to Department of Motor Vehicles records.

The car-service records were seized the day accountant Kenneth Geller and his family were whisked away from their Syosset, L.I., home and given new identities under the federal Witness Protection Program, sources said.

"If Ken Geller tells the truth," said Michael Persico's lawyer Judd Burstein, "Michael has nothing to fear. But he is already the victim of incompetent accounting, and I fear he is being set up by Geller. The guy is as crooked as the day is long. He stole millions of dollars, was about to be uncovered, and in another manifestation of his remarkable ability as a con man, he sold the government a bill of goods."

The FBI, the Brooklyn U.S. Attorney's office, and Geller's attorney declined to comment.

"Geller's a crook, too," conceded one law enforcement source, adding that the accountant decided to cooperate after FBI agents learned from informants that the Colombo mob had put out a contract on his life.

The source declined to say whether Geller wore a wire or if the car service was bugged.

None of Geller's investor victims or their lawyers could be reached for comment yesterday, but it looks like Geller turned his assets into cash that he took with him when he disappeared.

Gregory Messer, a trustee appointed by the federal bankruptcy court to seek out and attach any assets Geller has, told "Gang Land" he found several Geller properties, but none in which the equity is larger than the mortgage.

Messer suspects that Geller, who had given investors returns as high as 24 percent for about seven years, may have been legitimate when he began, but that once his investments turned sour he used funds from later investors to pay interest to his early ones until the money dried up.

"He certainly paid interest, some at very high rates, but my suspicion is he began making real investments, but when they turned sour it turned into a Ponzi scheme," said Messer.

Meanwhile, a few subpoenaed Colombo mobsters and associates showed up in court yesterday and quickly left when prosecutors refused to give them immunity to testify before a Brooklyn grand jury said to be looking into the mob war.

"None of my clients testified," said Marvyn Kornberg, "nor did any of the men represented by other attorneys I know. It appears, as we stated originally, that this grand jury business was a one-day circus and publicity stunt."

Dennis Hawkins, chief of the Brooklyn District Attorney's organized crime bureau, said a majority declined to testify but disputed assertions by Kornberg and other lawyers that none of the subpoenaed Colombo associates testified.

"The grand jury investigation is continuing," said Hawkins, insisting that the probe was only "one part of a multiorganizational effort" by his office, the police, and federal investigators.

Meanwhile, the latest word from the streets is that Persico loyalists and followers of acting boss Victor "Little Vic" Orena are holding fast and in for the long haul.

Word is that the Luchese and Gambino crime families still back the Orena faction but are pressing for a negotiated end to the conflict, perhaps through the appointment of an interim boss satisfactory to both sides.

Even Mob Thinks He's Got It Coming

Much of the underworld thinks the government will finally convict John Gotti, but a few diehards are sure the Teflon Don has an ace up his sleeve.

And while a gangster worth his salt always roots for the bad guys—at trial and even in the movies—some mobsters and associates believe Gotti deserves to lose and hope he is convicted.

Some even say that guilty or not, Gotti loses.

"If he gets acquitted, he's still got troubles," one underworld source observed. "The feds won't let up on him, and he's got a lot of guys upset about what he's been saying behind everyone's backs."

The mainly gloomy assessment stems from the spate of bad news for Gotti since he and his top two associates were arrested 13 months ago and jailed without bail.

- The case, it turned out, is based on hundreds of hours of secretly recorded conversations from the Ravenite Social Club, Gotti's Manhattan headquarters.
- His long-time lawyer, Bruce Cutler, was thrown off the case.
- His handpicked underboss, Salvatore "Sammy Bull" Gravano, became a government witness.

"My feeling is, how much of a fight can you still put up, when all the news is so bad," said another underworld source. "Losing Cutler hurts him. I don't know whether Cutler is a good lawyer, but I do know he has been a very good good-luck charm."

"John's got no one to blame but himself," said an associate of Gotti's Gambino crime family. "He said a lot of things a boss should never talk about—murders, Cosa Nostra. He should have never talked at the club; he should have got up and walked around the block."

The Gambino sources said many family members and associates are pleased with Gotti's predicament while at the same time worried about what else Gotti said on the tapes, "what other good fellows are in trouble that we don't know about yet."

"Maybe it's about time he got his, always badmouthing everybody behind his back, and whacking 'made' guys for no reason," the source added, pointing to the killings of mobsters Robert "DeeBee" DiBernardo, Louis Milito, and Louis DiBono. DiBono, a contractor/partner of Gravano's, was killed in a World Trade Center parking lot on October 4, 1990. The bodies of DiBernardo and Milito were never found.

Both complaints—Gotti's bad-mouthing and hair trigger—are documented in a conversation he had with co-defendant Frank "Frankie Loc" Locascio on December 12, 1989. The subject was murder; the reasons not befitting a Mafia boss.

"When DeeBee got whacked, they told me a story," said Gotti, with "they" a reference to now-dead Gambino capo Angelo Ruggiero, who owed DiBernardo $100,000. "I was in jail when I whacked him. I knew why it was being done. I done it anyway. I allowed it to be done anyway."

In discussing Milito, after Locascio agreed that he had never heard Milito speak badly about Gotti, Gotti explained why he approved his murder: "I took Sammy's word that he talked behind my back. I took Sammy's word."

Gotti told Locascio that Gravano "wanted permission" to kill DiBono for cheating him in a business deal. "I saw the papers and everything," said Gotti. "He didn't rob nothing. Know why he's dying? He's gonna die because he refused to come in when I called."

Mob hotheads like Gravano and Ruggiero have always killed at the slightest provocation, but big-time mob bosses are supposed to have restraint—and not supposed to bad-mouth the hotheads after giving them permission to kill.

"Paul (Castellano, the Gambino boss Gotti allegedly killed) never would have killed a guy for not coming in," said the source. "He wasn't screwing somebody's wife, or ratting anybody out, for Christ's sake."

The mob is not a monolith, however, and some gangsters think a gambler like Gotti can never be counted out. He might win on pure luck, or because he's holding a secret card—Gravano.

The latter view holds that Gotti is running his best scam yet—to make the government believe Gravano will take the stand and testify against him when in fact in the end Gravano will say that Gotti is just a peace-loving plumbing salesman.

"I feel that Sammy was put up to do it," said an associate of several mob families.

"(Gotti's) gonna beat this one, too," said another. "He's coming home. Past performance means a lot in horse races and trials. Sammy's definitely with the government, but I'm counting on him not being too credible. He killed a lot of people. Him turning around may be the best thing to happen to Gotti."

Sam Bull: Rat in Shining Armor?

Salvatore "Sammy Bull" Gravano may be a lying rat to John Gotti and a key witness for federal prosecutors in Brooklyn, but the feds across the river in Manhattan hope Gravano will be a white knight for them.

"Gang Land" hears that Manhattan federal prosecutors hope Gravano, Gotti's former underboss, can help them revive a racketeering and drug case against a Brooklyn-based Sicilian faction of the Gambino crime family.

The case, which is in danger of falling apart, stems from a 1988 arrest of a dozen reputed drug dealers at a Bensonhurst nightclub that allegedly served as the headquarters for reputed Gotti capo Giovanni "John" Gambino and his brother Giuseppe (Joseph).

The case has taken many turns, mostly bad for the government, including the acquittal of four defendants at one trial and the government's branding of its key informer in the case, William Kane, as a liar.

Now, the witness who was supposed to replace Kane—Giovanni "John" Zarbano—has accused FBI agents and federal prosecutors Andrew McCarthy and Frances Fragos of pressuring him to "testify falsely" against the Gambino brothers.

Zarbano, whose cooperation led to the inclusion of four murders in the case and the disqualification of a defense lawyer, says prosecutors tried to get him to lie to corroborate another witness's story and to involve John Gambino in drug deals and murders he did not know about.

"It's a fascinating development, consistent with what we believe to be the truth," said lawyer Charles Carnesi, who was disqualified from the trial by Judge Peter Leisure on information supplied by Zarbano that is now suspect.

Zarbano's lawyer, Howard Jacobs, told "Gang Land" that Carnesi wants to question Zarbano about the prosecutors. McCarthy could not be reached; Fragos said she would submit a response to Leisure as soon as possible, but declined other comment.

For years, Gravano and the Gambinos were virtually neighbors; Gravano's base of operations was in Bensonhurst at Tali's Lounge on 18th Avenue, the same street that was home to the Caffe Giardina, the Sicilian-faction nightclub operated by the Gambino brothers.

Since Gotti took over the crime family, Gravano and the Gambinos have often been spotted at each others' clubs, but some law enforcement officials doubt Gravano will be much help to the Manhattan case.

"They're on the same block, but their clubs are worlds apart," said one investigator.

Law enforcement sources, however, said McCarthy and Fragos are interested in talking to Gravano about a murder he's revealed to the FBI. In doing so, Gravano implicated himself, Giuseppe Gambino, and Carnesi's client, co-defendant Lorenzo Mannino, in the killing.

"I would not be surprised," said Carnesi. "You expose one liar and they plug in another one, like the proverbial boy in the dike."

———

The doors to the cells of two of the most prolific killers in gangland history appeared to clang shout forever last week when an appeals court affirmed the convictions of Joseph Testa and Anthony Senter.

Testa and Senter were members of a Gambino family crew that pillaged New York for nearly a decade before a federal strike force led by former Manhattan prosecutor Walter Mack snared them in a massive racketeering case.

The case was ultimately divided into two trials; Testa and Senter were acquitted in the first, which featured former Gambino boss Paul Castellano as a co-defendant, but were convicted in the second of several murders and sentenced to life.

The two trials brought one of the longest federal investigations ever to an end. They were bedeviled by many dramatic events, including the murder of Castellano during the first, and the heart attack death of the lead defendant in the second.

The leader of the mob crew, Roy DeMeo, was murdered before the trials began. The FBI has said that the DeMeo crew is suspected of killing 200 people from the early 1970s to the early 1980s.

While the convictions of Testa, Senter, and four other crew members were affirmed, the appeals court set aside the fraud convictions of two lesser defendants, Wayne and Judith Hellman, on grounds they should have been tried separately.

FEBRUARY 4, 1992

Doing In Dapper Don from the Grave

John Gotti, who is accused of ordering or approving 11 mob killings since December 16, 1985, may be undone by the ghost of a mobster whose murder he had nothing to do with.

Edward Lino, a Bonanno associate said to be "made" by Gotti after he allegedly took over the Gambino crime family, was killed as he sat in his 1990 Mercedes parked in Sheepshead Bay, Brooklyn, on November 8, 1990.

Salvatore "Sammy Bull" Gravano, who has not hesitated to link Gotti to murders, says Gotti had nothing to do with Lino's killing, but did have a lot to do with bribing a juror who helped get him acquitted of heroin trafficking a few months before his death. Lino's killing remains unsolved.

After a four-week trial, Lino and his co-defendants were jubilant when the jury acquitted them—in less than 90 minutes—of charges they supplied heroin to Gene Gotti, Angelo Ruggiero, and other Gambino mobsters in 1982.

"Eight years we were with this. It's the end of a horrible nightmare," said Lino, who along with co-defendants Giuseppe "Joe" LoPresti and Gerlando Sciascia, whistled and applauded the jurors as they left the courtroom.

"Thank you very much. God bless you," said LoPresti, a reputed Montreal mobster who allegedly was taped discussing large quantities of heroin, cocaine, and Quaaludes he supplied to Gotti, Ruggiero, and others.

Truth is, the case was weakened a great deal when the trial judge ruled out tapes referring to coke or Quaaludes. The first vote was 9–3 for acquittal, said one juror. And, as one defense lawyer, Paul Bergman, recalled, his colleague "Ben Brafman destroyed their expert witness" about the meaning of the hard-to-hear heroin-dealing tapes that remained in the case.

But, as prosecutor John Gleeson stated yesterday, to the agreement of Judge I. Leo Glasser, Gotti can be convicted of juror bribery even if he tried to pay off a juror and the conduit—who "was in fact, ripping (Gotti) off"—kept the cash.

In 1982, Lino was making a very good living dealing drugs and did not want to be "made," because then-Gambino boss Paul Castellano was so opposed to drug dealing that an infraction called for the death penalty.

"What do I need it for, I'm gonna get myself killed," said Lino in the bugged basement of Ruggiero's home, adding that he might feel differently if "Johnny becomes the boss."

Sources said that following the execution of Castellano, Lino was true to his word, and became an important mobster for Gotti, so important that Gotti, in the words of Gleeson, "did, in fact, bribe a juror" in Lino's case.

So far, said Gleeson, the FBI has not identified the tainted juror, but has identified the juror Gotti allegedly bribed to win a racketeering acquittal in 1987 that catapulted the so-called Dapper Don to Teflon Don.

There's a little bit of larceny in every reporter's heart … at least the ones who are any good at all.

But to call us petty thieves, safecrackers, and aiders and abettors seems a little much, even for Judge Glasser, who has indicated a bias against the press that goes back to 1941, when as a young reporter, his city editor at the *Journal American* had staffers steal bottles of milk from stoops to try and find germs in them.

Yesterday, in an apparent reference to a *Daily News* exclusive story that reported that prosecutors believe Gotti and Gravano were together in a parked car near the Castellano murder site, Glasser "wondered" whether reporters who based the story on information from people *he* ordered not to discuss the case, could be charged with aiding and abetting the crime of contempt of court.

Referring to reporters from four newspapers who found documents marked "submitted under seal" publicly filed and used them to write stories upping Gotti's alleged murder victims to 11, Glasser said it was like cashing a check received by mistake or cracking a "symbolic safe around the documents."

Presiding over the racketeering trial of Gotti has been an awesome task, one that has meant difficult rulings about pretrial detention, lawyer disqualifications, and juror anonymity and sequestration.

"Gang Land" wonders whether Glasser really meant what he said. Or was he merely venting frustration similar to that of reporters who often feel prosecutors, defense lawyers, and judges conspire to make covering the Gotti trial more difficult than it should be.

MARCH 3, 1992

It's a Day of See or Be Seen

F. Lee Bailey was seated in the front row yesterday, squeezed in with familiar faces from the John Gotti support group: Peter Gotti, Jack D'Amico, and Joseph De-Cicco.

New York FBI boss James Fox and supervisor Bruce Mouw, the boss of the FBI's Gambino squad, were seated two rows behind.

And in the row between was Joseph D'Angelo, a young sandy-haired Staten Island man said by a very interested spectator to be "almost an adopted son to Sammy"—Salvatore "Sammy Bull" Gravano, the reason why everyone was packing this particular Brooklyn federal courtroom.

Yesterday was unlike any previous day in the history of the Mafia in New York or the United States—an underboss would testify against his boss, in this case, John Gotti.

Gravano would break *omerta*, the vow of silence, and his Mafia soul would burn like the picture of the saint that Paul Castellano set afire in Gravano's hand when Castellano "made" him a member of the Gambino crime family in 1976.

Despite the public reasons they uttered, Bailey, the two FBI bosses and nearly all the other spectators were there to see and hear Sammy.

For a time, D'Angelo was squeezed into the first row, on the aisle, where Gravano would be sure to spot him as soon as he took the witness stand.

D'Angelo's position was so obvious that at the request of the prosecutors, Judge I. Leo Glasser ordered D'Angelo out of the first row.

"Your honor," complained U.S. Attorney Andrew Malony, "he's there for one reason, to intimidate and try to make Mr. Gravano perhaps clam up."

Several hours later, after the prosecution called a surprise witness to Castellano's homicide, after some shouting between the judge and the defense lawyers about it, and after lunch, Gravano took the witness stand.

In his two hours on the stand, Gravano did not disappoint his FBI sponsors; D'Angelo did not disappoint his sponsors, whoever they were.

Shortly after Gravano gave his age, 46; the ages of his children, 19 and 16, and his education, eighth grade, D'Angelo, who was wearing a gray-and-white pullover sweater, stood up and slowly made his way down the aisle, and, even more slowly, walked out of the courtroom.

D'Angelo, not much taller than Gravano, had been sitting on his leg before that, but between the complement of suits in the first spectator row and the eight FBI agents seated in front of them, was not doing too well—if intimidation was his game.

Gravano followed him with his eyes as D'Angelo left the courtroom. Moments later, when he returned, Gravano's eyes followed him to his seat. Still, Gravano continued on his mission, to satisfy his current bosses in hopes of possibly getting out of prison, alive.

That would be a marked contrast to the fate of Joseph "Joe Piney" Armone, who was buried yesterday after being waked at the same Brooklyn funeral home where Frank DeCicco, Gotti's first underboss, was laid out when he was blown up and killed in 1986.

Since Christmas 1987—when Armone was convicted of racketeering and opted for federal prison rather than denounce the Mafia—until last week when he died of natural causes at 74, Armone had been in federal prison.

Along with Gravano, Gotti, and DeCicco, Armone was a member of "the fist," the Gambino mobsters Gravano said plotted for more than eight months to kill Castellano before they succeeded a few days before Christmas in 1985.

Armone, like the current underboss sitting next to Gotti, Frank "Frankie Loc" LoCascio, was "made" before the "books were closed" by Mafia bosses in 1957 after a nationwide conclave in upstate Apalachin, N.Y., was raided by the law.

Back then, mobsters, even those like Joe Piney who occasionally dabbled in drugs, were more aware of the Mafia tradition than Gravano ever was, according to his testimony.

Yesterday, after Gravano had testified that he couldn't get "made" because the books were closed from 1957 to 1975, Prosecutor John Gleeson asked: "Did you ever learn a reason for that?"

"No," said Gravano.

Gleeson, who looked somewhat surprised by the response, pressed with two follow up questions, but realized that Gravano had mastered neither books nor Mafia tradition while he was growing up in Bensonhurst, Brooklyn.

Give Sammy a Grammy
for Song

For an eighth-grade dropout, Sammy Bull Gravano has more than held his own, parrying the biting questions of high-priced defense lawyer Albert Krieger during his cross-examination at John Gotti's murder and racketeering trial.

And yesterday, he held his own with his former boss, staring down Gotti's killing eyes in the first extended eye contact between the former friends and associates since Gravano took the witness stand last week.

At that point, Krieger was searching for a transcript of a conversation the two mobsters had on December 13, 1989, one day after Gotti ripped Gravano in a lengthy discussion with co-defendant Frank "Frankie Loc" Locascio.

It was the first time Gravano allowed himself the luxury of expressing visible anger toward his former boss, an unmistakable sign his confidence has reached the saturation point.

By the end of the day, shortened by the death of a juror's father, Gravano's confidence had turned dangerously close to

arrogance and contempt as Krieger badgered him about his prior testimony about the plot to kill Paul Castellano.

Earlier, Krieger focused Gravano on the murder of Robert "DeeBee" DiBernardo and asked if it weren't true that Gravano had assumed control over Teamsters Local 282 "only after DiBernardo was killed."

"No," said Gravano.

Gravano listened, and read along patiently, as Krieger read from a December 12, 1989, conversation in which Gotti bad-mouthed Gravano to Locascio, complaining how his underboss had gotten control of 282 President Robert Sasso after DiBernardo's murder.

When he concluded reading that conversation, Krieger moved to one the following day between Gotti and Gravano and asked if they were talking about "what took place on December 12. Right?"

"No," said Gravano, again looking toward Gotti, "I don't know what took place on December 12 until I read these transcripts and heard the tape."

As Krieger read a transcript of a December 13 conversation and tried to imply that Gravano and Gotti were talking about the previous day's conversation, Gravano said he didn't "know nothing about that conversation he had with Frankie on December 12."

As Gotti frowned and shook his head back and forth in disagreement, indicating no, Gravano looked at him and nodded yes, with a knowing look that seemed to say, "I know you're a backstabber."

When Krieger gave up that line and moved back to his original theme—one he has advanced throughout his cross, that Gravano plotted and committed each murder for his own personal gain—again Gravano resisted.

"DeeBee was killed, and you got Bobby Sasso, right?"

"No."

"You didn't get Bobby Sasso?"

"I always had Bobby Sasso," insisted Gravano, who thwarted Krieger's efforts so easily that it seemed to go to his head when Krieger moved his questioning to the centerpiece of the case, the Castellano homicide.

Using large fly charts with some 22 reputed mobsters listed in red letters, Krieger checked off their names as Gravano agreed they were aware of the plot to kill Castellano.

When Krieger named Colombo and Luchese mobsters who Gravano said last week were sought out for tacit approval before the killing, Gravano denied it, then became overly combative, even when confronted with his prior words.

After Gravano conceded he had spoken to Luchese leaders Vittorio Amuso and Anthony Casso, Krieger asked if their response was, "They were behind it."

Gravano resisted, saying "their response was we wouldn't have any problems with those people."

When Krieger accurately read his prior remarks, "They were behind it," Gravano said that was the "same answer."

Gravano made similar retorts during Krieger's questions about the Colombo leaders, but by the time he got to the Bonanno family's awareness of the murder plot, Gravano was back on track, disagreeing with Krieger only when he moved afield from his prior testimony.

"I'm not trying to be cute," Gravano said at another point, "I'm trying to focus in on what you're talking about."

"I don't think that it's that important, but go ahead," he said during another exchange.

If Gravano finishes up as well as he's begun, you can bet prosecutors won't reach out for Philip Leonetti, the former Philadelphia underboss who'd add little to the case except for the 10 murders he's committed.

Don't Know Beans About Frank

Frank "Frank Leo" Locascio is a co-defendant at John Gotti's racketeering and murder trial, but he is certainly not Gotti's co-star.

Occasionally, Locascio gets mentioned in the FBI's taped conversations between Gotti and former right-hand-man-in-crime Salvatore "Sammy Bull" Gravano, and once in awhile he even says a few words on the tapes.

Yesterday, for example, in one lengthy conversation that prosecutors say clearly demonstrates efforts by Gotti & Co. to obstruct justice, Locascio was heard muttering words that a maître d' or head waiter might say.

"Heat up them meatballs, Norman," said Locascio, adding seconds later, "What (do) they want?"

That discussion was one of five that took place two flights above the Raventine Social Club in an apartment that was home to a widow of a former Gambino soldier. Locascio was obviously hungry at the time.

In another long, drawn-out discussion among seven alleged co-conspirators that lasted a half-hour and took 42 pages to transcribe, Locascio said fewer than 15 words, doling them out carefully, a few words at a time.

"You got a fireplace?" was one utterance. "Jerking us over" was another. "Customer" and "ex-cop" were two others, and for his grand finale, "Ain't doing nothing together?"

And in another conversation among five persons, just a little shorter than the previous one, Locascio did not make a sound—not even a cough—as Gotti and Gravano quizzed convicted lawyer Michael Coiro about his corrupt source in the Nassau County District Attorney's office.

Locascio's lack of participation was so glaring—the excerpt played for the jury ran 37 pages—that prosecutor Laura Ward found it necessary to remind the jury that Locascio was there during her questioning of the FBI's tape expert.

"Frankie's from the old school, he doesn't say much," said one law enforcement official, in the understatement of the trial.

When prosecutors played several hours of silent FBI videotapes of comings and goings around the Ravenite, Locascio could usually be seen walking and talking with Gotti, Gravano and others, but not heard by the jury, of course.

Locascio is accused of taking part in one of the five murders in the indictment, but during the tapes that have been played so far, Locascio is a heavy listener who says little, if anything, to incriminate himself.

Even in one long conversation in which Gotti says he killed two mobsters for Gravano and was going to kill another who failed to "come in" to see him, Locascio does little more than listen to Gotti rant and rave about Gravano's greed.

In the one murder in which Gravano testified that Locascio played a supporting role, Locascio never said a word as he drove up, opened the car trunk from the inside, and drove away with the body of Robert "DeeBee" DiBernardo.

Under questioning from prosecutor John Gleeson, Gravano said Locascio never volunteered any details about the disposal of the body, and Gravano never asked: "It was none of my business."

Under cross-examination by Anthony Cardinale, Gravano also said Locascio never received any money from two gambling operations and one loan-sharking business allegedly controlled by Gotti.

Locascio lives quietly in the Bronx, raises and trains horses on an upstate New York farm, and has no major convictions.

According to the tapes, however, Locascio was "made" back in the 1950s, when Carlo Gambino was boss, and under Gotti became a capo, acting underboss, and in 1990, the crime family's acting consigliere, or counselor.

Locascio often attends sidebar conferences called by Judge I. Leo Glasser, invariably returning to his seat with a big smile on his face and a thumbs-up gesture to his son and other supporters in the audience.

Yesterday, after one sidebar, before he gave his usual smiling thumbs-up to the audience, he whispered his report to Gotti, who took it all in, then turned to reporters, pointed to Locascio, and said with a smile, "Counselor."

Gotta Give the Don His Due on Gripe

John Gotti has consistently complained that the FBI, the Brooklyn U.S. Attorney's office, and the trial judge have combined to stack the deck against him.

The prosecution rested yesterday in Gotti's murder and racketeering case, and it's pretty hard for "Gang Land" to disagree with the Dapper Don's assessment.

This is not to say that the prosecution did not put forward an overwhelming case against Gotti. The FBI tapes and testimony, most importantly that of Salvatore "Sammy Bull" Gravano—which linked him to 11 murders and much mayhem—were devastating.

However, to "Gang Land" it looks like prosecutors used clever legal games to deprive Gotti and his co-defendant of lawyers that, in hindsight, they had a right to hire. And yesterday, Judge I. Leo Glasser made a ruling that seems fundamentally unfair to the defense.

"Gang Land" takes no issue with Glasser's disqualification of Bruce Cutler. Prosecutors effectively used his taped conversations with Gotti to prove that Gotti was head of a nationwide criminal enterprise. Yesterday, for example, jurors heard Gotti tell Cutler to serve as a "messenger" between the Gambino family and the boss of the New England Mafia family.

When Cutler was disqualified, however, prosecutors stopped Gotti from hiring James LaRossa. Later, they prevented LaRossa's law partner from questioning witnesses on behalf of Gotti's co-defendant, Frank "Frankie Loc" Locascio.

Last August, after Cutler was disqualified from the trial, Gotti personally complained to Glasser that lead prosecutor John Gleeson had also eliminated "Mr. LaRossa, my friend," by subpoenaing him as a witness.

"Ask him, he knows," said Gotti, pointing to Gleeson, when the judge said he had no idea what he was talking about.

Gleeson and Glasser ignored Gotti that day, but a few weeks later, the prosecutor stated that LaRossa "will be a government witness at trial ... an important witness to significant facts."

Gleeson said LaRossa, who represented Gambino boss Paul Castellano when he was killed, would give "particularly significant" testimony about the murder of his client and "Gotti's motive" to kill Castellano.

The prosecution maintained that position until last week when without explanation it dropped plans to call LaRossa, a move that can only be interpreted as a move to keep LaRossa out of the case.

Gleeson, who has refused to discuss the case with reporters, most likely wanted to deny Gotti the tactical advantage of having the attorney for the murder victim representing the man accused of killing him.

Unable to come up with a legal basis for that concern, the government appeared to have invented other ones.

Yesterday, Glasser also refused to allow the defense to reopen its cross-examination of a key eyewitness to the Castellano homicide who identified longtime Gotti pal John Carneglia as one of four one-the-scene shooters.

The witness, Jeffrey Davidson, lied about his reasons for embezzling more the $13,000 from two employers, lied that his convictions were removed from his record, and lied that he had made restitution, according to police records uncovered by the defense.

During his testimony, Davidson said he stole the money to pay for medical care for his wife and newborn child and his wife's ailing grandmother when the defense lawyers blindly asked whether it was for a drug or gambling problem.

In fact, Davidson told police he stole money to cover an expensive honeymoon and to cover his stock market losses.

Since the defense lawyers were sandbagged to begin with and not given any background information about Davidson before he took the stand, it seems only fair that the defense should now be able to test his credibility again.

Glasser said no, however, on grounds there was "no substantial difference" in the two versions because there was "no further criminal activity" by Davidson.

No difference between stock market losses and family medical bills?

Gravano's decision to switch sides forced Gotti to choose a new underboss for his crime family and, for a time, he tried to keep it in his personal family, according to law enforcement sources.

Believe or not, Gotti threw up some trial balloons on how the family capos would be answering to 28-year-old John "Junior" Gotti, before naming a reliable old-timer who's pushing 80, Giuseppe "Joe" Arcuri, to the post.

Not only is Arcuri popular among other geriatric gangsters, he poses no threat to Gotti.

Finally, Judge Leo Roars Loud

For nine weeks, Brooklyn Federal Judge I. Leo Glasser, who is presiding over John Gotti's murder and racketeering trial, has looked like a steaming pressure cooker whose lid is about to pop.

Yesterday, Glasser's lid finally went into orbit.

The much anticipated explosion happened during the rebuttal summation of lead prosecutor John Gleeson, when defense lawyer Anthony Cardinale rose from his seat and said in his best Hopalong Cassidy imitation, "Whoa, whoa, whoa."

"Excuse me, Mr. Cardinale," said Glasser, his finger pointing menacingly, his body rising, his voice trembling.

"EXCUSE ME," Glasser shouted as Cardinale remained standing and objected that Gleeson had unfairly accused him of inventing evidence.

Sounding like a stern headmaster whose charges have finally bested his patience, Glasser intoned, "SIT DOWN. SIT DOWN. SIT DOWN!"

Two hours later, when U.S. Attorney Andrew Maloney shocked the entire courtroom by telling the jurors they had a right to be afraid to convict Gotti, Glasser was the calmest person in the room, his steam already released.

Glasser, a former law professor, seemed to be thinking how to prevent a mistrial that would force another trial and more confrontations with Gotti, his supporters, lawyers, prosecutors, sketch artists, and, maybe worst of all, the nagging presence of the media.

"Sustained. I'll ask the jury to disregard the last remarks," said Glasser, who later denied a motion for a mistrial and indicated he was likely to instruct jurors in detail to disregard Maloney's inflammatory statement.

Throughout the trial, however, the pressure cooker on the bench has been close to exploding on numerous occasions.

He has cited Cardinale for contempt, threatened to banish Gotti to a basement cell for gesturing and otherwise carrying on at the defense table, likened reporters to thieves and safecrackers, and warned sketch artists he would confiscate their work if they drew jurors even as unrecognizable stick figures.

He has also had harsh words for defense lawyer John Mitchell and expressed anger and frustration with the prosecution.

On Friday, for example, during a discussion about 4-by-8-foot charts Gleeson used during his closing argument, Glasser expressed anger with Mitchell, who complained that the charts would block the defendants' sight lines and asked the judge to "insure that we at all times are able to view the jury."

"Mr. Mitchell, excuse me," said Glasser, with pained agitation, adding that he couldn't "insure" anything, but "should the occasion arise, *sir*, when you are not able to see the jury, *please* call it to my attention."

But Glasser, who said he hadn't seen the charts before, turned his wrath toward Gleeson. "As a matter of fact," he said sarcastically, "it would have been helpful if I had, and we could have discussed this problem before this morning. What would have been a good idea is to take a video photo of those charts and put them on the screen. That might have been a good idea."

A few minutes later, as Gleeson began unfurling his charts in front of the jury box, Glasser pointedly told him: "Can you move that easel, perhaps, back there?" motioning toward the spectator section.

"Let's try it. Move the easel back there to the end of that (the prosecution) table. Move it back there. Try it," Glasser insisted sharply.

The judge doesn't like it when he thinks lawyers think he's angry. In fact, he gets angry about it.

On the second day of star witness Salvatore "Sammy Bull" Gravano's testimony, Glasser went to great lengths to deny an assertion from Mitchell that he was angry with him.

"One of the things I resent terribly is the kind of observation that I am being angry," Glasser said angrily.

"You are, sir," Mitchell replied.

"I am not angry," the judge answered back. "I am being as affirmative as I know how to be. Period."

That's the way Glasser ends a lot of his statements. Period.

Last Hurrah: Still All in the Family

John Gotti made it clear he was still the Godfather yesterday.

And he did it the way *the boss* always does it, by making others do his dirty work.

Although Gotti said nothing in court, the words of his consigliere and the riotous and bush-league actions by his son's mob crew left no doubt about the convicted don's intentions for the future of the Gambino crime family.

When Judge I. Leo Glasser asked whether he had anything to say, the defiant don smirked and shook his head no, as if to say, "You're not worth my time."

In court, Frank Locascio was Gotti's designated hitter, and he spoke his lines perfectly: "I am guilty of being a good friend of John Gotti. If there was more men like John Gotti, we would have a better country."

Outside the courthouse, Michael McLaughlin, who doubles as a bodyguard/chauffeur for reputed capo John "Junior" Gotti, manned a bullhorn to lead rowdy demonstrators in their chant for justice: "FREE JOHN GOTTI."

Gotti's son-in-law Carmine Agnello wasn't spotted, but a flatbed tow truck bearing the name of his Queens salvage company circled the courthouse honking its horn, leaving no doubt the demonstration was a Gotti family affair.

Steven Kaplan, a reputed member of Junior Gotti's crew, also was seen chanting "FREE JOHN GOTTI." Two years ago, Kaplan and Junior Gotti were arrested with six others for pummeling two men whose dates spurned advances by the wannabe gangsters at a Long Island bar. The assault charges were dismissed later when the victims suddenly forgot who hit them.

Junior's crew members Anthony Amoroso and George "Fat Georgie" DiBello, who runs Junior's Our Friends Social Club in South Ozone Park, were handing out placards and keeping up with a new chant: "What did he get? RAW DEAL. What do we want? FAIR TRIAL."

Norman Dupont, the former bartender and current caretaker of Gotti's Ravenite Social Club in Little Italy, was there to lend his support. Dupont, who was arrested in a brawl with cops outside the Ravenite last fall, didn't do anything yesterday to earn a follow-up arrest, at least nothing that anyone saw.

When the mini-riot ended with one car overturned, four damaged, and seven cops injured, seven residents of Howard Beach and South Ozone Park were arrested on assault and riot charges.

One arrested demonstrator, Richard Valley, 20, is an associate of Junior Gotti who frequents his social club, and another, Joseph Gotti, 22, is Junior's cousin. A third, John Gurino, is a Howard Beach deli owner whose acquittal of murder in 1984 earned his then-unknown defense lawyer, Bruce Cutler, a spot next to John Gotti.

It's a safe bet that Gotti will never take credit for yesterday's affair.

Nothing but bad things happened to the only other New York Mafia family whose flamboyant and publicity-minded boss authorized and encouraged protests.

Joe Colombo, who organized demonstrations outside the FBI building 20 years ago, was gunned down at a massive Colombus Circle rally of the Italian American Civil Rights League he founded.

Gotti's actions also resemble the efforts by Colombo's successor, Carmine Persico, to run the Colombo crime family from federal prison for the eventual benefit of his son, Alphonse.

The bloody war between Persico supporters and those loyal to acting boss Victor Orena has resulted in at least eight deaths and many injuries to rival hoods as well as innocent bystanders.

Gotti's ego has apparently made him decide to ignore his promise to step down as boss if he were convicted and sentenced to a long jail term. This decision—especially if it entails the ascension of Junior to the top spot—will surely be resisted by more traditional Gambino gangsters.

The resulting warfare could dwarf the Colombo family's internecine struggle, because the Gambinos are three times bigger and at least as violent. According to federal prosecutors, Gotti has a penchant for violence. He was convicted of ordering 11 murders from 1985 to 1990.

Stir-Ring Trouble from Jail: Don's Still the Boss

Running a crime family from prison is not a simple matter, but it can be done.

John Gotti, for example, is in Marion, the Illinois hellhole of federal prisons, but he's still boss of the Gambino crime family.

Gotti can make only two 15-minute collect phone calls a month and is allowed five seven-hour noncontact visits by up to three people at a time per month, but he's still running the largest, richest, and most powerful mob family in the country.

Granted, he's been there only three weeks, but a look at the Colombo mob shows that a boss—if his troops are loyal—can effectively wage a bloody war from jail.

And Gotti has every intention of maintaining control, according to law enforcement and underworld sources.

Since the Colombo war erupted in November, 11 persons, including two bystanders, have been killed—mainly on the streets of Brooklyn—and 16 have been wounded in the battle for the 100-man crime family.

"Gang Land" sources on both sides of the law say the two sides in the Colombo war are trying to arrange a lasting peace, but they caution that the current ceasefire could end without notice.

The uneasy truce is only one indication that Carmine "Junior" Persico—a Marion graduate still looking at 100-plus years—may be winning his war with Victor "Little Vic" Orena, who's been in jail the last few months.

For conventioneers, and other newcomers to "Gang Land," Persico wants the family to revert to his son Alphonse, a capo. Alphonse was convicted of racketeering with his dad in 1986 and is set to get out of prison next year. (The elder Persico got 39 years in 1986 and 100 more the following year.)

But Orena, whom Persico named acting boss in 1988, decided that he wanted the family for himself.

Early on, Orena loyalists had a decided edge, with the killings of Persico soldiers Rosario "Black Sam" Nastasa and Henry "Hank the Bank" Smurra. But Persico's gunmen have since killed key Orena moneymaker Nicholas "Nicky Black"

Grancio, the only capo to die in the war. A former Teamsters Union official, Grancio was hired by the Waldbaum's supermarket chain as a labor specialist shortly before he was killed.

And lately, the legal system has been much harsher on the Orena faction.

Vincent DeMartino, a suspected shooter in the Nastasa and Smurra rubouts, got four years for violating probation and faces 10 more for a federal gun conviction. Gabriel Scianna received 21 months for his federal rap, while Orena loyalist Michael Spataro, who was arrested with them, still awaits trial.

By contrast, Robert Zambardi, a suspected shooter in rubout attempts of several Orena supporters, was acquitted at his federal loan-sharking trial.

Meanwhile, Orena and reputed capo Pasquale "Patsy" Amato are in prison awaiting trial in September on murder and racketeering charges that could land them lifetime reservations in places like Marion.

Law enforcement and underworld sources say the Persico faction will get a big boost when Persico's long-time friend and enforcer, Hugh "Mac" McIntosh, is released from federal prison later this year.

"He's expected to bolster morale," said Zambardi's lawyer, Frank Lopez, who once employed McIntosh as a paralegal. "I hope Mac still has the gift of persuasion for which he is noted."

Wife Who Sits & Waits—in Jail

Rita Bologna always knew her husband wasn't the most faithful wiseguy a woman could love, but they raised three children who gave them three grandchildren.

So, after a divorce, many years apart and a second marriage that failed, she moved back in with him.

Now, two years later, the 51-year-old grandmother is caught in a prosecutorial power play, held in jail, like her former husband—Salvatore "Sally Dogs" Lombardi, a reputed mob capo—without bail on major league heroin-trafficking charges that could keep her there for life.

The Manhattan District Attorney's office would like her to testify against him, or for him to plead guilty, and it's playing legal hardball against both.

The judge in the case, a former drug prosecutor for the Manhattan District Attorney's office, seems to be pitching particularly high hard ones.

"Gang Land" is not shilling for Lombardi; a reputed Genovese capo with a number of dead men on his resumé, and a federal drug conviction on his rap sheet.

"Gang Land" also is not shilling for Bologna if—always a big IF—she is convicted of scheming to ship heroin to New York, last year from Spain, this year from Boston.

What's troubling, however, is that Bologna has been *remanded* without bail, and has spent time hospitalized at Rikers Island, where she has been treated for recurring asthma, while three of her husband's reputed mob co-defendants are free on bail awaiting trial for the same charges.

The men, with ties to the Genovese family allegedly carried heroin here from Spain and raised $120,000 to buy a cache in Boston. They're associates of Lombardi, not his paramour.

One is also awaiting trial on federal heroin charges in Brooklyn. All three were released on $1 million bail that was set by Supreme Court Justice Leslie Snyder over the objections of the Manhattan District Attorney's office.

Snyder, an excellent judge is very tough on crime and declined to discuss the case.

A few days after the arrests, lawyer Judd Burstein charged the district attorney's office with "seeking some sort of pressure or tactical advantage" by detaining Bologna and pleaded that his client be released on her own recognizance.

"She has aunts, uncles, nieces, nephews, brothers, and sisters in the community. She has serious asthmatic problems. I see no reason to detain a woman with these kinds of roots, this kind of physical condition, and this weak a case against her," Burstein argued in court.

"It's not a sexist argument, is it?" chided Snyder. "Do you argue that it would be okay to detain a man in this position but not a woman?"

"Absolutely not," responded Burstein, adding that, at worst, his client may have been present when illegal activity took place but was unaware of it. "The 'mere presence' defense was perhaps invented for this situation."

After hearing counterarguments and additional secret arguments later from prosecutors that Bologna was intimately involved in Lombardi's alleged drug dealing and would flee if released, Snyder ordered Bologna held without bail.

Transcripts of the secret proceeding, which Snyder allowed because prosecutors asserted the information could jeopardize ongoing probes, were recently unsealed. Burstein charges that Snyder was "misled by what can only be characterized as a fraudulent representation" by prosecutor Eric Herschmann.

In court papers, Burstein said an examination of nine boxes of electronic surveillance logs and documents seized by prosecutors showed that Herschmann made many "false claims."

These included his statement that Bologna signed "a slew" of $9,000 and $9,500 checks that Lombardi used to pay drug-dealing expenses, that she paid rent and other bills for a Lombardi drug partner, and that they kept $350,000 in their children's names and $150,000 in another account.

"In my view the DA's office is attempting to gain some unfair advantage against Mr. Lombardi by unfairly continuing to incarcerate Ms. Bologna," Burstein said yesterday.

Herschmann has not yet filed his response and could not be reached for comment.

A high-level source in the district attorney's office conceded that Herschmann misspoke about the "slew of checks" but insisted that all of Burstein's other claims "were a matter of interpretation."

"This is standard stuff, attacking the prosecutor when you don't have the facts, but 95 percent of what (Herschmann) said was accurate and we still think we're on pretty solid ground and that the judge did the right thing," said the source.

Lombardi, after allegedly dragging his former wife into a drug indictment, may have finally done the right thing by her.

In an affidavit, Lombardi said Bologna had no "knowledge about my business dealings, whether legitimate, or as the government alleges, illicit," and would testify to that effect, if she had a separated trial.

If Snyder wished more details, he added, Lombardi would give "the substance of the testimony" at a secret *in camera* session—like the one the prosecutors used to keep the mother of his children in jail.

Is It the Shoes?
Only He Knows

The economy is so bad these days that top mobsters are looking to get their sandals wholesale.

And they're willing to talk about it.

Take the recent testimony of Joseph "Joe Butch" Corrao, a reputed Gambino capo charged with racketeering and bribery along with former Detective William Peist, the Gambino family's alleged mole in the police intelligence division.

Corrao allegedly was overheard passing along secret information he got from Peist to John Gotti on an FBI bug at the Ravenite Social Club. He is free on bail—with some restrictions, such as not frequenting any Gambino family social clubs.

At a hearing where prosecutors sought to modify his bail conditions, Corrao testified that when he stopped his jeep outside the Veterans and Friends Social Club in Bensonhurst on June 7, he wasn't there to see James "Jimmy Brown" Failla, he was looking for bargain on shoes, specifically white sandals.

Prosecutors had cited Corrao's appearance at the club, and another at the Hawaiian Moonlighters Social Club on Mulberry Street a month earlier, and asked that he be placed under house arrest except for visits to his lawyer or doctor.

Failla, one of three capos said by FBI informants to be running the family for Gotti these days, may have been inside, but Corrao told Brooklyn Federal Judge I. Leo Glasser he never went inside.

"I was simply riding down the street past the Veterans and Friends Club when I noticed someone I know who sells shoes at a discount price, who I know as 'Paulie Shoes,' to tell him that I was looking to buy some shoes," Corrao said.

"Paulie, do me a favor; see if you can get some white sandals for me," Corrao recalled saying to the street shoe salesman.

Corrao admitted talking to Louis "Louie Fats" Astuto as he "was looking through the (shoe) catalog," but noted that the reputed Gambino soldier is not on his list of restricted persons.

Besides, Corrao said in an affidavit, Astuto had merely "walked over to say hello and asked me how I was feeling."

Whether Astuto discussed Gambino family business with Corrao is conjecture, but Louie Fats surely asked how Corrao was feeling because Corrao's health is no laughing matter.

Corrao, who has severe diabetes, undergoes dialysis treatment three days a week for kidney disease that has reached a crisis stage. Last year, his body rejected a kidney donated by a sister. He is on a waiting list for another kidney transplant.

In court papers, lawyer James LaRossa has asked that Corrao be severed from the case, arguing that the dialysis treatment, which Corrao receives Monday, Wednesday, and Friday mornings, would make him unable to attend trial those days since he needs bed rest after treatment.

Prosecutors concede the legitimacy of Corrao's illness, but propose that he receive treatment Tuesday, Thursday, and Saturday afternoons, which would allow three full days and two mornings of trial each week.

Glasser has not ruled on the severance issue and refused to restrict Corrao to his house, even after prosecutor John Gleeson said Corrao had been spotted during several surveillances around the city that day.

Glasser noted he had seen so many video surveillance tapes "that sometimes I feel I'm an honorary member" of the Gambino crime family. He told Corrao to stay away from the outside of social clubs and let him off with a stern warning.

"What I'm going to say to you, I'm going to say to you just once," Glasser said. "In the future, I will detain you at the MCC (Metropolitan Correctional Center) or some other appropriate facility. The fact that you have physical problems will not deter me."

A tough law-and-order judge has refused to reconsider her decision that the ex-wife of a Genovese capo with no prior arrests should remain in jail without bail while several of her co-defendants with prior convictions are free on bail.

In upholding her ruling, Supreme Court Justice Leslie Snyder vilified defense lawyer Judd Burstein for making unwarranted "vicious personal attacks" against prosecutor Eric Herschmann in arguing for his client's release.

Snyder mildly criticized Herschmann for two "mistakes" in his recitation of relevant facts about Rita Bologna's alleged role in her ex-husband's drug business but said the mistakes were "a small part of the broader picture."

Snyder said tapes and other evidence appears "overwhelming" that Bologna was involved in a drug conspiracy run by Salvatore "Sally Dogs" Lombardi and that she "has every incentive to flee" if released on bail.

Burstein will appeal. "As we will allege in our papers," said Burstein, "Judge Snyder did not provide us with anything that remotely resembled a fair hearing …. One of the issues we will raise is whether the judge had unauthorized and improper *ex parte* communications with the prosecutor."

PART 3

The Mid-1990s

With John Gotti in Marion Federal Penitentiary, the feds started picking off some of his top wiseguys and set their sights on his handpicked acting boss, son John A. "Junior" Gotti, as superstar turncoat Sammy Bull Gravano got a sweet five-year sentence and freedom.

Meanwhile, the feds went after the Colombo mobsters who survived their bloody war, and a gaggle of Genovese gangsters were busted for corrupting the San Gennaro festival as their legendary leader, Vincent "Chin" Gigante, continued seeing shrinks and ducking his inevitable trial on racketeering and murder charges.

"Gang Land" kept on trucking. There were columns about *Lefty Guns*, the *Barber of Brooklyn*, and *Ray's Pizza*. The column came to the defense of a federal judge in Brooklyn and tweaked another in Manhattan for telling lies from the bench.

From September 1995 through June 1996, "Gang Land" spent an academic year of study at Stanford University as a John S. Knight Fellow. Going away to college ended the column's run in the *News*, but gave way to an even longer run on the World Wide Web.

JANUARY 5, 1993

Theories Abound in
Scarpa Slay Try

Gregory Scarpa, the Colombo capo with AIDS, was ambushed last week by mob rivals who discovered he's an FBI informer.

That's what "Gang Land" hears from usually reliable underworld sources who credit a rival Colombo capo with luring the AIDS-stricken capo into a hail of bullets a few blocks from his Dyker Heights, Brooklyn, home.

But, according to current and former law enforcement officials, Scarpa has been an informer for two decades.

Investigators say there may be many reasons, including his suspected informer status, for the most recent Scarpa rubout effort.

Scarpa's lawyer, Joseph Benfante, said the notion Scarpa was shot because he was an informer was "absolutely absurd. He learned his son was in trouble and was shot when he left his house to try and protect his son."

Police and federal authorities have heard this, too.

Supposedly Scarpa's son Joseph, 21, was having a dispute over $500 with "wannabe mobsters minutes before the elder Scarpa was shot in the eye.

But the feds have known for some time that mobsters loyal to acting boss Victor "Little Vic" Orena suspected Scarpa, who remained loyal to jailed Colombo boss Carmine "Junior" Persico, was an informer.

And even Persico had doubts about Scarpa's trustworthiness. During an IRS sting operation 15 years ago, he expressed them when he was asked about Scarpa by an agent pretending to be corrupt.

"We're not too sure about him," said Persico, who reportedly became very certain about Scarpa's loyalty, as well as his abilities with a gun, a year ago, on January 7, 1992.

That day, at the height of the bloody insurrection by Orena followers to oust Persico as the family's "official" boss, capo Nicholas "Nicky Black" Grancio was sitting in his all-terrain vehicle near his social club in Gravesend.

A few minutes earlier, Grancio, who was aligned with Orena, was overheard muttering to associates, "Yeah, we're trying to make peace. We gotta stop all this stupid s--t."

"This one's for Carmine," said a gunman, identified by law enforcement and underworld sources as Scarpa, who stuck a gun behind Grancio's ear and blew his brains out.

Grancio is the only capo to die in the war, which has claimed at least 12 lives, including two bystanders.

Law enforcement sources said Scarpa picked out Grancio for execution after he failed to locate his main target that day, Alfonse "Funzi" D'ambrosio, an Orena loyalist with whom Scarpa has had a long-running feud.

"One day, they're each driving down Avenue U in different directions," an underworld source told "Gang Land," "when they see each other and start shooting. They drive a little more, make U-turns and start shooting again when they pass each other."

Neither man was hit in the fusillade, said the source.

Sources on both sides of the law said the man most likely behind the attempted rubout of Scarpa is Orena capo William Cutolo, whom Scarpa is accused of conspiring to kill in June.

Cutolo, who's called Wild Bill by the feds and Billy Fingers by the mob, was the target of an aborted hit by Scarpa last year, according to conversations that were picked up in the home and car of Joseph "Joey Brains" Ambrosino, a Scarpa crew member who was arrested in June and became a cooperating witness.

———

Orena may be the acting Colombo boss, and Pasquale "Patsy" Amato may be a capo but they're "low-level hoodlums" to the federal judge who presided over Orena's trial and began picking a jury yesterday for Amato's trial.

"This is not John Gotti, these are just low-level hoodlums" said Brooklyn Federal Judge Jack Weinstein as he rejected a request by prosecutors for an anonymous and sequestered jury for the men at a pre-trial proceeding.

The Colombo mob may well be merely "a gang," a derogatory term Weinstein often used during the trial, but they sure used some pretty sophisticated means to track down rival mobsters they wanted to murder.

When Orena was arrested at his home, along with body bags and a small arsenal, the FBI seized telephone toll records of mobsters and their girlfriends, as well as reverse directories that can be used to locate addresses.

Amato is charged with taking part in the 1989 murder of Colombo mobster Thomas Ocera. He was severed from Orena's trial after prosectors conceded they had little evidence linking him to the Colombo war.

———

Bruce Cutler's New Year's Eve session before Federal Judge Thomas Platt was cut short and put over until Thursday because of stomach problems—not his or the judge's, but his lawyer's.

Halfway through his arguments why criminal contempt charges against Cutler should be thrown out, Fred Haffetz took ill and Platt agreed to an adjournment.

Cutler said there has been a "tremendous show of support from lawyers all over the country" who plan to attend a fund-raiser for him at Tavern on the Green later this month. "I'm very happy about it."

Stickup Plan Got Stuck: Couple's Spree Short, Not Smart

Thomas and Rosemarie Uva should have known better.

Both were ex cons. Both had seen *Goodfellas.*

And to make matters worse, they rented an apartment in Ozone Park, Queens, where John Gotti and his brothers became infamous as operators of the Bergin Hunt and Fish Club and Our Friends Social Club.

From last summer until Christmas Eve, however, the Uvas behaved like a very dumb Bonnie and Clyde, holding up mob social clubs like the Hawaiian Moonlighters in Little Italy and the Veterans and Friends in Bensonhurst, Brooklyn.

These are the private domains of some pretty big mob capos: Joseph "Joe Butch" Corrao and James "Jimmy Brown" Failla.

Just like the banks of the Roaring '20s, before armed guards and video surveillance cameras, the men in the social clubs on Mulberry Street and 86th Street seemed like easy marks.

So did the men who regularly hang out at two no-name clubs two blocks from the Veterans and Friends Social Club on Bath Avenue.

After all, the patrons usually have thousands of dollars in their pockets and never carry hardware when they conduct their business in the intimacy of their clubs.

And these men, for the most part, are criminals who would *never* call the cops.

So with Thomas, 28, brandishing an Uzi submachine gun, and his 21-year-old bride/moll working as a wheel woman, the Uvas began a short career of ripping off mob social clubs shortly after Thomas got out of jail in May.

In almost every case, the doors of the storefront clubs were open, and Thomas walked in with his weapon out and ordered the men to deposit their cash in a bag and gently hand it over.

On one occasion, according to sources, an annoyed robbery victim warned Uva that he would eventually be found and killed.

"Everybody dies," shrugged Thomas Uva, like a seasoned revolutionary.

When Thomas hit the club a second time, the robbery victims ran out, gave chase and were impressed by Rosemarie's prowess as a getaway driver.

But as most New Yorkers know, guys like Corrao, Failla, George DeCicco, and Anthony Spero have investigative techniques that rival those of the FBI and NYPD.

For the record, Corrao, who faces trial soon on racketeering charges, is proprietor of the Hawaiian Moonlighters; Failla, a former chauffeur to Carl Gambino, operates the Veterans and Friends; DeCicco, brother of slain Gotti underboss Frank DeCicco, runs the Bath Avenue no-name near Bay 13th; and Spero, who owns a nearby car service, operates the no-name near Bay 16th.

And while Corrao, Failla, and DeCicco—all reputed Gambino capos—and Spero, a reputed Bonanno consigliere, agree with many law enforcement officials about the necessity of the death penalty, they don't go along with things like jury trials.

And so, early Christmas Eve, as the Uvas were about to do some last-minute Christmas shopping in Ozone Park, they were executed for the crime of stupidity by assassins who shot them each three times in the head in their Mercury Topaz at the corner of 103rd Avenue and 91st Street.

Law enforcement officials told "Gang Land" they believe the killers "got the right guys."

The Queens District Attorney's office "is investigating the shooting," said Eileen Sullivan, chief of the prosecutor's organized crime and rackets bureau.

Last month, Colombo-mobster-turned-informer Al Quattrache gave testimony that helped convict acting Colombo boss Victor "Little Vic" Orena of murder and racketeering charges and others on murder conspiracy charges.

Under cross-examination, he conceded that he often exaggerated, like the time he said he drove a fork through a loan-shark victim's hand so ferociously that the guy couldn't lift his hand from the table.

Quattrache was never confronted about a statement he made January 20, but "Gang Land" can assure you that, except for some silly reference to a payroll, "Gang Land" would like to think he was telling the truth when he was over-heard commenting about a participant on a CNBC television show he had just seen.

"They just had Jerry Capeci, the *Daily News* writer, he knows more about the f------g Mafia than any Mafia guy I know. We follow him to know what's going on. He gets more information."

"How does he get the information? Wiseguy rats. They're on his payroll. They tell him everything. He knows everything—to the T … (inaudible) about our meetings …."

"The stuff that he prints we did, to the T, he knew. How it was broken up … (inaudible) into the unions."

In His (God)father's Footsteps

It was summertime 1990, and John Gotti, the ultimate family man, was concerned how his oldest son would be able to provide for his budding brood.

Son John A. "Junior" Gotti, a full-fledged Gambino mobster, was certainly not struggling to make ends meet. He owned his own trucking company and got a ton of money from family friends who attended his gala wedding reception at the Helmsley Palace.

Young John and his bride got down to the business of raising a family, and, well, you know how some men feel about grandchildren. The day after he became a grandfather in 1984, the Dapper Don bought his grandson a $20,000 bond. "Second day of his life, the kid has $20,000," said Gotti to a fair-weather friend wearing a wire. "Me, I had two f--n' cents."

The elder Gotti also did what any self-respecting father who was also chief executive officer of any huge conglomerate would do: He decided to make his son an executive of the company—a capo in the Gambino crime family.

He called Frank "Frankie Loc" Locascio and Salvatore "Sammy Bull" Gravano to a top executives–only meeting in an apartment above the Ravenite Social Club in Little Italy and asked if they would recommend young John to be a capo.

The discussion took place long after the FBI removed its bug from the apartment, but according to sources familiar with the conversation, Locascio and Gravano reacted as expected, fighting each other to get the words out first: "Sure." "Great idea, John." "Great choice."

Locascio and Gravano wasted no time. Later that day, they met Junior Gotti and told him that their boss wanted him to be a capo with his own crew.

That night, they took young John and formally presented him to his father.

"This is your new *caporegime*," they said.

Turning to the new capo, "This is your *representante*," they said, using the word that gangsters in Sicily would use to describe the boss.

Then, father and son, *representante* and *caporegime*, embraced.

Later, Locascio and Gravano introduced the young capo to the capos who had the good fortune to be at the Ravenite that evening.

Despite some resentment from fellow capos over his favored-son promotion, young Gotti has surprised many with his staying power. The true test, however, will come if—make that when—his father's conviction is upheld on appeal.

So far, however, he has weathered all criticism, including hot-tempered finger-pointing by supercapo James "Jimmy Brown" Failla, a former chauffeur/body-guard to Carlo Gambino.

In fact, the only black mark on Junior's mob resumé thus far is the unavenged death of Bartholemew "Bobby" Borriello, the former chauffeur/bodyguard for the elder Gotti who was gunned down after joining Junior's crew.

(Bruce Cutler, lawyer and friend of the Gottis, said Junior Gotti, who visits his father regularly, "is an honorable young man loved like his father is, is not part of any mob, and has no black marks.")

Borriello was shot to death in front of his Bensonhurst, Brooklyn home in April 1991 and according to law enforcement and underworld sources, the man who killed him was Preston Geritano, a mob associate and onetime Borriello pal.

The men, who hailed from South Brooklyn, had been feuding, according to "Gang Land" sources, for many years. A few years ago, after Borriello pulled a gun

and fired at Geritano but missed, the Gambino and Genovese families had two high-level sit-downs to iron out the feud and determine which family was responsible for Geritano.

At first, between Genovese underboss Venero "Benny Eggs" Mangano and Gravano, Mangano conceded that Geritano was "with the Gambinos" and that they had right to kill one of their own.

But he asked that Geritano be spared, as a favor. In return, Geritano would be put "on record" as a Genovese associate and "not cause any more trouble."

Soon after, Geritano began "mouthing off" that he was going to retaliate, according to sources familiar with Gravano's statements to the FBI, and Gravano warned Genovese capo Michael Generoso to "get him in line or kill him."

A few months later after Gravano and Gotti had been jailed to await trial for murder and racketeering, Borriello was killed, and Gotti sent word to the Genoveses that he expected Geritano to be killed.

The Genoveses agreed, Gravano reported, but months later, with Geritano still alive, an annoyed Gotti told Gravano, "If they don't do it soon, I'll have my people do it."

At the moment Geritano is apparently still alive but smart enough to make himself scarce.

Lucheses Keep It All in the Family

Along the way, the top members of the Luchese crime family probably watched a lot of James Bond movies or read a book or two about the CIA.

They have moles scattered throughout the law enforcement community. They carry beepers and have a rigid telephone security procedure. They're into disguises, notably beards. And they use a spy-like vocabulary.

For example, they use the term "dry clean" to describe precautions they take to avoid being followed and the term "crystal ball" to refer to a paid law enforcement informer.

A month before the feds filed racketeering charges in the so-called Windows case, Luchese leaders Vittorio Amuso and Anthony "Gaspipe" Casso beeped then-capo Alphonse "Little Al" D'Arco to a Sheepshead Bay, Brooklyn, clam bar for an emergency planning session.

"Something's going down, and we might have to take off," Amuso told D'Arco, adding that any communications should go through the Canarsie, Brooklyn, home of a relative of Anthony Senter, according to what D'Arco told the feds. Senter, along with Joseph and Patrick Testa, were recently inducted Luchese mobsters who earned their stripes as killers-for-hire under Gambino mobster Roy DeMeo.

On the weekend before the Windows indictment was filed, Casso told D'Arco under the Verrazano Bridge near the big cannon at the Fort Hamilton Army base that Amuso had already "gone on the lam." Casso then left in what D'Arco described as an "emotional departure."

D'Arco spoke to Casso and Amuso often via telephone and met them five times while they were fugitives. The first meeting was at the New Jersey home of a mobster whose family was out for the night. Both men were "starting to grow beards," D'Arco said.

D'Arco was accompanied by capo George "Georgie Neck" Zappola—still a fugitive and said to be "like a son" to Casso. A bar in Scranton, Pennsylvania, would be their emergency rendezvous point. Amuso and Casso drove off in a black Jeep, wearing baseball caps and sunglasses.

A few weeks later, D'Arco got an untraceable car from Patty Testa, owner of a used-car business, and met Zappola near Canal Street. D'Arco was to drive to Scranton and stay at a motel. D'Arco checked in, using an assumed name, and paid cash.

The next day he drove to a supermarket and waited. Casso, now sporting a full beard, arrived in a Jeep and led D'Arco to a house on a tree-lined street on which people were jogging. Amuso had a full gray beard.

Shortly before Christmas 1990, D'Arco met his fugitive bosses again. He met Testa, who drove around for a while in his Cadillac to "dry clean ourselves" before dropping him off for the meet in Canarsie.

After they took care of some routine family business, Amuso and Casso told D'Arco where to host the Luchese family Christmas party.

A few weeks later, on January 9, 1991, after going through the same ritual, D'Arco met them again in the same house in Canarsie. Still sporting full beards, Amuso and Casso named D'Arco acting boss after he passed along a $50,000 Christmas gift from a Luchese-controlled contractor.

Shortly before Amuso was arrested in July 1991, D'Arco—this time with acting underboss Anthony Barratta and supercapos Frank Lastorino and Salvatore Avellino—met them for the last time, in Staten Island.

Amuso and Casso were now clean shaven. They reduced D'Arco and Barratta to capo, told the four capos to run the family by committee, and left.

The Lucheses get much secret information about investigations and pending indictments from three key law enforcement officials controlled by Casso, Avellino, and Lastorino, D'Arco told the feds.

D'Arco says Amuso is the only one who knows anything about Casso's contact.

Avellino meets his source—someone "close to the FBI and detectives working the Gambino family"—somewhere on Long Island the first week of every month and pays him $4,000.

Lastorino meets his source, said to be a Latino named Tony who has a girlfriend in the Brooklyn District Attorney's office, in Canarsie near a car wash that Lastorino controls, according to D'Arco.

The Luchese and Genovese gangs had a peculiar problem in 1989 involving an informer's girlfriend, and it almost led to blood in the streets.

It happened when the girlfriend of Vincent "Fish" Cafaro—once a highly trusted Genovese soldier who became a major federal witness—failed to repay $50,000 borrowed from the sister of Luchese family associate.

Top gangsters in the Luchese family wanted the girlfriend dead. But Cafaro's son, Tommy, interceded on her behalf. That made D'Arco furious.

"Who the hell is this guy? Where does this guy get off saying anything? He's nothing but the son of a rat," D'Arco screamed during a sit-down with Genovese capo Michael Generoso.

"You ain't killing nobody," Generoso told D'Arco with enough emphasis to keep Fish's girlfriend from getting whacked like any other gangster.

Apparently the Genoveses aren't as bloodthirsty as their Luchese cousins, who are suspected of putting out a contract on informer Peter "Fat Pete" Chiodo's sister.

FEBRUARY 16, 1993

Mob Firebug Gets Warm Bed—in Jail

Thomas Masotto is a respected pillar of his upscale community Glen Head, L.I., where he raised four children. He has a degree in business administration and a profitable carting business.

Masotto, 57, is also an associate of the Gambino crime family, a hijacker, and an arsonist, according to the FBI, which claims Masotto burned them—literally.

Three days before Christmas, Masotto began cooling his heels at the Metropolitan Correctional Center, charged with burning down a secret FBI surveillance post on Woodcleft Avenue, not far from the Guy Lombardo Marina, in the heart of the Freeport, L.I., waterfront.

According to the feds, the building was gutted and surveillance videotapes the FBI had made of Masotto walking and talking with other reputed Gambino mob types were destroyed.

The arsonist, Joseph Lucas, did such a good job, he told the feds, that members of John A. "Junior" Gotti's crew hired him a year later to burn down a gay bar in Smithtown, L.I. that competed with one they owned a block away.

In February 1991, Masotto learned the FBI was using the waterfront building to investigate him for loan-sharking and other crimes and allegedly agreed to pay Lucas $2,500 to torch the place.

Lucas did the job on February 22, 1991. Two days later, Masotto stiffed him, paying him only $1,000, according to Masotto's 10-count arson conspiracy indictment.

That March, apparently buoyed by Lucas's torch work, Masotto directed three truck hijackings in Queens and Long Island in which drivers were threatened, tied up, and blackjacked by gun-toting robbers, according to the indictment.

Masotto, a reputed associate under Gambino capo James "Jimmy Brown" Failla, received a portion of the loot from the hijackers, according to court papers filed by Assistant U.S. Attorney Mark Wasserman.

Masotto is a distant cousin of Carlo Gambino. But defense lawyers Michael Rosen and Alan Futerfas say "there are no provable allegations of organized crime here, just hype and smoke and mirrors on the government's part."

The lawyers point out that Masotto has no prior arrests and assert that their client is being implicated in crimes by an admitted lifelong criminal "with a history of arsons who is trying to save his own neck."

Masotto, however, knows a little about arson himself, according to court papers. He is heard on a tape-recorded conversation last May 13 "discussing how to go about destroying competitors' trucks by arson."

Judge Thomas Platt, who read through transcripts of FBI wiretaps and bugs, grand jury testimony, and other exhibits, said, "The evidence (against Masotto) is very substantial."

With all that stacked against him, Masotto was ready for a break, and seemed to get one. Platt, usually a tough, government-oriented judge, seemed swayed by letters from friends and relatives, and proposed strict "house arrest" conditions for Masotto to be released from prison to await trial.

The conditions were substantial: house arrest, a $5 million promissory note, a $2 million bond, ankle bracelet, security cameras, etc. But before Platt's proposal could be acted upon, the Second Circuit U.S. Court of Appeals reversed a judge who had granted bail to Colombo boss Victor Orena. Prosecutor Wasserman rushed Platt a copy.

After reading it, Platt took back his "house arrest" proposal, stating that the appeals court "virtually mandated" that no conditions of bail would protect the public from "dangerous defendants" like Orena and Masotto.

"We believe that house arrest is a viable alternative for bail, and we believe the Circuit did not rule to the contrary," said Futerfas.

"The judge thought the ruling was a red flag, but we see it only as a yellow marker on the road, one you can go around, with caution," said Rosen.

Tomorrow, the lawyers will try to convince the appeals court that Masotto and Orena—who was convicted of racketeering the week Masotto was arrested—are different. Wasserman, of course, will argue they're the same.

Son Also Wises: Feds Target 'Acting Don' Junior Gotti

John A. "Junior" Gotti's almost-overnight rise to the top has gotten the ultimate law enforcement compliment: a full-scale federal grand jury probe of Junior and his junior henchmen.

The grand jury is probing Junior's role in the current hierarchy of the Gambino crime family: the loan-sharking, protection, and labor rackets he is said to control and his quasi-legitimate interests in several bars and nightclubs in Queens and on Long Island, said "Gang Land" sources who declined to provide specifics.

Gotti, a reputed Gambino capo since 1990, has been functioning basically as acting boss, visiting his father regularly at the federal penitentiary in Marion, Illinois, and relaying orders to the other Gambino family capos, sources said.

The young, muscle-bound Gotti holds court every Wednesday night at the Our Friends Social Club in South Ozone Park, Queens, for the 25 reputed mobsters and associates under his control.

About a dozen young members of his crew have been hit with subpoenas by a Brooklyn federal grand jury that's headed by the same prosecutors who sent the elder Gotti away for life—John Gleeson and Laura Ward, sources said.

The outspoken Bruce Cutler, attorney for father and son, was taking it all in stride.

"We're aware of the government's targeting of John Gotti's son, the way they targeted the father," he said. "If charges are brought, we'll meet them head on."

Also subpoenaed by the grand jury was John "Jackie Nose" D'Amico, a reputed capo who was a regular spectator and kibitzer during the murder and racketeering trial last year of John Gotti, *the father*.

D'Amico, a veteran of these kinds of judicial invitations, invoked his Fifth Amendment rights and refused to testify, sources said.

Junior Gotti has not been subpoenaed and—befitting his status as a main target of the probe—won't be asked to testify before the panel.

Not so lucky—or very lucky, depending on your point of view—is Junior's brother-in-law, Carmine Agnello, a successful junk-car dealer/millionaire businessman who has been tabbed for testimony by the grand jury.

Agnello is trying to beg off, claiming that scar tissue lodged near his brain has dulled his powers of recall so badly the feds might as well subpoena one of his rusted-out clinkers for all the help he can provide.

Agnello's reputed memory problems are documented in sealed court papers filed with Brooklyn Federal Judge Eugene Nickerson, who has put Agnello's grand jury appearance on hold for the time being, the sources said.

A cynical view among some investigators has Agnello preparing a defense to possible charges of criminal contempt, perjury, or obstruction of justice for trying to stymie the federal panel.

Yesterday, we tried to raise the cynical view with Agnello's lawyer, Anthony Cardinale of Boston. But Cardinale, a defense team member at the trial of John Gotti, the father, refused comment, as did Gleeson, Ward, and D'Amico lawyer James DiPietro.

Speaking of Juniors, Ralph "Don't Call Me Ralphie" Scopo Jr. got a big win the other day, the only court victory Colombo mobsters have managed since they began killing one another 16 months ago in a bloody intrafamily war. Scopo, son of jailed mobster Ralph "Little Ralphie" Scopo, was arrested soon after the shooting started when he changed lanes without signaling and two detectives spotted a gun in "plain view" on the backseat of his car.

As his rights were read, an angry Scopo told his co-defendant: "F--k those A-B-C (by the book) men, they promised my father 10 and they gave him 115." That's only a slight exaggeration of the 100-year sentence his father received in 1987 for racketeering.

With the gun and Scopo's statement as evidence, federal prosecutor Andrew Weissmann felt good about the case, but he underestimated the resourcefulness of Scopo's attorney, James DiPietro, who represents D'Amico.

DiPietro charged that on January 17, 1992, detectives on a state-federal "Colombo strike force" had used a minor traffic violation 2 miles before as a "pretext" to stop Scopo and illegally search his car for weapons without obtaining the required search warrant.

After a hearing, Brooklyn Federal Judge I. Leo Glasser agreed, ruling that the search of Scopo's car was "pretextual." He ordered the gun and statement suppressed from the case as "fruits of this unconstitutional behavior."

Besides the nasty behavior by the detectives, Matthew Higgins and Benjamin Gozun, Scopo also objected to being referred to in court papers as Ralphie—a nickname Glasser dutifully omitted atop his 34-page opinion.

APRIL 13, 1993

Colombo Consigliere Singing for Fed Captors

After nine months on the lam, Carmine Sessa finally found religion on Palm Sunday—right outside St. Patrick's Cathedral.

Sessa, the Colombo family consigliere, became the latest top Mafia turncoat and began cooperating with the FBI when he was nabbed with the brother of the family's imprisoned boss, the *Daily News* learned yesterday.

The defection by Sessa, a major player for Carmine "Junior" Persico in the bloody Colombo family war in Brooklyn, has already led to the arrests of three Colombo capos who are being held without bail, law enforcement sources said.

And one ecstatic high-ranking law enforcement official predicted, with perhaps just a touch of hyperbole, "Sessa will help us dismantle the entire Colombo mob."

Sessa, 42, has headed the Persico faction of the Colombo family since mobsters allied with acting boss Victor "Little Vic" Orena opened fire on November 18, 1991, against a car they thought was being driven by capo Gregory Scarpa Sr.

"This is a lot of trouble," one usually reliable underworld source told "Gang Land" yesterday. "I still can't believe it. He's been in it since Day One. He knows where all the bodies are buried."

FBI supervisor Lindley DeVecchio, who heads the FBI's Colombo squad, and Assistant U.S. Attorneys George Stamboulidis and Andrew Weissmann, prosecutors in the Brooklyn case, refused to confirm or deny Sessa's cooperation.

But sources said that Sessa offered to cooperate "10 minutes after he was arrested" by a team of FBI agents who were tipped that he would be meeting with capo Theodore "Teddy" Persico outside St. Pat's early on Palm Sunday.

As worshippers inside received their symbolic palm, Sessa, Persico and associate Frank "Frankie Blue Eyes" Sparaco were handcuffed and taken away.

However, only Persico, 55, and Sparaco, 37, both charged with conspiring to murder members of the Orena faction of the Colombo mob and of harboring the fugitive Sessa, were arraigned in a public proceeding, after which they were jailed without bail.

On Thursday, capos Joseph "JoJo" Russo and his cousin Anthony "Chuckie" Russo, capo Robert "Bobby Zam" Zambardi, and soldier Joseph "Joe Monte" Monteleone Sr. were arrested on charges they also conspired to murder Orena loyalists.

The following day, Persico and Sparaco were released on $1 million bail each and were put under house arrest, under electronic monitoring.

Today, Stamboulidis and Weissman will argue that the four were involved in several murders, are dangers to the community at large, and should remain in jail while awaiting trial.

Meanwhile, Sessa awaits his debut as a witness and becomes part of a mob sell-out that includes former Gambino underboss Salvatore "Sammy Bull" Gravano and former Luchese acting boss Alphonse "Little Al" D'Arco.

As reported elsewhere in today's *News*, there was another installment of Sammy Bull's one-man demolition of the Gambino crime family yesterday.

By now, of course, his reputation precedes him. The jury in the tiral of the family's alleged drug-dealing Sicilian faction barely seemed to stir when Gravano calmly noted that he had pleaded guilty to 19 murders after he became a government witness.

More surprising to some jurors was Gravano's remark that the only things of value the government had given him since the deal were a cheap watch and a cheap pair of glasses. "Together, they're worth about $40," he said.

Gravano was wearing an expensive John Gotti-style suit, but even Gotti's lawyer, Bruce Cutler—who will cross-examine Gravano later—conceded to the *News'* Gene Mustain that Gravano bought it with his own money.

Time's Running Out for Persicos

For two years now, Colombo mobsters loyal to Carmine "Junior" Persico have been waging a bloody mob war so his son Alphonse could take over the crime family when he was released from prison.

Alphonse, a capo, is due out next month after serving a six-year stretch. But with nine mobsters and associates killed in action and two dozen more in jail or on their way, there's not much left, in firepower—or brain power.

So instead of trying to pump new life into the crime family, and thinking of ways to fulfill his father's wishes, Alphonse should be looking for a good lawyer.

That's because, in the cruelest of ironies, Alphonse—who "Gang Land" hears never really wanted his father's business anyway—is squarely in the sights of the feds and their newest high-level mob turncoat, reputed consigliere Carmine Sessa.

And the feds are working on tight deadlines to make two racketeering cases—one for Alphonse, and another for his uncle, Theodore Persico, a reputed capo who was nabbed with Sessa outside St. Patrick's Cathedral on Palm Sunday and charged with harboring Sessa, a fugitive for nine months.

The feds have until May 4 to indict Theodore, who is under house arrest under charges filed in a criminal complaint. They want to indict Alphonse before May 30, when he is due out of a federal prison in Milan, Michigan.

In a June 1991 phone call he made from Milan to the home of a Colombo mobster, Alphonse involved himself in the early stages of the war between his father and mobsters loyal to acting boss Victor "Little Vic" Orena.

According to FBI documents, Sessa arranged the call to tell Alphonse that Teddy and reputed capos Joseph "JoJo" Russo and Anthony "Chuckie" Russo did not attend a four-crime-family meeting to iron out the war and to ask Alphonse to get them to attend the next one.

Using a simple code in which Carmine and Teddy Persico were "Papa Bear" and "Teddy Bear," and the Russos were "the cousins," Alphonse promised Sessa and reputed capo John Pate he would bring "Teddy Bear" and the cousins in line.

The next day, Pate flew to Michigan and visited Alphonse, according to cooperating mobster Joseph Ambrosino, who earned the name "Joey Brains" years ago when, while fleeing from cops, he led them to a social club full of mobsters.

Ambrosino, who has testified against Orena, reputed Orena capo Pasquale "Patsy" Amato, and several Persico loyalists, has spared no one, not even his wife, Lucille, in his tales of mayhem and madness to the FBI:

- Late one night in 1989, Ambrosino was tipped off that detectives were "down the street," so he had his wife put a load of guns, knives, and ammunition he was storing in his house on his next-door neighbor's back porch. They intended to wake at 5 A.M. and remove them.

  But they overslept and were awakened by cops who came to his neighbor's home after she called and told them she had found a garbage bag full of weapons.

- During the war, Ambrosino, Michael Sessa, and three other mobsters ended an unsuccessful stakeout for an Orena soldier and drove to Coney Island. There, they practiced their marksmanship at a boardwalk shooting gallery and topped off the night with hot dogs at Nathan's Famous.

- One morning, five shooters were staked out at the Staten Island home of another Orena loyalist when a resident seemed suspicious of the stolen car that three of them were waiting in. They fled without alerting two cohorts, who were waiting up the street. These two would-be assassins finally fled two hours later after they were spotted by a friend of their intended victim.

- During the war effort, the Persico faction always used stolen cars, which allowed reputed crew members like Frank "Frankie Steel" Pontillo and Lawrence Fiorenza to earn a few extra bucks. After stealing an Audi whose owner had left the engine running while buying a newspaper, Pontillo and Fiorenze told Michael Sessa they bought the "stolen car" for $300, which Sessa forked over.

- Many of the same Persico mobsters held a big sitdown about the war at a restaurant in New Jersey. The only problem was they all sat at different tables, capos with capos, soldiers with soldiers, associates with associates. No one knew what was said at the others' tables, but everyone paid with stolen credit cards.

FBI agents are sure to ask Carmine Sessa for his version of the 1987 killing of Colombo mobster Joseph Delmonico, son of a Gambino soldier with the same name who goes by the name of Joe Brewster.

According to Salvatore "Sammy Bull" Gravano, the younger Delmonico "fell out of favor" when he refused to "do a piece of work" (a contract killing) for reputed capo Gregory Scarpa, and worse yet, became a born-again Christian.

After the hit, the elder Delmonico sought to avenge his son's death, but since the killing was a Colombo family matter, "there was nothing the Gambino family could do to protest the murder," Gravano told the FBI.

JUNE 9, 1993

Judge Got Bum Rap For Biased Remark

There's a few people out there who owe Brooklyn Federal Judge Jack Weinstein an apology.

Weinstein was excoriated two weeks ago when he proclaimed at a sentencing of three Colombo family killers that a "large part of the young Italo-American community … should be discouraged" from becoming mobsters.

Weinstein recalled that during the trials of acting boss Victor "Little Vic" Orena and two capos, "accomplice witnesses detailed how young, impressionable males in the Italian-American community have been lured into the destructive life of these mobs before they are able to recognize the better opportunities available to them."

Criticisms came from people like Bill Fugazy, chairman of the Coalition of Italo-American Associations, who blasted the judge for a "ridiculous choice of words" that smeared "an entire ethnic group." He demanded an apology.

The next day, a stung Weinstein amended his remarks, noting that only "a miniscule percentage" of Italian-Americans were gangsters. Fugazy and many callers to "Gang Land" were pleased by the judge's clarification.

At the time, "Gang Land" was pondering a new record we received a few months ago by wanna-be rapper Lou "Big Lou" Ferrante, who sang rhyming praises to John Gotti.

In his rap, Ferrante describes former U.S. Attorney Andrew Maloney as a drunk, lead prosecutor John Gleeson as someone who "wears lingerie and high-heel pumps," and Salvatore "Sammy Bull" Gravano as a "punk rat."

The record, which includes real sound bites of Gotti lawyer Bruce Cutler and TV reporter John Miller in the background, favorably compares Gotti with John F. Kennedy, the Rev. Martin Luther King, and Malcolm X.

And about halfway through his rap, Ferrante compares Gotti to Jesus Christ:

Sittin' in a cell is the cross he's carryin'

No blinkin' eyes, no beads of sweat.

I played the song a few times in disbelief, then tried hard to forget about it. But the record remained on a dining room

125

server—with Gotti's angry stare filling the room—and this ridiculous rap would just not go away.

While it's not selling like hot cakes, there have been far too many sales of "Justice Not Found: The John Gotti Story" to suit a lot of people, including Fugazy.

At Liberty Records in Ozone Park, for example, manager Joe Chavez reports sales of "over 100 copies in the last two months," to youngsters, mostly male and mostly Italian-American.

Adam Shrem, owner/manager of the Music Stop in Gravesend, reports that during the same period, he sold "maybe 40 or 50 pieces." Shrem said record buyers were "boys, mostly Italian."

"Those are big numbers," said Fugazy, who sounded a lot like Weinstein as he went on. "This is wrong. Parents should make sure their children don't buy it. I don't want young kids thinking that Gotti is a martyr sitting in jail. This is terrible."

Fugazy conceded that the Gotti rap records sales indicate that maybe Weinstein was right, but he declined to back off, explaining that Weinstein's remarks "singled out" Italian-Americans.

"Unfortunately," said Fugazy, "too many youngsters of all ethnic backgrounds use criminals as role models. We should all strive to stop that."

Neither Ferrante nor Freedom Records returned calls to "Gang Land."

It's a safe bet that many fans of Ferrante's record—the youngsters both Fugazy and Weinstein were talking about—took part in the well-orchestrated protest that turned into a minor riot at the federal courthouse in Brooklyn on June 23, 1992, the day Gotti got a life sentence.

One of the protesters was Paul Orena, youngest son of the acting Colombo boss, who was in prison awaiting his own trial for murder and racketeering—the trial that led to his conviction, a life sentence, and Weinstein's remarks.

Early that morning, Victor Orena told his son in a monitored telephone conversation to attend the Gotti rally.

"Be careful," the elder Orena cautioned. "And make sure you introduce yourself to Joe Butter (Gotti associate Joe DeCicco) so he knows you were there."

JULY 4, 1993

Lefty Guns & FBI Pal Back on Street

They were the best of friends, and then the worst of enemies.

Joe Pistone was a hero FBI agent with his life on the line as he tried to infiltrate the mob. Benjamin "Lefty Guns" Ruggiero was a Bonanno soldier who sponsored him for membership in La Cosa Nostra.

Eventually, Ruggiero was sent to prison while Pistone, the most famous undercover FBI agent in history, quit the bureau, wrote a book about his exploits, and tried the private-eye business.

Lefty Guns is back on the street. And Pistone, 54, is back on the job, under yet another new alias, not the Donnie Brasco name he used while Lefty Guns was teaching Donnie how to walk and talk like a real gangster.

Neither Pistone nor Ruggiero would talk to the *Daily News* about their former friendship. But more than a dozen years after their relationship soured, the FBI was apparently still worried the mob would try to get even.

"What are you nuts?" Ruggiero told two FBI agents who recently visited his lower Manhattan apartment and warned him not to "even think about" settling an old score with Pistone, according to sources.

"The idea of me wanting to hurt an FBI agent is so f-----g ridiculous that you wasted your f-----g time to come and see me," said Ruggiero, now 67 and suffering from cancer, and scheduled for surgery next month.

"If Donnie learned anything from his six years on the street, it was one thing: Street guys don't go after cops," he added, before shooing them away.

After he resigned in 1986, Pistone realized that he missed the FBI, not the undercover role that took him away from his wife and daughters for five years, federal officials said.

"I really miss the organization, the people I worked with," Pistone told surprised FBI officials last year after he asked to go back on the FBI payroll.

His former supervisors told him he would have to go through training again.

And so, 14 months ago, Pistone began the FBI rigid 16-week training course at Quantico, Virginia, alongside agents less than half his age with no idea they were competing with an FBI legend.

"At his age, he deserves an awful lot of credit," said FBI supervisor William Doran, adding that the FBI gave Pistone "no special consideration" for his previous heroics.

Pistone has told Doran and other FBI friends that he's enjoying his second FBI career so much that they'll have to drag him out at age 57, when he reaches mandatory retirement age.

"Joe was a trailblazer," said Barbara Jones, chief assistant to Manhattan District Attorney Robert Morgenthau and the former federal prosecutor who tried Ruggiero and spoke fondly about the impact Pistone had on the jury.

"From the witness stand, he gave us an honest man's look inside the mob, not the look from an accomplice carrying along criminal baggage," said Jones.

His work also had a lasting effect on the mob status of the Bonanno family, which was bounced from the Commission, the mob's board of directors, according to recent testimony by turncoat underboss Salvatore "Sammy Bull" Gravano.

"They were involved with dealing with an undercover FBI agent, Donnie Brasco. They almost made him a made member in their family," said Gravano, adding that as punishment, the Commission "put that family on restriction"—a restriction that still exists.

Ah, When Mobsters Were Mobsters

John Gotti must be banging his head against the bars of his prison cell at Marion, Illinois, wondering if there are real mobsters left.

Gotti is still boss of the Gambino family, but each week his influence diminishes.

Take the case of Pasquale "Patsy" Conte, a reputed capo and accused heroin dealer charged with killing mobster Louis DiBono on Gotti's orders.

He has retained Jay Goldberg, one of the "erudite, professional, egghead types" that Gotti and his lawyer Bruce Cutler said they despise—on tape.

What's worse, Goldberg, a Harvard Law grad who lists Donald Trump, Riddick Bowe, and Willie Nelson as clients, informed on a mob associate in a $7.9 million armored-car robbery and helped send the guy to prison with his testimony.

If Gotti were walking on Mulberry Street instead of pumping iron in Marion, Conte never would have hired Goldberg.

Meanwhile, other Gambino mobsters are ignoring an ironclad Cosa Nostra rule that Gotti strictly enforced: Don't admit

anything, don't plead guilty without permission.

"They're doing things that would have gotten them killed three years ago," said one "Gang Land" source.

They are pleading guilty to assorted crimes and membership in the Gambino crime family in record numbers, a violation of the secrecy oath of *omerta* that mobsters take when they swear allegiance to the crime family, the sources said.

In the old days, these guys probably would have been whacked, the sources said.

Conte is charged with killing DiBono in a World Trade Center parking lot for much less. On an FBI tape, Gotti says: He's gonna die because he refused to come in when I called. He didn't do nothing else wrong."

Goldberg, who won an acquittal for sewage contractor Andy Capasso and was voted "the best pure trial lawyer in town" by 40 criminal lawyers, was hired by Conte last month, soon after his bail was revoked.

Conte selected Goldberg after he won an acquittal for another Gotti mobster at a trial in which capo Thomas Gambino was convicted of racketeering.

By all accounts, his defense work was excellent, but it was aided immeasurably when Salvatore "Sammy Bull" Gravano testified that he didn't know much about Goldberg's client.

"My destroying Gravano's credibility on the witness stand may well imperil the Gotti verdict," Goldberg, who is not shy about his ability, boasted after the trial.

Goldberg, however, was quick to downplay the impact his testimony had in convicting Joseph Coffey of taking part in a $7.9 million robbery of a Wells Fargo depot in 1984.

The robbers used pickaxes and sledgehammers to bust open an armored car they had loaded up with cash before fleeing.

Coffey, according to Goldberg, approached him to represent Jeffrey Grubczak, a Fulton Fish Market worker who helped the robbers break open the armored car.

Goldberg—who was described as a "hostile witness" by the prosecutor in the case—never implicated Coffey.

But when "Gang Land" pointed out that Goldberg's testimony was the only difference in the cases against Coffey and his two co-defendants—who were acquitted of all charges at the same trial—Goldberg conceded the obvious with an explanation.

"I'm not a mob lawyer, but when their lives are on the line, many alleged organized crime figures go to the best, and that's why they hire me. I am a lawyer first. I was granted immunity and ordered to testify. There is no lawyer-client privilege for third-party payments for legal fees, and Coffey, who served four years in prison, bears me no ill will. I was not going to commit perjury or refuse to testify," said Goldberg.

It's true that Goldberg was compelled to testify, but FBI documents state Goldberg approached the prosecutor and offered to cooperate *during* the earlier trial of Grubczak, who was convicted and sentenced to 25 years in prison.

"I'll help you in any way I can. I'll testify in the grand jury," Goldberg told then-prosecutor Steven Kaplan while Grubczak's trial was under way, a year before Coffey was arrested.

Goldberg told "Gang Land" he doesn't recall making that statement, but if he did it would have been because he knew even then that he would have no legal recourse but to name Coffey as the person who hired him to represent Grubczak.

During Coffey's trial, his lawyer, David Breitbart, accused Goldberg of failing to do his best for Gubczak out of fear he would be prosecuted for helping Grubczak concoct a phony alibi, a charge Goldberg vehemently denied in a robing room conference after his testimony.

In a shot at Breitbart, who has a Police Department "carry" permit and likes to talk of his marksmanship, Goldberg said *he* wasn't a mob lawyer who carried a gun.

"If it walks like a duck, talks like a duck, and smells like a duck, then it's a duck," Breitbart said yesterday. "Defense attorneys fight gallantly for their clients. An informer, in most cases, just to save himself, is willing to trade everything, even his client and his self-respect. With the facts as we know them, it's not difficult to put him into the appropriate category."

"Gang Land" wonders what category John Gotti would put him in and what he would tell Patsy Conte.

Justice Imperiled
When Judges Lie

In some trials, the search for truth begins with a lie.

Miriam Cedarbaum has been a federal judge for seven years now, supposedly dispensing justice and searching for truth.

With all due respect, Cedarbaum has either failed in her odyssey or gotten sidetracked along the way.

Yesterday, she told a panel of 100 prospective jurors for the racketeering trial of two reputed gangsters named Joe that their identities would be kept confidential to protect them from "being contacted by members of the media who might improperly contact them during the case."

What a whopper.

In the last few years, there have been quite a few trials in which jurors have been bribed or threatened, but none in New York in which a reporter—to our knowledge—has done the nasty deed, or even been accused of trying to reach a juror for any reason, even a story.

Cedarbaum ordered that the jurors remain anonymous to protect them from tampering, or worse, by persons linked to the defendants, not the media. Her ruling

came on a motion by the prosecutors and over the objections of defense lawyers.

Federal judges have been doing that since 1978, when an anonymous jury was selected for the drug trafficking trial of notorious Harlem drug merchant Leroy "Nicky" Barnes.

Even if the potential jurors were from Mars and had absolutely no idea why their names were kept secret yesterday, they surely figured it out after reading the questionnaires Cedarbaum told them to fill out. For example:

"Do you believe that there is an alleged association referred to as 'organized crime,' the 'Luchese family' the 'Mafia,' or 'La Cosa Nostra.'?"

"Do you have a bias or prejudice for or against Italians?"

"Is there anything about the word 'racketeering' that would prevent you from being a fair and impartial juror in this case?"

"Do you have any beliefs or attitudes about Italians that would prevent you from fairly evaluating the evidence?"

"Have you or any member of your family or any close associates ever had any contact with anyone you believed or later learned to be a member of an alleged organized crime group?"

After 62 questions, no one but a moron could believe that Cedarbaum was trying to keep a horde of pencil-chomping, notebook-waving journalists at bay.

While it's upsetting that Cedarbaum smeared reporters, the real problem "Gang Land" saw and heard yesterday in courtroom 506 was the judge destroying her own credibility with jurors on the first day of a six to seven week trial.

How can any conscientious juror follow her instructions about the evidence, or the law, when the juror knows the judge lied about an important point on the very first day of trial?

Cedarbaum declined to discuss the matter.

Her instructions were a "very dangerous proposition that could even hurt the government," said a legal observer. "If the jury gets the feeling they are being treated like children, and if jurors believe they're being lied to by the judge, of all people, it could start them thinking that nothing's on the level."

A prosecutor not connected to the case agreed that jurors could take out their anger with a judge on the prosecution, but said the judge had "an impossible situation. She could not tell the jurors the real reason—the defendants are a danger to you—because that would prejudice them."

All defendants do deserve a fair trial. And as long as the Supreme Court says anonymous juries can be fair, why couldn't a judge say something like: "For reasons that I cannot go into, in order to insure a fair trial for all parties, you will serve anonymously. Sometimes this happens in federal cases. If it affects your ability to serve, I urge you to let us know."

The defendants in the case—reputed Luchese mobster Joseph "Joey Bang Bang" Massaro and associate Joseph "Joey K" Kerns are charged with racketeering, extortion, arson, loan-sharking, and the murder of Joseph Fiorito in 1990.

Prosecutors David Kelley and Randall Bodner charge they killed Fiorito because they believed he was an informer.

Defense lawyers Harry Batchelder and David Liebman are expected to claim that admitted triggerman-turned-informer Patrick Esposito killed Fiorito with no help from their clients.

Before the trial plays out, turncoat Luchese acting boss Alfonso "Little Al" D'Arco and hero undercover FBI agent Joe Pistone are to take the witness stand for the prosecution.

For a time, up to 1991, D'Arco served as Massaro's boss; in the late 1970s and early 1980s, Pistone, playing the role of a Bonanno associate, met Massaro a few times.

He Ducks Feds & Rivals — Usually

For nearly two years now, mob capo William "Wild Bill" Cutolo has managed to avoid any serious brushes with two adversaries who want him badly—the feds, and rival mobsters in the warring Colombo crime family.

A few weeks back, however, Cutolo brought on a little grief for himself with police when he stepped on the toes of two cops who arrived at the door of his Brooklyn social club in hot pursuit of three suspects in a minor assault.

His actions cost him his first arrest in 18 years—a misdemeanor rap for obstruction of governmental administration—as well as some aggravation stemming from what one law enforcement official called "legal harassment."

Cutolo, who was standing in front of his club at the corner of 63d Street and 11th Avenue in Bay Ridge, stepped in front of the pursuing cops and blocked them from entering.

His ever-present bodyguards, Joseph Campanella and Joseph Russo—who are obviously quick on their feet—followed suit. Very soon, a large, noisy crowd gathered and began to harass the outmanned, and probably outgunned, cops.

Looking to avoid a major confrontation, the cops retreated, went back to the 68th Precinct stationhouse, forgot about the guys they were chasing, and picked out their protagonists for detectives, who quickly got arrest warrants for Cutolo and the two Joes, said Detective Sgt. Anthony Celano.

By then, however, Cutolo, Campanella, and Russo—like the three assault suspects—had also disappeared. But Celano and Detective Thomas Dades knew how to make them reappear.

For three days, detectives kept showing up and leaving messages for Cutolo at the nearby Hotel Gregory and Granita Restaurant, where the 44-year-old capo regularly meets with his crew members and where Cutolo's son is a manager.

"He obviously got the message and surrendered," said Celano.

Cutolo's crew members are mainstays of acting boss Victor "Little Vic" Orena's faction and are believed responsible— by both the feds and Cutolo's mob rivals—for firing the opening salvos in the shooting war that's claimed 11 lives.

In November 1991, Cutolo crew mobsters ambushed mobster Greg Scarpa in an unsuccessful rubout attempt, and followed that with successful hits against two mobsters loyal to imprisoned boss Carmine "Junior" Persico, according to court records.

In four trials, witnesses from the Persico faction have described how they tracked and trailed Cutolo to no avail. In April, turncoat consigliere Carmine Sessa said Cutolo was still marked for death by the Persico crowd.

A score of Persico and Orena loyalists, including members of Cutolo's crew, have been convicted and sentenced to heavy jail time, but through it all, Cutolo has remained free, although sources say that a federal grand jury in Brooklyn has him in its sights.

In 1974, when he got a message that a young hood was fingering mob bookies and loan sharks for robberies, Cutolo allegedly shot the hood to death, put the body in a 55-gallon oil drum with eight holes in it, and dumped it into the East River.

A year later, after the drum floated to the surface and Cutolo allegedly was heard to say that the next time he killed someone he would puncture the victim's lungs so the body would stay submerged, he was charged with murder.

With lawyer Martin Light leading the defense, Cutolo was acquitted, and while many around him have fallen, including Light, who was convicted of drug trafficking in 1985, Wild Bill Cutolo is still riding high. For now.

SEPTEMBER 21, 1993

Gotti's Stamp on N.Y.: Gambinos Peddle Stolen Postal Goods

Just when the feds thought they had John Gotti licked, some of his guys have begun selling U.S. postage stamps, wholesale.

While Gotti serves a life term in the federal pen in Marion, Illinois, associates in his Gambino crime family recently have done a banner business peddling stolen rolls of 29-cent first-class stamps to local candy stores and newsstands in many neighborhoods in Brooklyn, Queens, and Manhattan, sources told "Gang Land."

Guys with street names like Fat Bobby, Leo the Book, and Flash have flooded stores and stands in Bensonhurst, Bay Ridge, Borough Park, Gravesend, Red Hook, Astoria, Ozone Park, and Little Italy with discounted 100-count rolls of the familiar American flag stamp.

The outlets, whose proprietors claim to sell stamps as a "courtesy" to regular customers, still add on their usual 6- to 11-cent service charge, raising the price of 29-cent stamps to 35 to 40 cents each.

To do otherwise would raise suspicions of most New Yorkers, and many shopkeepers were advised not to lower their prices for just that reason, sources said.

Some merchants and small businesses also have been given cut-rate deals on the $9.95 Express Mail stamps used for small packages.

Most insiders, who pay $11 for the 100-count rolls and $4 each for the Express Mail stamps, are selling the $29 rolls for $18 to $20 and discounting the Express Mail stamps for $7.

Sources say the stamp pushers, who include a few teen mob wanna-bes, have invoked the names of several Gambino soldiers—including the street name of reputed Gambino soldier Philip Mazzara—when asked for their affiliation by local hoods looking to protect their turf.

"I'm with Philly Dogs," is the usual reply.

Mazzara is a reputed stalwart under James "Jimmy Brown" Failla, a high-ranking Gotti capo. Along with Failla and four others, Mazzara allegedly killed mobster Thomas "Tommy Sparrow" Spinelli in 1989 when Spinelli was thinking of telling the truth to a federal grand jury, and is awaiting trial on racketeering and murder charges.

According to turncoat underboss Salvatore "Sammy Bull" Gravano, Mazzaro drove Spinelli to a glass factory in Brooklyn, where he was killed, and then transported his body to Staten Island, where it was disposed of.

Lawyer Charles Carnesi told "Gang Land" that Mazzara maintains his innocence in the federal racketeering and murder case, but he declined to comment about the wholesale stamp business.

Sources said the stamp pushers began selling the stamps near the Bay Ridge and Bensonhurst hangouts of Mazzara and his cronies, and later expanded to other sections of Brooklyn, Queens, and Manhattan.

"It's hard work," said one source. "No one's getting rich, but some guys are making a hundred and fifty to two hundred a day."

"We're aware there are some stolen stamps out there, and it's under investigation," said Postal Inspector Mike Kmetz, who echoed what some mob stamp pushers have said while pitching the stamps to potential customers.

"We've had quite a few burglaries of stamp stock in recent years," said Kmetz, "but there are no special markings on stamps, so it's hard to tell where they came from. Stamps in California are the same as those in New York."

Late yesterday, "Gang Land" got an unconfirmed report from a usually reliable source that the mob's supply of 100-count rolls was dwindling, but "now they have books of 20 for $4."

———

John "Sonny" Franzese, the imprisoned 76-year-old Colombo capo who was disgraced when his capo son Michael turned informer, still has enough clout to impose the death penalty for those who cross him.

At least that's what the FBI believes.

Franzese, who's doing a third—or is it fourth?—stint for violating federal parole on his 1967 bank robbery conviction, has put out murder contracts on three old associates of his son from his cell in Petersburg, Virginia, the feds say.

The reason: Associates Frank Cestaro, Louis Fenza, and Frank Castignaro have switched from the Colombo faction aligned with Victor "Little Vic" Orena to the one loyal to Carmine "Junior" Persico.

It seems to us that Sonny Franzese would be more upset about Michael's betrayal of family ties than the affections of three guys who, unlike Michael, shut their mouths and did their time when they were indicted with him.

After learning of the threats, however, FBI agent Dan Reilly visited Cestaro,

Fenza, and Castignaro and warned all three that Sonny, who's due out of prison April 22, had marked them for death.

Forget It, This Book's a Fantasyland

That book "Gang Land" warned readers about earlier, the one that has nothing to do with us even though it's called *Gangland*, has made it into bookstores posing as a true crime book.

It belongs either in the consumer fraud section or on the fiction shelves.

From its illogical beginning to its outright dishonest ending, this supposed nonfiction book about John Gotti contains at least 50 factual errors—we found roughly one error every six pages before we got tired and stopped counting.

There are also 50 or so instances in which the author quotes tape-recorded conversations out of context, puts tape-recorded remarks in the mouths of others, and imagines thoughts of people he never interviewed, such as Gotti and his turncoat underboss, Salvatore "Sammy Bull" Gravano.

First, we must point out that "Gang Land" has co-authored two Mafia books with *Daily News* colleague Gene Mustain, including one about Gotti. A third book—a rise-and-fall story about the Gambino crime family under Gotti and Gravano—is well under way. For that

reason, "Gang Land" bit his tongue about a copycat book that purported to cover the same territory as our first Gotti book.

But Howard Blum (who will be referred to simply as the author), this wanna-be competitor, had to call his book *Gangland*, even though he admitted he knew this would cause confusion in the marketplace—a tactic he blamed on his publisher.

"Don't blame me," he said the other day after introducing himself to "Gang Land," the column, in Sal's Pizzeria on Second Avenue. "I'm only the storyteller."

The stories he tells—through a maze of factual errors, made-up dialogue, and movie-of-the-minute fakery—are whoppers.

Gangland loses its credibility in its nonsensical beginning, a January day in 1990; groping for drama, the author portrays FBI agents as afraid that Gotti was "invincible" and "forever beyond their reach."

The truth is, agents penetrated Gotti's inner sanctum two months earlier and had already taped Gotti admitting a slew of crimes—three murders, for instance—and knew they had the mob boss dead to rights.

The author apparently started the book there—spending his first six chapters on January 17, 1990—to shoehorn in material he used in a magazine article last year about a crooked cop.

The cop gave up many law enforcement secrets, but none about the FBI's investigations of Gotti. And that's what this book claims to be about.

The book begins with Gotti in the middle of his 1990 trial in Manhattan for assault and erroneously portrays him as confident because he had "an edge" with the jury that "guaranteed" a "good" verdict.

Gotti had no edge on that jury, and the transcripts of the FBI tapes of Gotti clearly show the Gambino boss making plans to turn over power to Gravano because he was worried he was going to lose the trial.

"I'm gonna go to jail and leave him (Sammy) in charge. Soon as anything happens to me, I'm off the streets, Sammy is the acting boss," said Gotti.

The author never even tries to show how Gotti had an edge. But the book is like that—it never adds up.

For example, in several chapters, the author says that for years FBI agents were aware of the growing hostilities between Gotti and former boss Paul Castellano. Yet, the agents' boss, Bruce Mouw, is portrayed as astounded that Gotti might be behind Castellano's murder.

Forget any portrayals of the gangsters. All you get in *Gangland* are cartoon goons. Gotti drives a Mercedes around and Gravano whips up some pasta while hiding out.

The author says he read the record of all of Gotti's trials. So it must be pure coincidence that after sifting through the 18,000 pages of transcript from Gotti's 1987 federal trial he ended up using only the quotes "Gang Land" and Mustain used in a book published in 1988.

This is not a book so much as a bad movie "treatment." The author tips his real intention in his afterword, when he fawns over a producer and insults FBI agents who, he says, talked to him after they learned that Tom Cruise might portray them.

Unable to find the real drama of this story, however, the author is reduced to desperation. He makes up scenes that Hollywood producers might like—such as a leering account of a conveniently unidentified woman's kinky bedroom antics with an unidentified gangster.

He also makes up an ending that's pure Hollywood hokum—a scene in which agents go to prison to collect Gravano, who has just decided to become an informer, and the guards bring down Gotti instead. It never happened.

The afterword provides final proof of the phony baloney in *Gangland*. The author goes on and on about all the reporting know-how he used to get the home telephone number of Mrs. Michael Cirelli, who lived in the apartment Gotti used as an inner sanctum. He needed secret documents, secret sources.

Anyone who wants to be spared this indulgent nonsense should just look on page 148 of the Manhattan White Pages.

NOVEMBER 9, 1993

Really Long Wait for Sign from God

You might say that Joey Bang Bang shot himself in the foot the other day while waiting for God to tell him not to pull the trigger.

In fact, Joseph "Joey Bang Bang" Massaro, 50, essentially put two behind his own ear when he sentenced himself to life in prison, bypassing a chance to do just 10 years.

Massaro—a made member of the Luchese family since 1985—was found guilty after a two-month trial, of racketeering and murder charges, which according to federal sentencing guidelines mandates life in prison.

He also was convicted of extortion and using arson and the threat of arson to take over several Long Island topless bars in the early 1980s during a feud between the Luchese and Bonanno families.

Since Massaro was convicted of putting two in the head of a mob associate, his life sentence is fitting, but he would have done much better if he took cues from his lawyers and co-defendants and copped a plea.

Instead, Massaro waited for a sign from God.

A former boxer with pretty good punching power, and known for his prowess with a gun, Massaro was the only one of six mobsters and associates of the so-called Harlem Crew to go to trial on the 16-month-old indictment.

The others, including Harlem Crew leader Anthony "Bowat" Baratta—who also served briefly as acting Luchese family boss—copped plea bargains that will allow them to walk out of jail instead of being carried out in a pine box.

"There will be a light at the end of the tunnel, eventually," is how Baratta's lawyer, Bruce Cutler, explained his client's decision to plead guilty in a deal that means a sentence of between 121 and 151 months in prison.

Baratta and the others will learn their exact prison terms next month; Massaro will get the news, officially, in February, from Manhattan Federal Court Judge Miriam Cedarbaum.

Sources on both sides of the law told "Gang Land" that Massaro had been offered basically the same 121-to-151-month deal during his trial—which began the day after Labor Day.

There is some disagreement between law enforcement and defense sources over the exact terms of the deal, but without question, Massaro would have been home at least three years before his 65th birthday, when most people retire.

But when defense lawyers Harry Batchelder and Brad Leventhal told Massaro of the prosecution's offer during the trial, they told Massaro the deal would mean a maximum of 10 years and urged him to accept it.

According to knowledgeable sources, Massaro wasn't willing to take a day more than five years, "unless I get a sign from God."

With that, Batchelder told him a long story about a drowning man who told would-be rescuers—two Coast Guard boats and a helicopter—he was waiting for a sign from God. At the Pearly Gates, St. Peter was shocked to see him.

"I was waiting for a sign from God," said the drowning victim.

"We though two boats and a helicopter was enough of a sign," said St. Peter.

Massaro also should have recognized a bullet that prosecutors fortuitously located a day before the trial—three years after he fired it into his victim's head—as a sign to plead guilty.

Dubbed the "magic bullet" by Batchelder, the slug was found in the car Massaro used to transport his dead victim—by a man who bought the car years after police had searched it and hadn't found the bullet. He found the bullet after an FBI agent located the car shortly before the trial, searched it, and didn't find it either.

According to prosecutors David Kelley and Randall Bodner, Massaro fired it as a "be sure" shot to make sure his victim, Joseph Fiorito, was dead.

The trial included brief testimony by FBI agent Joe Pistone, who said he learned of a 1980 sit-down between the Bonanno and Luchese families over a topless bar dispute while he worked undercover from 1977 to 1982.

Neither prosecutors nor defense lawyers would discuss the plea offers.

"I'm confident the verdict will be reversed on appeal," said Batchelder, who cited the "magic bullet" and Pistone's testimony as two "prime areas of our appeal."

"Pistone's testimony was a legal historical walk on the wild side of no relevance. The FBI had just hired him some late-inning relief to see if he could still hit the corners of the plate," said Batchelder.

State Takes Fourth Shot at Cop-Slay Suspects

After eight years and three false steps, prosecutors have set their sights again on the only mobster believed to have killed a New York City cop.

In the face of daunting odds, Queens prosecutors have decided to prosecute Genovese soldier Federico "Fritzi" Giovanelli and associate Steven Maltese on murder charges—again—in the brutal slaying of Detective Anthony Venditti.

Venditti was gunned down as he came out of a Queens diner while working undercover on a joint state-federal task force investigating Giovanelli as head of a Ridgewood bookmaking and loan-sharking operation. His partner, Kathleen Burke, was wounded.

The case drew widespread attention because of the unprecedented mob killing of a cop—and because Burke came under heavy criticism from some police officers for failing to respond quickly enough to save her partner.

The 1986 shooting outside the Castillo Diner has been the focus of three trials and one federal appellate court ruling.

Two state murder trials for the men ended in mistrials with hung juries. A third defendant, Carmine "Buddy" Gualtiere, was acquitted at the second of the trials.

The case was moved to federal court so that all three could be charged with murder and racketeering. They were convicted, but the murder counts were thrown out by a federal appeals court in 1991 because of technicalities.

Authorities decided to retry the men on state murder charges last month, just before Maltese was freed January 11 from federal prison on bookmaking charges and Giovanelli neared his mandatory release date.

"The fact that Maltese is already out and Giovanelli will be out next year played a big part in the decision to restore the case to the calendar," said one law enforcement source.

Asked about the likelihood of a conviction so long after the killing when juries in two prior cases were hung, Queens District Attorney Richard Brown said: "Obviously, it's not an easy case, but it seems to me that I have an obligation as a prosecutor to continue to bring those responsible for the murder of a detective to justice."

"Three trials, one federal appeal, and five years in jail, and now we're starting all over, as if nothing happened?" scoffed Maltese's lawyer Jay Horlick, who argued the successful appeal of Maltese's federal conviction.

Lawrence Hochheiser, who represented Giovanelli at the three trials, called the planned state prosecution "totally unfair, since it has been 5½ years since the last hung jury and a crucial witness for the defense has died."

Hochheiser said he's filing papers opposing the retrial, arguing that the move puts Giovanelli at risk of double jeopardy and violates his right to a speedy trial.

"More importantly," said Hochheiser, "is the concept of fair play. It's much a bigger issue than whether Freddy Giovanelli is prosecuted for the death of a policeman.

"If we sell out the most venerated principle of a fair trial in order to purchase vindication of the death of Detective Venditti, we'll get neither justice nor vindication."

Barber Of B'klyn Sings Aria to Feds

In literature, Figaro was the barber of Seville, a self-important type who became a valet to Count Almaviva after he helped the nobleman win the hand of the lovely Rosina in the comic opera by Gioacchino Rossini.

In gangland, "Dino" is the Barber of Gravesend, an immigrant from Palermo, Sicily, who cut hair for Don Carlo Gambino, sang at weddings and bar mitzvahs, and became a murderous mob associate who kicked people when they were down.

Today, the barber—Corrado "Dino" Marino, 52—sings for the feds against a slew of Luchese family mobsters who planned to make him part of the West Side Highway.

At 17, he immigrated to Brooklyn, working as a barber. In 1969 he opened up his own place—Mr. Dino Hair Styling Salon.

While cutting the hair of neighborhood "shoemakers, butchers, and undertakers," he also served customers like the legendary Gambino—and Luchese consigliere Christopher "Christy Tick" Furnari. He sold the shop in 1979.

Millionaire businessman Frank Arnold, who sports a hairpiece, was also a regular at Mr. Dino—an important one at that, Marino testified last week at Arnold's racketeering trial in Brooklyn Federal Court.

In fact, Marino said, the businessman was so important, he built a partition for him "because when a guy like Mr. Arnold takes off his hairpiece, he doesn't want to take (it) off in front of 15 people."

It was after meeting at Marino's shop that Furnari—who was convicted of racketeering in the historic Commission case and is doing 100 years—befriended and became a conspirator with Arnold, according to Marino and prosecutors Patricia Notopoulos and William Gurin.

They were such good friends that when Furnari was arrested in 1985, Arnold posted $1.75 million so Furnari could remain free during his trial.

Now it is Arnold on trial, charged with extortion, making cash payoffs to union officials, and using threats in 1989 to force former painters union official James Bishop not to run for reelection.

In 1990, Marino testified last week, he had his own experience with Bishop. He helped mobster Richard Pagliarulo and Michael DeSantis kill him when they learned from Luchese underboss Anthony "Gaspipe" Casso that "Bishop went bad"—became an informer, he said.

In 1992, while Marino was vacationing on the Greek island of Kios, he decided that the Lucheses wanted to do to him what they did to Bishop.

It happened this way, he said. Pagliarulo, who had been honeymooning in France, flew to Greece, put his arm around Marino, told him the Lucheses wanted to induct him, and said, "Let me give you a bit of advice so you don't get scared."

"You're going to be put in the backseat of a car between two people, be driven around a few streets to make sure (cops aren't following), and then you're going to be taken to a place where you're going to be sworn in," said Pagliarulo, according to Marino.

"I drew a conclusion I was not going to be made a member of the Luchese family. I was probably going to become a part of the West Side Highway," said Marino.

Soon after, Marino returned to Brooklyn, was indicted, and fled to Europe, telling Arnold's lawyer David Breitbart he "had to leave—(I was) dealing with a psychopath like Mr. Casso who killed because (Casso) dreamed the night before they were cooperating."

In graphic detail, Marino told of a frightening incident in which he drove Arnold to a Staten Island warehouse and watched in horror as, under orders from Casso capo Peter "Fat Pete" Chiodo, Pagliarulo put a shotgun to Arnold's head.

Pressed for details of the discussion, Marino said: "You know, you have to understand one thing, I was looking at the barrel of that shotgun. I was not aware of what was going to happen from one minute to the next. I paid some attention to the conversation, but ..."

"I want you to know that Mr. Arnold defecated because there was a smell in the room, and I, uh, was scared. I don't know how I didn't do the same thing because I was scared."

Breitbart, who began his defense case yesterday, has argued that the feds have had a vendetta against Arnold ever since he put up Furnari's bail money in 1985.

Arnold, asserts Breitbart, is a scrupulously honest businessman who was often threatened by mobsters but was afraid to notify authorities because the Lucheses had a law enforcement mole—code-named "Crystal Ball"—who often tipped them to informers.

Casso, who learned about an impending indictment and fled days before it was filed in 1990, was captured last year, and begins trial next month on murder and racketeering charges.

Last May, after eight months on the run, Marino was arrested in Belgium.

After three months of sleeping on the floor in prison, he decided to cooperate and called the FBI.

"I am not a dummy," he said last week.

Loan Shark Flaps His Jaws

Carmine Sessa returned to Brooklyn last week for the first time since he found religion outside St. Patrick's Cathedral last Palm Sunday.

In a flat monotone the highest-ranking Colombo family convert told a federal court jury about the bloody two-year mob war that left 11 dead, and how he personally killed 13 others, including a woman, during a life of crime.

In chilling detail, as his mother sat and listened impassively, Sessa described participation in the murders he committed and told why the shooting war between the Carmine "Junior" Persico and Victor "Little Vic" Orena fractions was bad for his loan-shark business.

"Sometimes I was just there; sometimes I was the shooter; sometimes I would wrap the body up," said Sessa when federal prosecutor George Stamboulidis asked about the different roles he played.

Sessa, the former cosigliere, recounted how he helped kill a woman in his clubhouse to prevent her from giving up the hideaway of a fugitive gangster, and how his failed effort to kill Orena in June 1991 was the official start of the Colombo war.

Besides littering the streets with bodies—including two bystanders—the war damaged his loan-shark payments. "It was harder to get around to collect your money. Guys were shooting at each other," said Sessa.

In a week of testimony, Sessa, 43, linked four reputed capos, one soldier, and one associate—all alleged Persico fraction allies on trial on murder and racketeering charges—to slayings and other war crimes in 1991 and 1992.

Before Sessa finished, one of the reputed capos, Richard Fusco, was severed from the trial when his blood pressure shot up so high that doctors feared he would have a stroke.

Sessa tied the others—capos Theodore Persico, Joseph "JoJo" Russo, Anthony "Chuckie" Russo, soldier Joseph "Joe Monte" Monteleone, and associate Lawrence Fiorenza—to murder conspiracies that mean life in prison, if convicted.

During cross-examination, Sessa admitted that he lied all his life, even to the FBI after he began cooperating, as defense lawyers tried to convince the jury that Sessa was lying about their clients to save himself.

He conceded that he hoped to avoid at least some of the life sentence he faces on his guilty plea to racketeering charges.

For the most part, Sessa spoke softly and calmly stuck to his guns, even while admitting to Persico's lawyer, Joel Winograd, that he snorted coke, cheated on his wife, and had an affair with the daughter of a gangster friend.

But Sessa lost his cool only once—throwing up his hands and appearing to begin to rise out of the witness chair—when Winograd pressed him and asked him twice if he had finished reading a document he had been given.

"Not yet," said Sessa, his voice rising. "Take it easy, take it easy. Talk. I'll give you all the answers you want when I'm finished reading."

"Wait a minute, hold on," said Judge Charles Sifton, who then told Sessa: "If you feel that you are losing your temper or losing control of your feelings, just tell me you need a recess."

Even before the trial began, Sifton was concerned about the possibility of a Sessa outburst—not from the witness stand, but the spectator section.

During Sessa's first day, Sifton called Sessa's mom, Jacqueline, up to the bench and warned her privately, she told her friends, against making any outburst during her son's testimony.

When "Gang Land" inquired about the conversation, Sifton placed this on the record: "I said I had received what I would characterize as rumors that she was going to do something to disrupt the proceedings, that I had absolutely no reason to think that that was true but that I thought that my obligation under the circumstances was to ask for her assurance that nothing of the sort would occur and she had given me that assurance, and that was the whole thing."

Early on Sessa detailed his induction into the Colombo family in March 1987, his promotion to capo the following year, and his elevation to consigliere by the spring of 1990.

Sessa's meteoric rise from associate to consigliere illustrates the talent shortage for top executives in today's mob. It is akin to an assembly line worker becoming chief operating officer in three years.

And like any corporation that doesn't take the time to train its top managers, the mob is losing its market share, as Sessa and dozens of others defectors leave the Mafia gasping for life and new leaders.

APRIL 26, 1994

A Closet Full of Turncoats

The feds have so much mob-informer firepower these days they've decided they don't even need their top-gun turncoat when three Luchese mobsters go on trial for murder and racketeering next month.

Instead, sources have told "Gang Land," former Luchese underboss Anthony "Gaspipe" Casso will be used in two labor racketeering investigations into the private carting and trucking industries and a sensitive police-corruption probe.

Our sources declined to spell out details of these labor probes. But in prior cases it's been established that the Luchese family controls much private carting—especially on Long Island—and maintains trucking company interests in the Garment District. The Lucheses are also known to have strong Teamster clout at Kennedy Airport.

Law enforcement officials brushed off one defense lawyer's claim that the feds are "very reluctant" to use Casso at next month's trial because FBI supervisors had previously described him as a psychopath.

"That's nonsense, combined with wishful thinking," said one official.

Even without Casso, the trial will feature more Luchese killers on the witness stand than accused killers at the defense table.

Prosecutors believe they have an overwhelming case against capo Frank "Big Frank" Lastorino and mobsters Michael DeSantis and Richard Pagliarulo.

While they've informed Brooklyn Federal Judge Eugene Nickerson that they will hold back Casso, prosecutors still intend to use recent Luchese turncoat Thomas "Tommy Irish" Carew at the Brooklyn Federal Court trial.

Prosecutors Charles Rose and Gregory O'Connell said they will also use former acting boss Alphonse "Little Al" D'Arco, capo Peter "Fat Pete" Chiodo, and associate Corrado "Dino" Marino at the May 16 trial.

Last week, Nickerson agreed to sequester the jury for the entire trial because of allegations from Casso that the defendants were planning to use private eyes to identify anonymous jurors, then use Luchese associates to seek them out and offer them $100,000 bribes to vote for acquittal.

That jury-tampering scheme was a fallback plan in case several escape efforts—including an armed assault by Luchese associates on a prison van—failed, according to court papers.

As the *Daily News* reported last month, the U.S. attorney's office is also probing allegations that Casso used NYPD Detectives Lou Eppolito and Steve Carcappa as law enforcement moles—and as hit men in the 1990 slaying of Gambino capo Edward Lino.

Eppolito and Caracappa, both retired, deny the allegations.

Of all the recent turncoats, Gaspipe's defection is remarkable for both the mob and law enforcement. Officials vilified him while he was on the lam, pointing to gruesome details of many murders of many mobsters.

Acting boss D'Arco considered many of Casso's murder schemes so bizarre that he ignored them. In 1991, however, D'Arco stopped ignoring Casso when he learned he himself was marked for death. He walked into an FBI office in New Rochelle and made a deal for himself and his family.

────────

Prosecutors used the same strategy—holding back a key witness—in the recent murder/racketeering trial of five Colombo wiseguys involved in a bloody two-year mob war that left 11 dead.

The Luchese prosecutors hope they do as well as their colleagues.

Last week, Colombo prosecutors Andrew Weissmann, George Stanboulidis, and Ellen Corcella won convictions across the board, likely meaning life in prison for capo Theodore "Teddy" Persico and his four co-defendants.

Persico, Joseph "JoJo" Russo, Anthony "Chuckie" Russo, Joseph Monteleone Sr., and Lawrence Fiorenza were convicted on the testimony of four major witnesses, including former consigliere Carmine Sessa.

The Colombo prosecutors held out turncoat capo John Pate, saving him for the trial in June of Teddy's nephew, Alphonse Persico—son of in-prison-for-life boss Carmine Persico.

Alphonse was the reason for the mob war—all four witnesses said Carmine Persico wanted his son to take over when Alphonse got out of prison last year—but only Pate can testify about talks he had with Alphonse during the war.

Pate visited Alphonse in prison several times during the height of the war, according to court records.

Now Pate's fresh for his stint at Alphonse's trial.

JUNE 14, 1994

No Tipping the Capo to Legendary Mobster

At the end Greg Scarpa went to his grave unrespected.

A made man for four decades, a feared enforcer, a Colombo capo powerful enough to single-handedly start a bloody family war, he might have rated a funeral no less extravagant than the great flower-bursting mob send-offs of yore.

But as it turned out, Greg Scarpa had lived two lives—one of them as a federal informant who spun dark mob secrets for 20 years. And cops surveilling the old man's wake Sunday saw not a single confederate come with lowered head to kiss his coffin and bid him farewell.

"Bless the body of Gregory," said the Rev. Eugene Coyle over the polished golden oak coffin at St. Bernadette's Church in Bensonhurst yesterday morning. But he addressed only family and neighbors who had come in a procession totaling five cars.

"None of us lives as his own master," Coyle said. "And none of us dies as his own master."

Greg Scarpa's resume is the stuff of mob legend.

In the 1960s, with budding Colombo boss Carmine "Junior" Persico, he helped then-boss Joe Profaci beat back an ambitious rebel faction headed by Crazy Joe Gallo.

In 1971, he was hauled before a Senate subcommittee for grilling about an airport theft ring, and he smiled broadly and took the Fifth more than 60 times.

One day in the late 1970s, one Dominick Somma complained about screwups that Scarpa's son Greg Jr. had made during a bank job, and Scarpa shot him on the spot. The memory always riled him later. "I'd like to dig him up and shoot him again," he once snarled.

In 1991, discussing a small business matter, he coolly faced down—all by himself—two rival capos who were backed up by nearly 50 heavily armed torpedoes.

Later that year, as the Colombos blew apart in civil warfare, he personally whacked three rivals, one of whom was putting up Christmas decorations on his home at the time. "I love the smell of gunpowder," Scarpa said.

And in late 1992, when his left eyeball was shot out in an ambush, he matter-of-factly refused to seek treatment until after he'd attended to some business, gone home, and had a Scotch.

"He was a unique individual," says his lawyer, Joseph Benfante. "If he'd lived 400 years ago, he would have been a pirate."

Just before he died last week at 66—of AIDS contracted during surgery in 1986, when a member of his own crew helpfully donated bad blood—Scarpa dictated a final revelation, a potentially explosive document that could wreck the feds' case against Colombo capo Alphonse "Allie" Persico, son of Scarpa's old friend Junior Persico.

Much discussed yesterday in Brooklyn Federal Court, the deathbed affidavit absolves Allie of any participation in the deadly 1991–1992 Colombo war, for which he is set to go to trial later this month. It was Scarpa's own war, the dead man insists.

Rival hoods "shot at me while I was in a car with my daughter (Linda) and 2-year-old grandchild," says Scarpa's affidavit. "I was so upset over this that my only intention was to retaliate …. I had no instructions to retaliate from anyone, especially Allie Persico …. I did not need anybody's permission to act …. Allie Persico had nothing to do with any of these events."

If he is cleared—and he might be—feds fear that the college-educated Allie will turn the now virtually moribund Colombo family into a viable operation again.

And such could be the final legacy of Greg Scarpa, helping from beyond the grave to rebuild the mob that yesterday gave him no respect as he went to the earth.

"Human reasoning is defective," Coyle offered yesterday, considering the eternal mysteries as the few mourners quietly wept. "We come up with the wrong answers as often as we come up with the right answers."

O.J. Shamus Digs for Gotti

What does John Gotti have in common with O.J. Simpson?

(No, this is not another bad O.J. joke.)

Answer: John McNally, ex-NYPD detective and private eye extraordinaire.

In Los Angeles, McNally's been hired to do heavy lifting for the ex-football star, responsible for rooting up evidence that would acquit him of killing ex-wife Nicole Brown Simpson and her pal Ronald Goldman.

But here at home, his top celebrity client these days is mob star Gotti—and he's been busy digging up dirt on Gotti's number one nemesis, Salvatore "Sammy Bull" Gravano.

The P.I.'s work is so respected—and has been so successful, sources say—that it's given Gotti's pal Joseph Watts the courage to reject a sweet deal that would close the books on four murders in exchange for seven years in jail.

Watts, a long-time Gambino family associate, was on the scene at the spectacular 1985 rubouts of Mafia boss Paul Castellano and his aide Thomas Bilotti, as well as mob hits in 1989 and 1990, according to Gravano.

Five other men, including powerhouse Gambino capos James "Jimmy Brown" Failla and Daniel Marino, have played it safe, pleading guilty and taking the seven years.

But Watts decided to shoot for the moon when McNally uncovered evidence linking Gravano to crimes he never admitted, sources say, including murders and drug dealings—crimes that could undercut his informant's credibility with jurors.

No way, says Gravano's lawyer. The feds won't say anything. But Gotti lawyer Bruce Cutler says McNally's terrific, and he says he's optimistic about a new trial.

So is Gotti, who is in "great spirits" in prison, Cutler says.

Los Angeles confirmed McNally's worth yesterday when the county Criminal Defense Investigators Association asked a judge to kick him out of town for working without a license.

The court will make that call. But McNally says he doesn't need the local ticket because he was hired by a California attorney—and two decades ago, when he was hired by California lawyers representing kidnapped-heiress-turned-terrorist Patty Hearst, he had the same problem with local P.I.s, and things got resolved his way.

————

Once a burly, swaggering tough guy, Colombo gangster Gregory Scarpa Sr. was a wraithlike 50 pounds on his deathbed, barely strong enough to write his name.

The graphic description of the AIDS-stricken Scarpa's last days in a federal prison hospital in Minnesota was given by prison official Dennis Bitz, who was summoned to appear as a defense witness at the Alphonse Persico trial in Brooklyn Federal Court.

On June 7, the day before Scarpa died, Bitz was asked to witness Scarpa's signature on an affidavit prepared by Persico's lawyers. That affidavit is crucial to Persico's defense, since it absolved him of any murder and mayhem during the bloody Colombo family war and put the full blame on Scarpa's own emaciated shoulders.

"Mr. Scarpa had very great difficulty moving his hands," Bitz told the court. "(He) appeared to be in a great deal of pain. His movements were very slow and measured. At various points he closed his eyes—excuse me, I mean his eye—Mr. Scarpa only had one eye."

Scarpa, an amazing gangster who loved the smell of gunpowder and lived a 30-year double life as an FBI informer, left his other eye on a Brooklyn street after a 1992 shootout.

————

The FBI is investigating whether a low-level wiseguy from Brooklyn helped fugitive con man/gangster/informer Kenneth "Kenny the Rat" O'Donnell make his daring escape from the Passaic County Jail.

The suspected accomplice visited O'Donnell weeks before his May 14 bust-out and may have provided him with clothes and cash, sources say.

O'Donnell, still on the lam, has boasted to "Gang Land" that he didn't need anyone else's help, that getting out of jail was "like eating a piece of cake."

FBI agents from New Rochelle, Newark, Manhattan, and Long Island are still searching for the elusive turncoat. They say they hope to find him before the mob does. Their way, he stays alive.

Playing Feds & Friends
Like Fiddle

He lived an amazing double life, both a top mobster and a key federal informant—and for more then 30 years he played both the mob and the FBI for suckers.

With the help of secret documents obtained yesterday, "Gang Land" now provides new details about double agent Greg Scarpa Sr., who was breaking the code of *omerta* as long ago as legendary mob informant Joe Valachi.

The documents—FBI informant memos going back to 1980 and sealed federal court records—show that the late Colombo big informed, usually to his own advantage, on everyone from his own son to top bosses in the faction-riddled crime family.

They paint John Gotti as an instigator of the bloody 1991–1992 Colombo war in which 11 people died. They reveal that Scarpa gave the FBI details of killings he committed during that war, without ever implicating himself.

Even after Scarpa was arrested for wartime killings and dropped as an active informant, he continued to tip the FBI to Colombo doings—including one "serious discussion" the family had about whacking the mother of a cooperating witness.

But, though he was "quite an asset to the FBI over the years," Assistant U.S. Attorney Valerie Caproni said in sealed remarks at Scarpa's sentencing December 15 that his value "doesn't mitigate the fact that he was a killer during the war."

"There is no question about that," agreed Brooklyn Federal Judge Jack Wienstein, handing Scarpa 10 years.

Scarpa had no hope of serving it out. He died of AIDS two months ago at a federal prison hospital in Minnesota.

The documents, when combined with information from law enforcement sources, show that Scarpa was a wily gangster who told of serious crimes by others—but threw the FBI mere crumbs about his own mob activities and those of his son Greg Jr.

In the early 1980s, Scarpa kept tabs on the constantly changing structure of the Colombo family, alerting the FBI to big decisions by frequently jailed boss, Carmine "Junior" Persico.

Since 1980, Scarpa was the eyes and ears of the FBI's Colombo squad supervisor, Lindley DeVecchio, regularly giving insight and details about the family's capos, soldiers, and associates, and their inductions, promotions, and deaths.

It was Scarpa who told DeVecchio as long ago as 1983 that Persico's son Alphonse was an "up-and-coming capo."

A year before the Colombo war began, Scarpa reported tensions between the elder Persico and acting boss Victor "Little Vic" Orena and said Persico was "trying to maintain firm control" until Alphonse got out of prison.

After Persico mobsters staked out Orena for a possible hit in 1991, Scarpa alerted the FBI—wrongly—that "this dispute will be settled soon."

But he was right when he predicted that he himself might be Orena faction's first target.

"Gotti has been manipulating Orena for a long time and is anxious to have this dispute resolved in Orena's favor so he can assume control of the Colombo family's activities," DeVecchio wrote after meeting Scarpa on November 4, 1991.

Gotti, then jailed and waiting trial on murder and racketeering charges, tried to assist Orena by ordering Gambino soldiers to end their business dealing with some 25 mobsters who backed Persico, Scarpa had told the agent.

Two weeks later, Scarpa was ambushed—but survived the attack—near his Brooklyn home, and the war was on.

As Gotti's trial began in 1992, his capo son John A. "Junior" Gotti urged an end to the "shooting war," Scarpa said, because the growing number of dead bodies of mobsters and bystanders would hurt his father's chances in court.

The warring mobsters ignored Junior. Scarpa kept killing Orena loyalists and was arrested in September 1992 and fired by the FBI.

Alan Futerfas, lawyer for convicted cap Anthony "Chuckie" Russo, says the documents prove that "during the so-called war, Scarpa was working for the FBI and was a government protagonist whose remarks should never have been used as evidence at my client's trial."

Futerfas told "Gang Land" that Russo failed to get a fair trial because the prosecutors used Scarpa's words without telling the judge, or defendants, that Scarpa was an informer.

"It's extraordinary for prosecutors to argue to the jury that Scarpa was a very active participant in the war when they knew all along that he was a government agent," said Futerfas.

Gotti's Lawyers Survive Hot Spell

The government has given up trying to find something on John Gotti's lawyers, Bruce Cutler and Gerald Shargel.

After four years of huffing, puffing, and poking into closets, federal prosecutors in Brooklyn have quietly shut down a grand jury investigation of Gotti's legal tag team—and notified both men that there will be no further action.

That means that Cutler and Shargel—the one-two punchers who kept Gotti out of prison longer then most other lawyers could have—will no longer have to ask their clients to sign embarrassing waivers acknowledging the probe.

"Gang Land" readers will recall that it was Gotti's own bombastic mouth—speaking into an FBI bug planted at his Ravenite Social Club in Little Italy—that caused prosecutors to suspect his lawyers might be hiding some secrets of their own.

On January 4, 1990, Gotti ranted to top aides about having had to pony up $300,000 in legal fees. "Where does it end?" Gotti demanded. "*Gambino* crime family? This is the Shargel, Cutler, and who-do-you-call-it crime family. I told

them yesterday, 'You know and I know that they (the feds) know you're taking money under the table.'"

But after painstaking inspections of the lawyers' bank and accounting records, the feds now acknowledge that they've come up dry.

Gotti prosecutor James Orenstein, who conducted the grand jury probe of the lawyers, yesterday confirmed the end of the game but had no other comment.

"I was always very confident about outcome," said Shargel. "But any investigation is cause for concern, so I'm extremely happy that it's over."

"It's good news," added Cutler. "Now that we have a clean bill of health, we can move forward on other fronts to help other people clear their names."

———

Is a Mafia boss mentally unfit to stand trial just because he likes to wear his pajamas outdoors?

For his part, Vincent "Chin" Gigante, who is the boss in question, will be present in Brooklyn Federal Court in October for a hearing before Judge

Eugene Nickerson to determine an answer to that.

But the same can't be said with certainty of either his prosecutors or a key government witness.

The prosecutors, Charles Rose and Gregory O'Connell, have resigned from the Brooklyn U.S. Attorney's office, and the Justice Department hasn't made a final decision whether to appoint them as special prosecutors.

And Anthony "Gaspipe" Casso, the latest top mobster to turn government witness, may be held out of the case by whomever the feds end up using as prosecutors, according to law enforcement sources familiar with Casso's FBI debriefings.

These sources say Casso, who was expected to testify that Gigante is quite sane, notwithstanding his penchant for wearing nightclothes on long walks outdoors, may never take the witness stand following a slight misunderstanding with his federal keepers. Reportedly, he held back information about two Luchese mobsters until FBI agents caught him at it—and threatened to void his cooperation deal.

The FBI and U.S. attorney's offices refused to talk about any of this yesterday.

As for Gigante: "No matter who the players are, we expect to proceed," says his lawyer, Barry Slotnick. "We believe nothing has changed since Mr. Gigante

was found to be incompetent four years ago."

Luchese mobster Anthony Grado should have followed the old Brooklyn adage: Loaning money to relatives only brings you grief.

It doesn't help if the relative is a drug dealer.

Back in 1991, Grado's drug-dealing cousin Robert Molini was strapped for cash and got a loan from Grado and mobster Thomas "Tommy Red" Anzeulotto.

Molini hadn't paid up a full year later, and Anzeulotto at one point allegedly put a gun to his head.

Today, according to Brooklyn federal prosecutor Neil Ross, Grado and Anzeulotto are being held without bail, awaiting trial on federal loan-sharking charges—thanks to Molini, who spilled his guts.

Molini—who has been promised relocation in the federal Witness Protection Program—also has told feds about a drug dealer he and several partners killed in 1992 for stealing $200,000.

But he still has some unfinished business with the state's Environmental Conservation Department. He's wanted for "illegal possession of wildlife"— namely Sasha, a 70-pound mountain lion he kept in his Canarsie, Brooklyn home three years ago.

"The suspect was seen walking the animal and had a litter box in his apartment," a Conservation official told the *Daily News* at the time.

Yesterday, spokesman Bill Hewitt told "Gang Land" that Sasha is doing well at her new home at the Holtsville Ecology Center in Brookhaven, L.I., and that Molini is a fugitive with "a warrant out for his arrest."

You can't make this stuff up ....

It's Deal Time for Gravano

Salvatore "Sammy Bull" Gravano has fulfilled his commitment to the feds. Now he wants his reward.

Gravano, the first and only Mafia underboss to testify against his boss, is looking for payback for three years of spilling his guts about John Gotti and hundreds of other gangsters, associates, corrupt cops, and union officials.

"My record speaks for itself," Gravano has told one "Gang Land" source.

The record says Gravano has been the most effective turncoat mobster in history, doing overwhelming damage to the mob—particularly the Gambino crime family.

His testimony has brought down one Mafia boss, an acting boss, nine capos, a corrupt NYPD detective, a corrupt juror, and the president of one of the most powerful Teamsters Union locals in the country.

"He's the best thing that ever happened to us," said one law enforcement official.

"I can't think of anyone who has accomplished more," agreed one veteran defense lawyer. "In most cases he stood alone—and everyone he implicated in crimes, who went to trial, was convicted."

And Manhattan District Attorney Robert Morgenthau rates Gravano in many ways as more important than even the celebrated Joe Valachi—the first to break with *omerta*, the Mafia's vow of secrecy.

Gravano, says Morgenthau, is "a more substantial guy, higher up in the organization than Valachi, and had more insights. In specific cases, Gravano is much more important that Valachi."

And so Gravano—despite the fact that he's personally owned up to 19 killings—feels he's earned a big reduction off the 20 years he potentially faces for murder and racketeering convictions.

Looking coldly at the numbers, any sentence that Gravano gets—even time served, which is less than four years for all his crimes, less that six months for each killing—is a steal for the feds.

In return for 30, perhaps 35 years of freedom—Gravano is 49—the feds have won jail terms totaling more than 200 years for dozens of other criminals, including a host of mob killers.

Gravano intends to keep his mouth shut when he appears for sentencing before Brooklyn Federal Judge Leo

Glasser, perhaps as soon as a few weeks from now.

But in private conversations with people "Gang Land" has talked to, Gravano has said he expects no more than 10 years, and he personally thinks the sentence that turncoat Philadelphia underboss Philip Leonetti got—6½ years, reduced from 45—should be a benchmark for him.

"He deserves tremendous credit for his historic contribution to law enforcement," says his lawyer, Larry Krantz.

Neither Morgenthau nor Gravano's federal sponsors would discuss with "Gang Land" the range of prison time they felt would be fair and just.

Meanwhile, Gravano is still slated to testify in three more trials—including the murder and racketeering case against Genovese crime boss Vincent "Chin" Gigante.

Rays of Light Shed on Pizza-Drug Link

It's a fact: The city is full of places called Original Ray's Pizza, but there's only one *genuinely* original Ray's, and it's on Prince Street in Little Italy, founded in 1959 by Ralph "Ray" Cuomo.

Don't confuse it with, among others, the Famous Original Ray's Pizza on Third Avenue, whose operators were charged last week with being part of a huge international drug ring.

It's a fact: Ray Cuomo has nothing to do with *that* operation.

However, the real original Ray is a full-fledged mobster in the Luchese crime family, according to law enforcement authorities and Mafia informers.

And, like the accused pizza pretenders nabbed last week, his secret specialty is supposedly also narcotics.

Cuomo, 57, officially got into the drug business in 1969, when the feds nabbed him and four others with 50 pounds of top-quality junk worth $25 million and convicted them all of heroin trafficking.

By that time, Ray's Pizza, at 27 Prince Street, a block and a half from the Ravenite Social Club, had been serving pizza by the slice for 10 years.

"We don't have to say 'Famous' or 'Original.' We leave that to the Johnny-come-latelies," manager Anthony Salvatore told an interviewer a few years ago. "And we have something none of them have. We have a Ray. The owner. Ralph Cuomo."

Cuomo opened his Ray's Pizza three years after being interrupted during an armed robbery of a Park Avenue eatery. He was bloodied by arresting officers, who shot one of his accomplices to death.

Since he finished his federal drug sentence in the late 1970s, Cuomo and his landmark pizzeria have been the focus of three separate, unsuccessful drug probes by the Manhattan District Attorney's office, sources say.

Bugs were planted, but Cuomo was never caught in any incriminating drug talk. Two investigations involved bugs secreted inside. Another used a bug placed outside the Prince Street Ray's. Today, he often can be seen on Prince Street, eating a slice inside or talking to friends.

But he's still in the drug business, according to authorities and former Luchese acting boss Alphonse "Little Al" D'Arco.

D'Arco told the FBI that Cuomo runs his heroin business from the pizzeria and often conducts criminal meetings in the basement, just like the Famous Original Ray's Pizza defendants allegedly did in their Third Avenue pizzeria.

To show he knew the turf, D'Arco described the pizzeria's cellar. "In the basement," said D'Arco, "there are actual tree limbs holding up the beams of the building. These trunks have a polished finish to them."

D'Arco was there many times—like the day in 1988 when he warned Cuomo and other Lucheses to be ready to duck whenever Anthony "Hickey" DiLorenzo, a Genovese mobster who frequented the place, was around. The Genoveses had marked him for death, but thankfully for Ray's, DiLorenzo was dispatched in front of his New Jersey home.

Neither Cuomo nor his manager were available to discuss pizza or anything else with "Gang Land."

Meanwhile, Rosolino Mangano, who controls 18 Famous Original Ray's Pizza stores and franchised a few others—including the one on Third Avenue—wants the New Yorkers to know that not every place called Ray's is a drug cover.

Mangano has a "personal hatred of drugs," said his spokesman, Steven Greene, and was "deeply disturbed" that he had sold a midtown franchise to alleged drug dealers.

He also has no use for Cuomo's claim that Ray's Pizza existed five years before Mangano opened his own first Original Ray's.

"He's got a little shop and he can claim whatever he wants," said Greene. "There is only one Original Ray's, and it was founded in 1964 by Rosolino Mangano."

His New Family Praises the Champion Turncoat

Three years ago, Salvatore "Sammy Bull" Gravano made the biggest bet of his life. Yesterday, he won it.

John Gotti's then-underboss made the wager in a secret meeting with three FBI agents and a federal prosecutor in a small room in the Brooklyn federal courthouse.

"The public and you guys both say John Gotti is the biggest mobster in the country," he told the four men that day in October 1991.

"That means that Sammy Gravano is the number two gangster in the country," he said. "Because I'm John Gotti's right-hand man.

"I could be a very important asset for the government," he said, "if we can make a deal and I cooperate with the government."

Prosecutor John Gleeson and FBI agents Bruce Mouw, George Gabriel, and Carmine Russo listened in amazement to the junior high school dropout from Bensonhurst, Brooklyn.

"I'm not here because I wanna get John Gotti," Sammy Bull told them. "I'm here for Sammy Gravano. I've thought this out, and I figure that this is the only shot I got to help myself, and maybe change my life around at the same time."

Yesterday, in the same courtroom where he pointed the damning finger that sent Gotti and a host of others to prison, the convicted racketeer and murderer heard a federal judge praise him as a hero—the number one witness against the Mafia in U.S. history.

Most importantly for Gravano, 49, he learned that—far from going back to prison for at least another 15 years—he should be a free man in six months, by his 50th birthday.

The judge, echoing assertions by 90 law enforcement agents cited in court papers, said Gravano's "assistance was invaluable" in sending dozens of killers—who would "never" have been prosecuted—to prison, some for life.

Judge I. Leo Glasser said he wasn't trying "to minimize" Gravano's participation in 19 murders, but he pointed out that each one of them was ordered by either Gotti, his predecessor Paul Castellano, or the boss of another crime family.

He praised Gravano for his truthfulness, his usefulness, the nature and extent of his cooperation, his timeliness in cooperating *before* his trial for racketeering and murder, and the lifelong potential danger to himself.

"It's commendable and remarkable what changes you have made in your life, by your conduct, not just lip service," the judge said.

The judge even denounced the media for calling Sammy Bull a "rat" and a "snitch."

In a courtroom packed with many federal and state law enforcement officials who supported a lenient sentence, Glasser rapped the media, which he said helps to glorify mobsters while denigrating mob witnesses who cooperate.

As prosecutors nodded in agreement, Glasser complained about the frequent media use of superlatives like "Godfather" and "Teflon Don" to describe Gotti—but "pejorative words" like "rats" and "snitches" to describe one-time mobsters, like Gravano, who elect to testify for the government.

A 'Bull Market'

List of those Gravano fingered. All were convicted:

John Gotti	Gambino Family Boss
Victor Orena	Colombo Family Acting Boss
John Riggi	DeCavalcante Family Boss
Frank LoCascio	Gambino Family Acting Consigliere
Venero Mangano	Genovese Family Boss
Benedetto Aloi	Colombo Family Consigliere
Robert Bisaccia	Gambino Family Captain
Thomas Gambino	Gambino Family Captain
Pasquale Conte	Gambino Family Captain
Joseph Corrao	Gambino Family Captain
James Failla	Gambino Family Captain
Daniel Marino	Gambino Family Captain
John Gambino	Gambino Family Captain
Ralph Mosca	Gambino Family Captain
Paul Graziano	Gambino Family Soldier
Anthony Vinciullo	Gambino Family Soldier
Domenico Cefalu	Gambino Family Soldier
Francesco Versaglio	Gambino Family Soldier
Orazio Stantini	Gambino Family Soldier
Phillip Mazzara	Gambino Family Soldier
Louis Astuto	Gambino Family Soldier
Dominic Borghese	Gambino Family Soldier
Joseph Gambino	Gambino Family Soldier
Peter Mosca	Gambino Family Soldier
Virgil Alessi	Gambino Family Soldier
Lorenzo Mannino	Gambino Family Associate
George Pape	Juror in 1986-87 Gotti Trial
Joseph Passanante	Gambino Family Associate
George Helbig	Gambino Family Associate
Peter Mavis	Gambino Family Associate
William Peist	NYPD Detective
Barry Nichilo	Gambino Family Associate
Robert Sasso	Teamsters Union Official
Michael Carbone	Teamsters Union Official
Michael Bourgal	Teamsters Union Official
John Probeyhan	Teamsters Union Official
Joseph Matarazzo	Teamsters Union Official

He could understand using "pejorative words" to describe informers for the KGB, Glasser said. And he said he doubted the media would have used "rat" or "snitch" to describe World Trade Center bombing defendants if they had cooperated, he said.

Outside the courtroom, Tony Caserta, 82, a retired Bensonhurst limousine driver turned court buff who remembered Gravano from the old days, agreed wholeheartedly.

"He's the best thing that ever happened, the best witness I ever saw," said Caserta, who has been watching proceedings even longer than "Gang Land" has been covering them.

"I'm Italian-American, and I think it's about time they finally started getting these guys," said Caserta. "They bleed you all the time, and then they leave you for dead. At least, now, he helped even his score."

"Gang Land," an Italian-American from Bensonhurst, couldn't agree more.

It's No Bull to Us, Say Mob Guys

Was it the biggest giveaway in the history of American jurisprudence?

Or was it a fair and equitable sentence handed down by a courageous federal judge?

Everybody has an opinion about last week's sentencing of Salvatore "Sammy Bull" Gravano.

We'll get to some of those in a minute, but there have been developments since Sammy Bull walked away with what was certainly a sweet deal for himself—about three months in prison for each of the 19 mob killings he admits taking part in.

Since then, at least one made mobster and several mob associates have called federal prosecutors who talk to "Gang Land" and have asked about making deals of their own.

Indeed, one of those prosecutors has even taken to answering his phone thusly: "This is not another Sammy Bull call, is it?"

The typical inquiry: "If Sammy Bull got five years for 19 murders and he cooperated *after* he got pinched, what could I get if I come in before I get pinched?"

So it appears that, so far as law enforcement is concerned, Sammy's five-year sentence is having the desired effect—and, by extension, society in general is reaping the benefits from that.

Other callers, meanwhile, include other cooperating witnesses who didn't happen to get the same light sentence Brooklyn Judge I. Leo Glasser gave Sammy—and who now feel they got screwed.

For example, one mob associate who killed five people and received a glowing report from prosecutors and agents about the "extraordinary" help he gave to the feds got 10 years, and he's been angrily complaining about the unfairness of it all.

Prosecutors generally think the Gravano sentence was too lenient ("a disgrace, a joke," said one), and defense lawyers generally think it was appropriate ("It's fair, he earned it"). All the judges "Gang Land" spoke to—on condition of anonymity—sided with the defense, agreeing that "a significant" reduction from the 20-year maximum was warranted under the circumstances.

"The loud message Judge Glasser sent to the underworld was simple," said one judge. "If you help the good guys against the bad guys, we'll reward you for your work."

"Most people don't understand how difficult it is to make cases against members of a criminal organization which is both sophisticated and ruthless," said another. "People like Gravano are critical to the process."

Another way to gauge Gravono's sentence is to compare his treatment with that of other notorious multiple killers who opted to testify for the feds.

"Gang Land" picked two nonmob guys who worked with the Mafia and were prosecuted and did their cooperating for the feds in Manhattan—former Harlem drug merchant Leroy "Nicky" Barnes and his successor, James Jackson.

Barnes, the former Mr. Untouchable, was given life without parole in 1978, but after working undercover in prison and helping put 44 drug dealers and murderers away, was rewarded with a sentence that will make him a free man in 1998.

Jackson, whose cooperation—like Gravano's—came before trial, and whose truthfulness has been attested to by the feds, initially received 25 years, later reduced to 18.

Zachary Carter, the Brooklyn U.S. attorney in charge of Gravano's case, said that it was "unique" in the history of organized crime prosecutions and that his sentence cannot be compared with those given Jackson or Barnes.

Mary Jo White, the Manhattan U.S. attorney, said Gravano's "cooperation was of historic significance" and that Glasser "was right to give him some not-insignificant reduction in his sentence."

"There is no one sentence that is fair," noted one federal prosecutor. "There are any number that could be fair.

"I think Glasser gave Gravano the lowest conscionable sentence that he could."

The Man Gotti Never Got

Spyredon "Spiro" Velentzas and John Gotti. The Greek Godfather and THE Godfather.

For decades, they were friends and colleagues, Velentzas working mostly in Queens, Gotti in Queens and beyond.

Their friendship also spawned one of the most colorful mob quotes ever: "You tell that punk, that I, me, John Gotti, will sever his f------ head off."

That "punk" was Spiro Velentzas.

While he got away with his head intact, Velentzas suffered the same fate as Gotti. Both men are now in federal prison for life—Velentzas in Terre Haute, Indiana, Gotti just 200 miles away in Marion, Illinois.

Gotti has stayed silently locked away. But two weeks ago Velentzas opened up, giving the *Daily News* his first ever interview—a candid and extensive look inside the New York mob.

"I was the king with my own kind—the Greeks," Spiro Velentzas said softly, without a trace of braggadocio. "We grew up together, everybody knew me. I gave the orders. I was the boss in Astoria."

John Gotti, who should know, stamps his approval.

"I know this Spiro good. He's the boss of the Greeks," he said in a taped chat with underboss Salvatore "Sammy Bull" Gravano in 1990.

"Unquestionably," Gravano agreed.

But Velentzas didn't do it all on his own.

The kingpin of organized crime in the city's Greek community amassed his fortune thanks to the backing of the real kingpins of organized crime in America—the Mafia.

"I work construction, I had restaurant business, I had pawnshop business, I had bagel business, I had a spaghetti joint," Velentzas said at the beginning of the interview. "I never lost one day of work."

But he conceded that for decades he made tons of money running lucrative illegal gambling rackets in the Greek community under an agreement with Gotti and other mobsters.

"I made a lot of money in gambling; I lost it all in the race tracks." He smiled—a smile that said he hadn't *really* lost it *all* playing the ponies.

He knew Gotti more than 25 years and frequently gambled with the Gambino boss at card games and Aqueduct and

Belmont race tracks. But, he says, it was the Luchese crime family that controlled him—lock, stock, and gambling parlor.

Under the Luchese umbrella, Velentzas, who emigrated from Greece at 14 and is now 59, operated horse rooms, ran all-night *barbut* or Greek dice games, and controlled the distribution of joker poker machines in Greek neighborhoods in Brooklyn and Queens, he said.

His working relationship with the Luchese family goes back to 30 years ago when he began driving his predecessor, Pete the Greek Kourakos, to meetings with the bosses in Brooklyn.

"When he died, I inherited the barbut game," said Velentzas.

In return for backing from the Lucheses, he paid tribute, and obeyed orders.

"The last four years, I gave them $10,000 a month—for the horse rooms, barbut games, and joker poker machines," he said, confirming what the feds say.

Indeed, during the jailhouse interview, Velentzas, who is not cooperating with the federal government, confirmed nearly everything that the feds and former Luchese mobsters say about him and his gambling operations.

The one thing Valentzas doesn't admit to is murder.

That's where he parts company with Peter Chiodo, the 400-pound former Luchese captain who fingered Velentzas for a 1988 killing that landed the Greek boss behind bars for life.

"Pete Chiodo set me up," said Velentzas. "In the whole world, I'm the guy he hates the most. He framed me."

Chiodo was also responsible, said Velentzas, for starting a near-fatal feud in early 1990 between him and Gotti.

That occurred when Velentzas, with Chiodo's backing, violated a long agreement between the Luchese and Gambino families and opened a barbut game near a high-stakes Gambino baccarat game.

The Greek dice game was cutting into Gambino profits, and Gotti was so engaged he sent his famous "sever his f---- head off" message to Velentzas.

Within days, Sammy Bull reported that Fat Pete, while blaming Velentzas, had apologized profusely.

"It was Fat Pete who opened it," said Valentzas. I almost got killed, and then he blamed me."

It was Chiodo's testimony that was key to getting Velentzas convicted of racketeering, including bookmaking, loan-sharking and extortion, in 1992. The jury, however, deadlocked on the 1988 murder of an old friend—and legendary jewel thief—Sarecho "Sammy the Arab" Nalo, voting 8–4 to acquit.

Mastermind of the $4 million Pierre Hotel robbery in 1972, Nalo was shot dead as he spoke on the telephone in Velentzas's office at a Queens travel agency. Velentzas, who was home, was on the other end of the line—and heard the shots that killed Nalo.

But Nalo died slowly.

"Get me an ambulance. I don't think I'm going to make it," he told police, according to court papers.

"Who did it?" asked one cop.

"Spiro Velentzas," he said. Nalo's dying accusation was not allowed into evidence at the trial.

But facing about eight years for the racketeering conviction, the lifelong gambler made the bet of his life when prosecutor Kevin McGrath said he would ask the judge to consider Nalo's murder in his sentencing of Velentzas, possibly adding years to his time.

Velentzas chose a retrial for the murder—and lost his bet. He was convicted and got life.

The life sentence is why Velentzas reached out to the *News* and agreed to discuss his mob dealings.

He said he was "hopeful" that underboss Anthony "Gaspipe" Casso, the latest Luchese defector, would exonerate him in his FBI debriefings.

"He knows what really happened," said Velentzas.

According to Velentzas, what really happened on October 26, 1988, is that Chiodo ordered the hit after Nalo failed to repay a $100,000 loan.

According to Chiodo, Velentzas wanted his old friend dead because Nalo "wanted a piece of Spiro's gambling business … and he was afraid for his life."

But Velentzas, if he expected the *News* to take him seriously, had to explain why Nalo fingered him, not Chiodo.

"For six months I was wondering why Sammy "the Arab" would say that," said Velentzas. "I guess at the moment he felt I set him up because nobody knew he was suppose to meet me but me."

From there, his explanation was tortured. He even conceded that, in fact, he had probably set Nalo up for the execution, albeit unwittingly.

Nalo was so secretive that no one knew where he lived. To meet, he would go to Velentzas's travel agency on Wednesday and Saturday evenings.

When Chiodo, trying to track him down to collect his $100,000, pressed Velentzas for his whereabouts, the Greek boss let it slip about the 6 P.M. office meetings. Chiodo then set up the hit there, Velentzas argued, to make it look like it had to be Velentzas's handiwork.

Like many convicts, Velentzas is plagued by what-ifs, and he rips his lawyers, blasting virtually everyone involved with his case as part of a "railroad job."

His situation now looks hopeless.

The Second Circuit Court of Appeals affirmed his conviction; Casso has confirmed that Chiodo's account of Nalo's killing is what really happened, and the *News* could find no proof Velentzas was wrongly convicted.

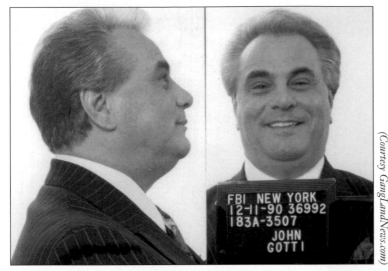

Gambino boss John Gotti, the late Dapper Don, mugs for the FBI camera on the day of his last arrest.

Underboss Sammy Bull Gravano on the day he was arrested with John Gotti.

Classic courtroom confrontation between Sammy Bull and John Gotti by sketch artist Ruth Pollack. "It was the most electric courtroom moment I ever felt," said Pollack.

The Junior Don, John A. "Junior" Gotti, son of the Dapper Don.

Onetime Luchese acting boss Alphonse "Little Al" D'Arco in a doorway on Grand and Mulberry streets in Little Italy in 1989.

Gambino underboss Sammy Bull Gravano and Luchese underboss Gaspipe Casso—both called the Florence Colorado Supermax Federal Penitentiary home in 2003—discuss family business on a Brooklyn street in 1989.

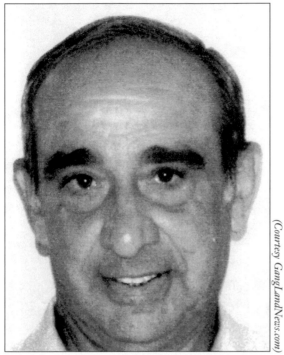

Jailed forever Colombo boss Carmine "Junior" Persico waged a bloody mob war because he wanted son Alphonse to take over the crime family.

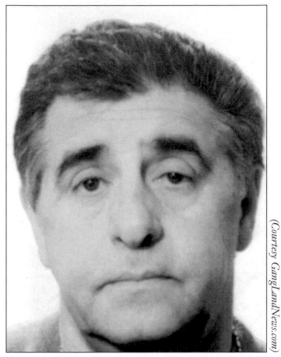

Onetime acting Colombo boss Victor "Little Vic" Orena lost his position, and his freedom, too.

College educated Alphonse Persico got the spot as acting boss, but lost his freedom.

Colombo capo William "Wild Bill" Cutolo moved up to underboss, then lost his life.

Greg Scarpa, Colombo capo who doubled as a top echelon FBI informer, circa 1977.

After a decade of freedom as Bonanno boss, Joseph Massino was nabbed for racketeering when his troops began to defect.

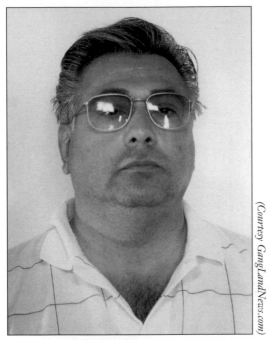

Capo Richard "Shellackhead" Cantarella was one of the main turncoats.

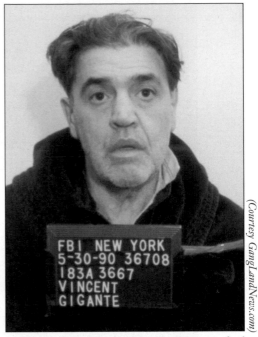

Genovese boss Vincent "Chin" Gigante is scheduled to be released from prison in 2010 at age 82.

Venero "Benny Eggs" Mangano, convicted Genovese family underboss is due out of prison in 2006, at age 85.

Cigar chomping Fat Tony Salerno, a onetime Genovese acting boss, who holds court outside his East Harlem social club here, died in prison at age 80.

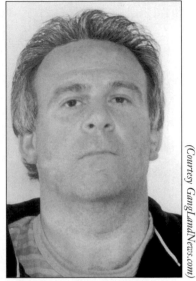

Capo Vincent "Vinny Ocean" Palermo was on a ruling panel that ran the New Jersey-based DeCavalcante family until he defected and decided to cooperate.

(Courtesy GangLandNews.com)

DeCavalcante soldier Joseph "Tin Ear" Sclafani was a real-life New Jersey gangster who loved *The Sopranos* and refused to cooperate with the feds.

(Courtesy GangLandNews.com)

Anthony Rotondo was a real-life New Jersey capo who loved *The Sopranos* but decided to cooperate.

(Courtesy GangLandNews.com)

Gambino Soldier Roy DeMeo squinting into the sunshine (*Left*) and under a chandelier in the trunk of his Cadillac (*Right*).

(Courtesy GangLandNews.com)

Young Colombo associate John Pappa, serving life for four mob hits, including the twelfth and last killing of the Colombo war.

Bizarre tattoo on Pappa's back, featuring the Italian words for "death before dishonor."

NOVEMBER 22, 1994

Both Sides of the Wire

Twelve years ago, Angelo Ditre of Red Hook bashed in the skull of a partner in crime caught wearing a wire.

So Ditre probably understands better than most why three dozen reputed wannabe mobsters and two mob molls feel like bashing *his* skull in with a tire iron. They've been nabbed in an FBI/police department sting in which Ditre was the informant.

For the last two years, "Gang Land" has learned, Ditre—who spent most of his adult life in prison—was the undercover operative behind last week's arrests of 38 mob associates for crimes from drug dealing to murder.

On April 20, 1982, however, two months after Ditre—then an elevator operator for the *Daily News*—planned and pulled off a daring $125,000 robbery of the *News'* Brooklyn plant, he found himself face-to-face with a wired-up informer.

"Ditre tore the recorder off the informant, smashed the recorder with a tire iron, and then attacked the informant with the tire iron," according to the prosecutor at his 1983 sentencing for the *News* robbery.

By then, Ditre was well into his criminal career—having been busted for robbery at age 17 and for being part of the kidnap/murder of a Queens bar owner in 1976.

"The defendant is an exceedingly violent and dangerous criminal. In fact, he is believed responsible for four homicides," the prosecutor added.

Because of that reputation—Ditre admits three murders, not four—the feds couldn't have picked a better person for a sting operation that targeted violent crews of thugs who killed innocent victims for profit and fun.

In one case of stunning brutality, for example, five men, including alleged ringleader Salvatore "Sal the Geep" Candela, are charged with murdering the son of a contractor whose home they invaded and burglarized. They then killed the family's dog for no reason.

Ditre "had a well-earned tough-guy reputation, and that certainly made it easier to get through the rough spots" in his new undercover role, said one law enforcement source.

One rough spot occurred in November 1992, soon after Ditre began wearing a wire, when crew member Thomas

Demetrio told Candela that he suspected Ditre of being an informer.

Rather than confront Ditre, Candela rebuked Demetrio and recounted to Ditre how Lorenzo Mannino, a trusted associate of John Gotti's, had introduced them.

Mannino may regret it.

Mannino, whom Gotti praised as a "man's man" on tapes made at his Manhattan headquarters, is currently serving 15 years in prison for a 1988 Gambino family murder contract.

Mannino and Gambino capos Louis "Big Lou" Vallario and Anthony "Sonny" Ciccone, are targets of a continuing investigation, sources said.

Many of the arrested defendants are alleged members of Vallario's or Ciccone's crews, according to former Gambino underboss Salvatore Gravano.

When Ditre began cooperating in late 1992, he continued a tradition he began 10 years earlier when he carried out the *Daily News* robbery—he brought along his younger brother, Michael, also a former *News* worker.

Angelo, who did the heavier work when they hijacked trucks and robbed their employer, also did the heavy work for the feds, though Michael supplied important details, too, sources say.

For example, after the brothers, along with Salvatore "Sal the Nose" Centore and since-slain crew member Richard Taglianetti, followed a truck from Brooklyn to Queens and hijacked it, Michael's job was to drive it back to Brooklyn for unloading.

But on the way back, according to court papers, Michael got lost and confused while driving along the Brooklyn Queens Expressway and drove over the Williamsburg Bridge and ended up on Delancey Street.

Eventually, he found his way back and they all enjoyed a few laughs about it.

But these days, only Angelo and Michael are laughing. They'll be getting new identities under the federal Witness Protection Program, while the others will likely be spending long stretches in prison.

DECEMBER 6, 1994

Hearts, Flowers, Bullets

Her name was Camille Colucci, and a Mafia capo's nephew wanted her for his wife.

She happened to have a husband already—but this is a Mafia love story. A couple of bullets to the back of the head soon removed Joey Colucci from the picture. And thereafter did Camille become Mrs. Thomas Spero.

That was nearly 25 years ago. Joey Colucci was the first man Salvatore "Sammy Bull" Gravano ever whacked. He did the job, the most infamous mob underboss in history testified at John Gotti's 1992 trial, because his then-Mafia supervisor, a capo, told him Colucci had threatened to kill the capo's nephew, Thomas Spero.

New, from law enforcement sources and with the help of Joey Colucci's still heartbroken relatives, "Gang Land" discloses the real reason Colucci died—gangland romance.

Colucci was 26 at the time, the father of a 6-year-old boy and a 6-month-old girl. On February 28, 1970, he was sitting in the front seat of a car driven by his buddy Spero. Gravano, a .38 caliber handgun at the ready, sat behind him.

"I shot him twice in the head," Gravano told the FBI. "Then three more times when his body was dumped out of the car on Rockaway Parkway." The order, he said, came from Spero's uncle, also named Thomas Spero.

Young Tommy Spero's marriage to the widow Colucci did not last forever. They divorced a few years ago. "Gang Land" could not locate either one of them, and it is not known if Camille ever learned that her first husband was killed on the orders of her second husband's uncle.

Colucci's mother, for her part, always suspected it.

Within weeks of the killing, Anne Colucci told "Gang Land," she was wagging her finger at the younger Spero whenever she encountered him in the neighborhood and openly accusing him of killing Joey: "You had something to do with it, or you know who killed him. How could you do this?"

It was a trying time. Because of a gravediggers strike, she couldn't give her son a proper burial. Meanwhile, she would regularly see the man she knew was responsible for making plans to marry Joey's widow.

Now 74, she still lives in Bensonhurst, in the same house in which she reared Joey and his sister, Jacqueline, the same house in which she and Jacqueline helped rear Joey's kids.

And both mother and daughter are furious that mobster-turned-informer Gravano will soon be getting out of prison—serving less than five years in the slaying not only of Joey Colucci but of 18 other people as well.

"I really feel the justice system sucks," Jacqueline said. "It really does stink. The justice system has finally hit rock bottom. It's a very sad day when a murderer is praised as a hero by judges and prosecutors and gets a gold pin from the FBI.

"Joey was it, my one and only brother. I feel like it happened yesterday. The hurt doesn't go away. The loss of my brother has caused heartaches that are still here after all these years. Our lives would have been different if he weren't taken from us.

"Sammy's wife and kids are supposed to be waiting for him," she said. "He's getting out in four months and my brother is still dead, and his kids still have no father. My brother was no criminal. He was the only one in the neighborhood who got up early to go to work. He was a bricklayer.

"Sammy had to prove that he could be a hit man," she said bitterly. "That's what they all have to do. And so he killed his friend so Tommy Spero could move in on his wife."

"When you're a budding Colombo associate like Sammy was, and you get an order to kill someone, you don't question it, you do it," agreed one law enforcement official. "Sammy did it."

And indeed, Gravano made his "bones" with the Colucci killing—proved he had the stuff to be a "made" man. It was the only time in his long career as top enforcer for the mob and, ultimately, John Gotti, that he actually pulled the trigger himself.

Wiseguy Looks for 2M Leg Up

Johnny G. must have been looking over his shoulder for gun-toting Luchese mobsters when he tripped over a crack in the sidewalk and broke his leg.

John "Johnny G." Gammarano, an alleged tough guy in John Gotti's Gambino crime family, was around the corner from his Bensonhurst, Brooklyn, home when he lost his battle with the concrete on 13th Avenue in 1991.

He broke his leg and did what 2,800 or so New Yorkers do every year when they hurt themselves on city sidewalks—he sued the city and the owner of property adjoining the sidewalk for $2 million.

Gammarano was in a cast for months, then underwent surgery, and during months of follow-up therapy spent some $5,000 for medical care, according to documents filed by his negligence lawyer, Joseph Levine.

But that didn't affect his criminal activities, according to the feds.

To win his lawsuit, Gammarano had to testify under oath.

So Gammarano, who normally prefers to remain in the shadows, testified about the events of July 11, 1991, in a pretrial deposition obtained by "Gang Land."

Gammarano, who said he sells construction materials and brokers construction jobs, said his injury didn't cost him any earnings, but claimed it caused him "excruciating pain."

The feds don't know about Gammarano's pain and suffering, but they agree wholeheartedly with the contention that his injuries didn't hurt his earning power.

In May 1992, the same month he made two follow-up visits to his doctor, Gammarano helped set up a $10 million scheme in which New Orleans mobsters cornered the market on the distribution of Joker Poker machines throughout Louisiana, according to the feds down on the bayou.

By June, he was well enough to travel and spend five days in the Big Easy "for the purpose of meeting with" the boss and underboss of the New Orleans mob to iron out details of the scheme, according to the indictment.

Gammarano is set for trial in New Orleans this fall, but first he'll have to deal with federal charges in Brooklyn in which he and mobsters from three other families are accused of extorting $500,000 from a builder of modular homes.

A few months before he broke his leg, that scheme nearly cost Gammarano his life during a simmering feud between the Luchese and Gambino families over the spoils from their joint rackets, according to FBI documents.

As Luchese mobsters "armed with handguns and submachine guns" lay in wait expecting trouble, Gammarano turned over $30,000 the Lucheses had coming and Gammarano got a firm hand-shake instead of hot lead, former Luchese acting boss, Alphonse "Little Al" D'Arco told the FBI.

Six months later, Johnny G. had his misstep.

"I was walking," said Gammarano, groping for the right words. "I hit … the front of my foot got caught in a little area, a little crack, or whatever you call it."

Gammarano remembered that he was wearing leather dress shoes during the mishap, but not how old they were at the time or whether he still owned the pair.

"I don't know, I couldn't tell you that. I have a lot of shoes," he said.

Gammarano, who went to barber school after high school, said he worked on a "strictly commission basis" selling construction materials for "five or six or seven years."

But he couldn't remember where the company was located.

"I go once in awhile," explained Gammarano.

"It's near Metropolitan Avenue, right off Metropolitan Avenue. It's confusing. It's near the major streets and lots there. You can get confused. I get lost myself."

He was dead certain, however, about one thing. "I was just in pain. I got to tell you, serious pain—the pain was excruciating," he said.

Levine would say only that he was close to settling the case.

Lawyers for the property owner, C.C. Equities Corp., would not comment.

The city thinks the property owner is at fault, said Eugene Borenstein, an official with the city corporation counsel's office.

Keeping Up a Gotti Tradition

Gotti boys just don't mix too well with bars. The gun possession arrest last weekend of John Gotti's 25-year-old nephew Peter Gotti Jr. continues a three-decades-old tradition—one that began when young John was nabbed breaking into a Long Island tavern in March 1965.

Seven years later, as a prison-hardened Gotti was about ready to make his bones for Carlo Gambino, he was arrested during a barroom brawl in Brooklyn. Inside a Staten Island bar a year after that, he killed a rival hood suspected of kidnapping and killing Gambino's nephew. And in 1984, he was charged with assault after slapping a refrigerator mechanic outside a Queens watering hole.

In 1989, chip-off-the-old-block John A. "Junior" Gotti, acting boss for his jailed father, was arrested—the charges were later dismissed—after he allegedly punched out two men and a woman in a Long Island disco.

Last Saturday, nephew Peter—son of the Dapper Don's brother Peter—was arrested with four others after a dispute outside the Palladium when cops found two semiautomatic pistols in their luxury car.

As it happens, though, despite his infamous name and a post as a shop steward for a mobbed-up construction local, Peter Gotti Jr. is not a gangster, according to "Gang Land's" sources.

"He may have gotten his job and his union post through his family's mob connections, but he actually goes to work," said one law enforcement official.

Added a source on the other side of the law: "Peter doesn't go to social clubs; he's been working for the same company for seven years. He's not a gangland kind of guy."

It was a very rude awakening the other morning for Frank "Frank the Wop" Manzo—even though the retired and ailing 70-year-old Luchese capo had been up and about for hours.

Manzo, recently out of federal prison, was nabbed for a 17-year-old crime as he returned to his Hollywood, Florida, condo after a walk with his wife.

He was charged with initiating a 13-year shakedown of John Quadrozzi, a concrete company magnate who claims to have forked over some $2 million to Manzo during the period.

The alleged crime began in 1978, a very good year for Manzo. That same year he and other good fellows from Canarsie and Queens shared in the proceeds of the daring $5.8 million Kennedy Airport robbery of Lufthansa Airlines.

Manzo was never arrested for the Lufthansa robbery, but years later, he was charged with running airport rackets for the Luchese family and improsined for what he told his sentencing judge would be a "death sentence," considering his many ailments.

He was wrong about that—but he could easily be right this time. Which probably explains why Manzo and his wife were "very upset" when FBI agents greeted them as they finished their walk.

It's déjà vu all over again. Reputed Bonanno hoodlum Joseph Cammarano Jr. has just lost his cushy job as a so-called Teamster working foreman.

Cammarano Jr. had been pulling down more than $100,000 a year checking union cards of drivers delivering supplies to a Staten Island condo project—whether he was there or not.

No more. After reviewing FBI reports, the Teamsters' independent review board found that Cammarano Jr., 25, a member of Local 282, was a Bonanno hood and recommended his ouster. The union bounced him yesterday.

Cammarano's father, Joseph Sr., also a former Teamster working foreman, was booted in November, also accused of being a mobster.

Trash Talk from Turncoat Will Dump on Garbage Deal

After 18 months on the shelf, top Luchese turncoat Alphonse "Little Al" D'Arco is set to resume his tales of mob mayhem now that federal prosecutors have turned their attention to a Pennsylvania garbage dump.

It's part of a complicated racketeering case, with 11 defendants—one mobster, five mob associates, a lawyer, and four operators of a landfill in Matamora, Pennsylvania—charged with numerous fraud, extortion, and tax-fraud counts.

D'Arco's main target this time is reputed soldier Peter Del Cioppo, an old buddy who cooked great burgers while working at D'Arco's Burger Palace on Elizabeth Street in the late 1980s. In addition to his talents with chopped meat and a spatula, Del Cioppo had expertise in arson and counterfeiting, and he stored "guns with silencers and a body bag" at the burger joint, according to D'Arco.

The body bag came in handy when D'Arco rubbed out Luchese mobster Michael Pappadio in 1989 and needed to transport the remains to their final resting place, D'Arco said, according to FBI documents obtained by "Gang Land."

During that year, Del Cioppo spent weekends at Matamoras—just across the New York border from upstate Port Jervis—making sure the mob's landfill partners weren't cheating the Lucheses out of their "fair share," says D'Arco.

Federal prosecutors Anthony Siano and Peter Gelfman charge that the landfill operated illegally from February to October 1989, raking in some $3 million in dumping fees—of which $500,000 was kicked back to the Lucheses.

Besides griddlemen, the Lucheses also employ barbers these days.

Long-time Luchese associate Angelo "Sonny Bamboo" McConnach, 68, seized on that the other day as he railed on about the decline of the Mafia to FBI agents who nabbed him and seven others on loan-sharking charges.

Pointing to co-defendant Frank "Frank the Barber" Pellicane, who allegedly accepted loan-shark payments at his Brooklyn barbershop, McConnach had everyone—except Pellicane—doubling over in laughter when he exclaimed:

"(Former Luchese boss) Tony Ducks 'Corallo' never got arrested with no f------ barber. That's how low we are now, we get arrested with f------ barbers."

The relationship between Salvatore "Sammy Bull" Gravano and his son has inspired the first novel by *Daily News* sports columnist Mark Kriegel, called *Bless Me, Father,* about a gangster who pushes his kid to be a boxer.

After hearing from trainer Teddy Atlas that the former Gambino underboss had forced his teenage boy into the fight game, Kriegel renamed them. According to early reviews, the result is, like Kriegel's Sunday sports column, "On The Mark."

Speaking of boxers, Vincent "Chin" Gigante still is fighting his murder and racketeering indictment, albeit in unorthodox style: He's contending he's too crazy to stand trial.

Gigante, a former boxer who often walks through Greenwich Village mumbling like he's punch-drunk, also claims he has an ailing heart. After listening recently to specialists, Brooklyn Federal Judge Eugene Nickerson decided he's heard enough about Gigante's heart and wants to learn about Gigante's mind.

"See when would be agreeable with everyone to come back here with the shrinks and give their testimony to me," he told the opposing lawyers.

Another ex-pug, Luchese mobster Angelo DeFendis, threw in the towel and pleaded guilty to extortion charges stemming from a one-punch knockdown over a contractor who was reluctant to fork over a $25,000 payoff.

DeFendis, a 1953 Golden Gloves middleweight champ and a 1957 contender for the light-heavyweight crown—and cohort Nicholas "Fat Nicky" DiCostanza—face 18 to 24 months on sentencing day later this month.

It's not all bad, though. The feds agreed not to object that DeFendis postpone serving his prison term until after his only daughter marries in June.

Serpico Gets the Last Laugh

Legendary hero cop Frank Serpico will get some sweet—if belated—revenge when Genovese capo Rudolph "Rudy" Santobello is sentenced for racketeering later this month.

Santobello was a young hoodlum when he was convicted of the 1950 murder of policeman Alfred Loreto. Because of his age—just 22—Santobello was spared the death penalty and sentenced to life in prison.

But 15 years later, after a U.S. Supreme Court ruling about illegal searches was applied retroactively to his conviction, he was released and went right back to the mean streets.

That's where Serpico collared him in 1968 as he pulled policy numbers from behind a removable brick in a South Bronx building.

In one of the most dramatic scenes in the 1973 movie about the bearded, bead-wearing cop who in 1970 blew the whistle on police corruption in New York, Serpico, played by Al Pacino, hauled Santobello to the station house and hand-cuffed him to a railing. After leaving the room for a few moments to attend to paperwork, Serpico returned to find that his fellow detectives had released Santobello and were laughing with him.

An outraged Serpico flung Santobello across the room, handcuffing him again as his colleagues told him to take it easy. "Rudy is good people," said one.

"This is who your friend is, he's a f------ cop killer," screamed Serpico as he threw Santobello's rap sheet at the detectives.

In real life, Serpico booked him, the Bronx district attorney's office got an indictment, and Santobello was sentenced to a year in prison.

But again, the Supreme Court came to his rescue. The high court upheld the claim that a newly assigned prosecutor was bound by a promise for leniency that a previously assigned prosecutor had given Santobello in return for his guilty plea.

Holding that plea bargaining was an essential element of the criminal justice system, the court ordered Santobello resentenced according to the original deal.

Now 66, Santobello has been convicted of running lucrative bookmaking and loan-sharking operations out of Club Arthur, his Bronx social club on Arthur

Avenue. He was found guilty of 10 counts of racketeering, including using violence to collect loans of up to $60,000 with yearly interest rates of more than 100 percent.

After each day of trial before Manhattan Federal Court Judge Robert Patterson, Santobello and his entourage would laugh and joke as they left the courtroom, according to the *Daily News's* man at the courthouse, Bill Kleinknecht.

But when the short, wiry, grizzled old gangster was pronounced guilty, his friends sat quietly, except for his two daughters, who sobbed softly.

The sobs turned to loud wails and hysterical moans after prosecutors James Johnson and Douglas Lanker—well aware of Santobello's many triumphs over justice—used the law to send him directly to jail.

"I assume there is no objection to bail being continued until sentence day," said Patterson.

Wrong, said the prosecutors, demanding that Santobello, who faces a maximum of 20 years and a likelihood of at least seven years under strict sentencing guidelines, be remanded while awaiting sentencing.

"Don't worry, I'll see you tomorrow," Santobello assured his family, assuming—quite incorrectly—that his lawyers would spring him quickly.

He's now in the federal lockup in upstate Otisville.

Mob Suspect's Wake-Up Call

Just because a guy's accused of taking part in a bloody mob war and he's too dangerous to be out on bail doesn't mean he shouldn't say his last good-byes to his grandmother.

And that's why, over the objections of federal prosecutors, a handcuffed Robert Gallagher got a six-hour pass from a federal detention center last week to attend his grandmother's wake.

Gallagher, charged with plotting to kill rival Colombo mobsters, had wanted to attend his grandmother's funeral, but Brooklyn Federal Judge Raymond Dearie rejected that idea.

Dearie required friends and relatives to post $2 million bail and made Gallagher pay for four guards who transported him to and from a Flatlands, Brooklyn, funeral parlor.

The trip went without incident, and "Gallagher was a perfect gentleman throughout," said former mob prosecutor Jeffrey Schlanger, whose private security firm was hired for the unusual detail.

It was a little crowded, but "Gang Land" heard no other complaints about the spectacular 10-hour-long wedding party that reputed Colombo capo William "Wild Bill" Cutolo threw for son William Jr. and his bride Saturday night.

About 300 mobsters, relatives, and friends attended the wedding reception at the Embassy Terrace in Gravesend, Brooklyn, which began about 6 P.M. with wine and cheese and ended about 4 A.M. Sunday with a complete breakfast.

In addition to his son's marriage, Wild Bill has a lot to celebrate these days, including his stunning acquittal on murder and racketeering charges and surviving a mob war that left 11 dead and 16 wounded.

For the 15th straight year, the Gotti clan has mourned the passing of a loved one with public expressions of private grief. On Saturday, Victoria Gotti, wife of the now-imprisoned Gambino family boss, and her surviving children placed notices in the *Daily News* expressing their love for Frank Gotti.

Frank, 12, second son of Victoria and John Gotti, was killed when he was struck by a neighbor's car. In a mystery that's never been solved, the neighbor disappeared and has been declared dead.

———

Matteo "Matty Square" Ruggiero must have been absent during American history when the teacher explained that since 1931, when 40 Mustache Petes were killed off by young Mafia rebels, mustaches are out for mobsters.

"That mustache will have to go," said Gotti way back in 1990, after Ruggiero was proposed for membership, recalled Salvatore "Sammy Bull" Gravano.

Ruggiero shaved it immediately, and he's kept it off. He was still clean-shaven when he was nabbed with 37 others late last year on federal robbery and gun charges, but he's still waiting for his button.

———

A son of an aging mobster has gotten an offer from the feds he just couldn't refuse—two years for murder conspiracy.

Rocco Miraglia Jr., whose old man ran with Mafia boss Joe Colombo in the 1960s, pleaded guilty before Brooklyn Federal Judge Edward Korman recently to getting involved in a murder conspiracy for the love of his father.

The plea can't be used against his co-defendants, and Miraglia will begin his sentence in November after he gets married, according to a deal worked out by lawyer James DiPietro and prosecutor George Stamboulidis.

Miraglia, 24, said that after he learned in 1991 that rival hoods had marked his father for death, "I agreed with my father that I would kill any individual who was aligning against my father."

Korman indicated he likely would approve the sentence, five years less than the most lenient ever given for murder conspiracy.

Though he did not take part in any mob-war activities, Miraglia was arrested during the war carrying a loaded .38 and wearing a bulletproof vest.

Fish Mart Rap's a Fluke, He Says

Genovese capo Alfonse "Allie Shades" Malangone wants everyone to know he's got nothing to do with the Fulton Fish Market.

As law enforcement presence intensified at the market in the wake of last week's arson, Malangone contacted "Gang Land" through his lawyer, of course to state unequivocally that authorities are mistaken about his involvement with the place.

"His son has a business there, but my client has no business there and hasn't been there in at least 10 years," said lawyer Alan Futerfas.

Law enforcement officials told the *Daily News* last week that Malangone, 58, of Brooklyn was one of two Genovese capos with a presence at the market. (Malangone didn't complain about the Genovese-capo part.)

His insistence that he's not connected with the market was backed up yesterday by two "Gang Land" law enforcement sources who said Rosario "Ross" Gangi is the day-to-day boss there.

Meanwhile, Carmine Romano, who ran the market for the Genovese family in the 1970s and early 1980s, is out of jail and back in the fish business in Boston, where he's stayed out of trouble with the law, at least so far.

———

Bonanno mobster Thomas "Tommy Karate" Pitera reached out to "Gang Land" from his maximum-security prison cell to say that old pal Frank Gangi has turned out to be a real crybaby.

Gangi, a nephew of fish market boss Ross Gangi by the way, "is a liar and a coward, but beyond that, he's a wimp and a crybaby," said Pitera, who's doing life for five execution murders.

What got Pitera sore was a mention here two months ago that Gangi, who testified against him, was looking for a reduction of the 10 years he got from the same federal judge, Reena Raggi, who sentenced Pitera to life.

"Gangi said he was sorry about killing five people and that he became an informer because he wanted to start a new life," said Pitera, who contacted us through his lawyer, Mathew Mari.

"He gets 10 years, a good deal, and he goes whimpering and weeping to the judge looking for a break. If you're really sorry for killing five people, you take your punishment like a man," said Pitera. Last week, to Pitera's glee, Raggi again refused a motion to reduce Gangi's sentence.

―――――

When you're a Genovese capo who did 15 years for killing a cop, and you've done a stretch for assaulting a federal agent, it's pretty hard to take bookmaking and loan-sharking charges too seriously.

So it's completely understandable that Rudy Santobello and his entourage laughed and joked during his trial for taking bets and pushing lots of money out of his Arthur Avenue social club in the Bronx.

But the 66-year-old Santobello turned dead serious at his sentencing last week after the feds asked Judge Robert Patterson to consider his lifetime of crime and sentence him to more than 11 years.

"This has been a very delicate situation for me," Santobello began, attempting to point out his many good qualities and seek a break.

"After getting married, having a daughter, I don't think I would be so foolish to subject myself to going back to prison at this stage of my life," he said. "I done my best to bring my daughter up in the right manner."

He argued that agents who testified that he was a ruthless Genovese capo were "prejudiced" against him and "got a personal vendetta against me."

In the end, Santobello was sentenced to 6½ years, about midway between the high and low points espoused by prosecutors and defense lawyers.

Feast Washout for Tony Waterguns

Crowds of smiling people were enjoying sausage and peppers, deep-fried calamari, and a host of other Italian goodies as they strolled up and down Mulberry Street over the weekend. But the San Gennaro Festival in Little Italy just ain't what it used to be.

Gone are the Big Six Wheel, the under-and-over table, and other gambling booths that Tony Waterguns allegedly controlled for the mob. Also missing from the Feast—which runs this year through September 22—is Tony Waterguns.

With 17 others, he awaits trial on racketeering charges stemming from the mob's alleged rip-offs of hundreds of thousands of dollars supposedly earmarked for charity.

Tony's given name is Anthony Pisapia, but everybody calls him Tony Waterguns. Even in an official court affidavit, the FBI called him Tony Waterguns when G-men were looking for court approval to raid his home last year to get the goods on him.

"Tony Waterguns is the Genovese crime family's representative who controls the Feast and other New York City feasts," said FBI agent Michael Campi. "A stand operator cannot participate in one of these feasts without Tony Waterguns' approval."

> "Tony Waterguns is the Genovese crime family's representative."

Armed with a warrant, agents raided the Waterguns home and seized records linking him to the San Gennaro Feast and other feasts in the New York metropolitan area. The raid also indicated that the old saying that most rich businessmen still have the first dollar they earned, surely applies to Pisapia, 57.

In addition to nine bankbooks with deposits of $940,263, agents seized many thousands of dollars wrapped and packaged in safes, plastic bags, and envelopes, indicating there was some sentimental value attached to them.

For example, found in several safes were $100 and $50 bills, 25 rolls of "silver" dimes, one $10 bill, one ripped $1 bill, four $1 silver certificates, one "gold" John F. Kennedy silver dollar, one 1971 $1 bill, and a white box of 15 gold coins.

In one yellow envelope, agents found 14 dimes, 5 pennies, 2 nickels, and 2 quarters. In a white envelope, they found a $1 bill, five silver dollars, three dimes, and two pennies.

Agents also found, and seized, the tools of his trade: four green money aprons and a box containing 15 waterguns—the kind you still see at the San Gennaro Festival and street fairs everywhere.

Another familiar Mulberry Street figure missed the 70th annual San Gennaro Festival. For the sixth straight year, John Gotti couldn't make it. In front of Gotti's old clubhouse, the Ravenite Social Club, guys were hawking "Free John Gotti" T-shirts for $14. They featured a smiling picture of the once Dapper Don—a photo similar to the one that's on the cover of *Gotti: Rise & Fall*, the book by yours truly and Gene Mustain. We couldn't resist the temptation and picked up a couple, which have tags saying they were "made in Russia."

Flying Dragons Clip Their Own Wings

Staring at a possible death sentence, two members of the Fujianese Flying Dragons blinked and opted for life without parole for the torture slaying of a Chinese woman immigrant they kidnapped in a failed ransom plot.

Chen Fu Xin, 21, and Chen Jia Wu, 30, pleaded guilty last week to the murder of a 38-year-old factory worker whose finger was chopped off with a meat axe, raped, beaten over the head with a TV set, and strangled a year ago.

A third alleged member of the gang, Peng You Zhong, 24, has elected to go to trial before Federal Judge Edward Korman despite the possibility of execution if convicted under a 1994 law.

Garbage Boss Gets No Respect

The feds wasted little time picking off the latest mobster to reach the top of the Colombo crime family—nailing Andrew Russo on racketeering charges.

Russo, a cousin of longtime boss Carmine "Junior" Persico, was arrested and charged essentially with being the mob muscle for a private carter who allegedly collected garbage from a Long Island town under "false and fraudulent pretenses."

Law enforcement sources say Persico recently stepped down to bring an end to a long feud with rival mobsters loyal to former acting boss Victor "Little Vic" Orena.

Russo, 63, is not charged with any violent acts in a 30-count indictment that lists crimes of mail fraud, labor racketeering, and money laundering—but federal prosecutors have managed to send him directly to jail while he awaits trial.

That's because the FBI spotted Russo meeting last May with reputed Colombo underboss Joel "Joe Waverly" Cacace, and Russo was also hit with violating parole restrictions against associating with organized crime figures.

The charges in the racketeering indictment are by no means penny ante, but normally they would not have resulted in Russo being jailed to await trial. In fact, a federal judge set bail at $3 million—which Russo was ready to post—but the parole warrant made the issue of bail a moot point.

The indictment alleges that Russo, who was in federal prison from 1986 to 1994, has been the power behind private carter Dennis Hickey, who has earned about $3 million a year picking up garbage in the town of Islip, Long Island.

The feds claim that Hickey's been doing that illegally since 1987, when he pleaded guilty to bribing town officials to use the Islip town dump without paying the required fees, and should forfeit $15 million in assets.

And Russo, who is identified in the indictment as an acting boss, is cooling his heels in the Metropolitan Detention Center in Brooklyn with no official recognition that he's the boss of the Colombo family.

Chin Goes Home to Mama

Meanwhile, Genovese boss Vincent "Chin" Gigante, who is charged with ordering eight murders and plotting to kill rival mob boss John Gotti, awaits his racketeering trial in the relative comfort of his mother's Greenwich Village apartment.

Gigante, who is due to appear in court for a status conference October 4, is being prosecuted by the same U.S. Attorney's office, the one that's based in Brooklyn and handles federal cases in Brooklyn, Queens, Staten Island, and Long Island.

As "Gang Land" followers know, Gigante was arraigned this month on racketeering charges that were lodged in 1990. That indictment came a decade after Gigante took over as Genovese boss. Then it took prosecutors six years to convince a federal judge that Gigante had been feigning insanity for 30 years and was competent to stand trial. After all

that, you'd think his prosecutors would seek to remand him, but they didn't.

Barney's Home Is Prison

In Manhattan, federal prosecutors broke off discussions with lawyers seeking bail for reputed Genovese acting boss Liborio "Barney" Bellomo and received more time to oppose a bail motion by Bellomo, who has been incarcerated since June.

Bellomo has passed two lie detector tests concerning the only act of violence he is charged with—a 1991 gangland–style slaying—and argues that a substantial bail package with strict house arrest provisions should be sufficient to ensure his appearance at trial next year.

Manhattan Federal Judge Lewis Kaplan has scheduled a hearing on Bellomo's motion for next week.

NOVEMBER 4, 1996

Greater Blouse a Three-Family Affair

Federal law enforcement officials in Brooklyn were reminiscing last week about the simpler, less violent times of the Gambino family—the days before John Gotti.

One memorable moment was May 6, 1983.

Gambino boss Paul Castellano was holding court with capos Thomas Gambino and Joseph "Joe Butch" Corrao in the big white house on Staten Island where he lived with his wife and his mistress/maid.

He often discussed family business at home with his blood brothers in crime. He had an unusually close relationship with Gambino, son of crime family patriarch Carlo Gambino and Castellano's nephew. Gambino was being groomed to succeed him as family boss.

Corrao was there to talk about a $50 raise he wanted for his brother Augie for a no-show job at the Greater Blouse, Skirt and Undergarment Association, a group of 300 garment center contractors that negotiated contracts with union workers.

During the discussion Gambino, who owned several Garment Center trucking companies, explained for his uncle Paul—and the feds who happened to be listening—that the Gambinos and the Genovese and Colombo crime families jointly controlled the association.

"There is three partners there. You got a third, the West Side has a third, and Jerry has a third," said Gambino. ("West Side" referred to the Genoveses; "Jerry" was Gennaro Langella, who, back then, was acting boss of the Colombos.)

Since those bygone times, Castellano was executed in front of Sparks steakhouse on Manhattan's East Side; Corrao and Gambino have been convicted of racketeering and are in federal prison; and the Colombos were wracked by a bloody family feud that left 12 dead on the sidewalks of New York.

But the three-family partnership lived on, according to an extortion indictment handed up last week against Joseph "Joe Notch" Iannaci, the Colombo family's reputed representative on the Greater Blouse payroll. He was charged with shaking down the group for $351,227 in the guise of salaries from 1989 to 1994, and $46,170 last year, when he "retired" from his position as assistant to the executive director.

Iannaci was arrested at his home in Reeders, Pennsylvania, and released on a $100,000 bail package worked out by federal prosecutor Laura Ward and defense lawyer Bruce Cutler.

Ward and Cutler have a little history between them. In 1990, they tangled briefly in the murder and racketeering prosecution of Gotti. Ward was part of the prosecution team that convicted Gotti. Cutler was bounced off the case because he showed up on too many FBI tape-recordings of Gotti to suit federal Judge I. Leo Glasser.

"It's sort of ironic that while we never used those conversations against Paul, or Joe Butch, or Tommy, we're using them against Joe Notch," said one law enforcement official.

But back in 1983, the feds' all-out assault on the mob was just beginning. And back then, John Gotti hadn't murdered his way to power, and he and his right-hand-man-in-crime Sammy Bull Gravano hadn't painted New York City blood red.

> "And today, it's tough to make a buck. And the expenses are more than they used to be. I even got to use a cell phone now."

Bookie Whines All the Way to the Bank

A longtime Brooklyn bookmaker is very close to the normal retirement age, but he won't be giving it up anytime soon. And after you listen to him explaining why and all the built-in difficulties he's got these days, you almost feel sorry for him. Well, almost.

"I got no pension, no Social Security, no nothing. I used to drive a truck, and I worked construction, but I always worked off the books. I never made my quarters, never made the contributions. So I gotta keep going."

"And today, it's tough to make a buck. And the expenses are more than they used to use a cell phone now. I know they're expensive, and … I know the feds can tap them in a second—I think it's even easier than landline phones—but I got no choice."

"For a while I got away with using quarters—I used to carry so many quarters I thought I would get a hernia. But now you can't find a damn phone that works anymore. It's a disgrace."

Two-to-one, this guy's got a little nest egg squirreled away somewhere. And even money some would-be wiseguy would love to buy up a piece of his action.

Watt's the Story on Joe

John Gotti's longtime pal, Joseph Watts, got to see Staten Island last Friday afternoon for the first time in a year, but not the ritzy Rosebank section he called home.

Watts took a short stroll in the island's St. George business district—from the Staten Island District Attorney's office to the Supreme Court. There, he pleaded innocent to kidnap and murder charges in the 1987 torture slaying of an emotionally disturbed man, who was thought to have pegged a shot at Gotti outside the Bergin Hunt and Fish Club.

After entering the plea in the April 29, 1987, slaying of William Ciccone, Watts was hustled back over the Verrazano Narrows Bridge to his home for at least the next couple of months—the Brooklyn House of Detention.

Watts, who pleaded guilty to federal murder charges in February, "was ordered by Gotti to kill Ciccone for allegedly shooting at the Gambino crime boss outside his South Ozone Park social club,"

said Staten Island District Attorney William Murphy.

Nine years ago, Gotti and his crew were at the top of their game and openly flaunted their gangster lifestyle at the club. That day, Gotti's pals heard a loud noise that sounded like a gunshot. They chased Ciccone, grabbed him, stuffed him in a car trunk, and drove him to Staten Island, where he was "tortured for several hours by Watts," and then shot in the head, Murphy said.

The case lay dormant until former Gambino mobster Dominick "Fat Dom" Borghese began cooperating with authorities and told them Watts had pumped six shots into Ciccone's head.

Watts, 54, will conclude his six-year federal sentence before his 59th birthday. If convicted of Ciccone's murder, however, he faces an additional 25 years to life in state prison.

Despite that very bleak possibility, Watts, looking elegant in a gray suit, white shirt, and black tie, was upbeat as

> Gambino mobster Dominick "Fat Dom" Borghese began cooperating with authorities and told them Watts had pumped six shots into Ciccone's head.

he strolled down Richmond Terrace, smiling and chatting softly with the detectives who ushered him along. A silver white mane had replaced the jet black pompadour that had been a Watts trademark. The federal lockup in West Virginia apparently doesn't stock Grecian Formula.

Don't Blame Jimmy the Gent for this Scandal

The recent betting scandal involving the Boston College football team brought back memories of another dapper and murderous gangster, James "Jimmy the Gent" Burke, who died of cancer in an upstate prison in April.

Burke, who bankrolled a point-shaving scheme with the help of BC basketball players during the 1978–1979 season, masterminded a daring, predawn $5.8 million robbery at Kennedy Airport's Lufthansa cargo terminal in the middle of the moderately lucrative betting operation.

The robbery was the focal point of the excellent gangster movie, *Goodfellas*, which starred Robert DeNiro in the Burke role. No members of the robbery team were ever charged with the heist, and none of the money was ever recovered. But Burke, three members of his operation, and a reserve forward on the BC Eagles were convicted of federal sports bribery charges and sent to prison.

While serving eight years on the federal rap, Burke was convicted of murder and died while serving a 20-year-to-life sentence.

Sonny's Back in the Soup

Legendary Colombo capo John "Sonny" Franzese is in better physical shape than many men half his age, but the 77-year-old gangster keeps pushing the envelope and is back in prison—for two more years.

Sentenced to 50 years in 1967 for heading a Queens-based bank robbery ring, Franzese has been released on parole more times than "Gang Land" can remember. Each time, however, he manages to do something to work his way back into the joint.

This time, it was a bowl of spinach soup he had back in February at a Great Neck, Long Island, restaurant with two Colombo hoods. That's a no-no. He's not supposed to associate with known criminals, even if they're pals.

Franzese got the news two weeks ago, but he's already served nearly nine months, so, with good time off, he could be home for the Christmas holidays—but not until next year.

Home Is Where the Heart Is

Vincent "Chin" Gigante may be a multiple murderer, and he may head the most powerful organized crime family in the country, but deep down he's still a mama's boy.

And where mama goes, Chin goes.

Last Friday, the reputed Genovese boss petitioned Brooklyn Federal Judge Eugene Nickerson for permission to move from his 94-year-old mother's Greenwich Village apartment to the New Jersey home where she recently moved.

Until recently, Yolanda Gigante had been caring for the 68-year-old Chin— short for Cinzino, "little Vincent"—at the flat. Even after she was mugged in July, she still tended to the needs of her Cinzino, who, she told the *New York Post*, was "very sick" and anything but a crime boss.

"Boss? No boss," she said. "He's boss of the toilet. My son is sick. Boss of shit. Six years he lives here with me. Every day I care for him. I feed him, I wash him, I cry over him."

Recently, however, according to Chin's lawyer, James LaRossa, she fell and broke a vertebrae and hasn't been able to take care of her little boy.

Gigante's sons and his brother, the Rev. Louis Gigante, started visiting him more, trying to pick up the slack. But Gigante feels lost without her and wants to relocate to New Jersey to be with her.

If you've been following Chin's story, this may not seem all that startling. But what is unusual is that Chin's mother moved in with Gigante's estranged wife, Olympia.

That's right. Gigante's estranged wife is nursing Gigante's ailing mother and Chin wants to move in.

Nickerson, who ruled two months ago that Chin has feigned insanity for 30 years with the help of his wife and mother, approved the move and Gigante was expected to make the trek across the Hudson River over the weekend.

Figuring one Olympia was enough for any man, prosecutors George Stamboulidis and Andrew Weissmann asked Nickerson to rescind an order granting Gigante permission to visit the East Side townhouse of his long-time paramour, Olympia Esposito. You can't make this stuff up.

Nickerson must be a romantic. He rejected their request and Gigante, who according to court records visits Esposito three or four times a week, will still be able to eat his cake and have it, too—so to speak.

However, Nickerson did order LaRossa to submit medical reports to back up his claim that Chin has an aneurysm which is likely to burst if he comes to court next time. Gigante, who

> "If it turns out to be true that he needs an operation, we wish him a speedy recovery so he can go to trial on March 17."

underwent heart surgery in 1988, needs another operation, according to his doctors.

So far, Nickerson has held fast to a scheduled March 17 trial date.

"If it turns out to be true that he needs an operation," Weissmann said, "we wish him a speedy recovery so he can go to trial on March 17."

Did You Hear the One About the Wiseguy Who …

Pete Bowles wasn't sure what to expect.

He could feel the penetrating eyes of John Gotti and Gene Gotti as Gambino mobster Leonard DiMaria walked over to him and handed him an envelope.

"I made a little gift for you in my jail cell, and I want you to have it. Here," said DiMaria, who was on trial in Brooklyn Federal Court with the Gotti brothers and four others a decade ago for murder and racketeering.

Bowles, a Pulitzer Prize–winning reporter for *Newsday*, protested, but DiMaria would not take no for an answer.

"C'mon, it's a little thing but it means a lot to me. The (deputy U.S.) marshals said it was okay," said DiMaria, who was serving time for an unrelated cigarette smuggling conviction at the time.

So as gangsters, reporters, marshals, lawyers, court officials, and court gadflies watched, Bowles opened the envelope and almost jumped out of his skin when it exploded in a "whirring noise that sounded like a rattlesnake," recalled Bowles.

"Lenny had rigged a rubber band, a paper clip, a button, and cardboard, like

when we were kids, and I jumped," said Bowles, who grew up in Oklahoma. "Gotti got a big laugh out of it. Everyone did."

While the seven defendants saved their best laughs for the end of the trial when they were acquitted of all charges, DiMaria had everyone but the prosecution team chuckling from the beginning.

His antics began during the weeks-long jury selection process. Each time the judge introduced a new panel of potential jurors, DiMaria, whose loud booming voice had been tape-recorded and would be played during the trial, would stand and squeak in a high-pitched voice, "Hello."

Later, after cops and FBI agents ended their testimony and stepped off the witness stand to walk out of court, DiMaria would rise, smile, and extend his hand and say, "Gee, thanks for coming." Many of the law enforcement types would shake his hand reflexively.

One time a bomb scare forced the evacuation of the courthouse. Reporters and others complained about standing out in the cold, but DiMaria said he didn't have it so bad. "They chained me to a steam pipe in the basement," he quipped.

DiMaria seemed to enjoy himself throughout the seven-month trial. He drew cartoons and passed them to the sketch artists, saying his work was better than theirs. He joked that FBI agents and detectives who testified about conversations they overheard "were riding the Erie again, yep, they're on the Erie," as he cupped his hand behind his ear. During testimony that the Gambino family "gave a pass" to a gangster marked for death, DiMaria turned to a reporter who had made a serious mistake in that day's paper, and mouthed the words, "Don't worry, we're gonna give you a pass."

The only person who never seemed to smile at DiMaria's antics was co-defendant and longtime buddy Nicholas "Little Nick" Corozzo, who is about to succeed Gotti as Gambino boss, according to underworld and law enforcement sources.

As disclosed in the *Daily News*, Corozzo, 56, will take over the crime family as soon as Gotti's latest appeal for a new trial is denied. DiMaria, 55, a capo, is Corozzo's right-hand man and has been there for three decades.

"I'm not surprised about Corozzo," said Bowles, "He never smiled and struck me as the meanest of the bunch."

> "They chained me to a steam pipe in the basement," (DiMaria) quipped.

DiMaria, Bowles said, "was the funniest defendant I've ever covered, but he had the hands of a fighter, large hands, and could take care of himself. I was almost hoping he had decided to go straight."

Bowles, 58, is still at *Newsday*, but he no longer covers the Brooklyn Federal Court. But if DiMaria ever winds up in the dock again, Bowles is sure to attend, if only to say thanks for the laughs and for sending him a get-well card from prison in 1989, when Bowles suffered a heart attack. "It was a terrible, ugly cartoon, but it said, 'Get well, Pete,' and was signed, 'Uncle Lenny.' I sent him a thank-you note, but I never thanked him in person," Bowles said.

Nearly 10 years after the stunning not-guilty verdicts in the Gotti trial—the only case in which a Mafia boss was acquitted of federal racketeering charges—only Corozzo and DiMaria remain as viable gangsters.

After his big win on Friday, March 13, 1987, Gotti had a run of a little more than three-and-a-half years as the Dapper and Teflon Don. But he was arrested on December 11, 1990, and since June 23, 1992, has been serving a life sentence in virtual isolation at Marion Federal Penitentiary.

His brother, Gene, and good buddy John Carneglia didn't last quite as long as their crime boss, although for them there is light at the end of a long tunnel. After two mistrials, both were convicted of heroin dealing in 1989 and sentenced to 50 years. With good time, they're scheduled to "max out" of federal prison in about 2014.

Gotti pal Anthony "Tony Roach" Rampino lasted less than four months as a free man. A heroin addict, Rampino cleaned up his act during the trial, but quickly went back to his old ways and was nabbed selling a load of heroin to an undercover cop in late June 1987. Rampino's doing 25 to life and won't be out until 2012, at the earliest.

All of them are better off than Wilfred "Willie Boy" Johnson, who was exposed in the case as having been a top echelon FBI informer. Johnson was shot to death as he left his house for his construction worker job on August 29, 1988, demonstrating that mob life is more than fun and games, no matter how comical it seems at times.

PART 4

The Late 1990s

In its new venue, "Gang Land" reached a much wider audience. The column chronicled the aftermath of the bloody battles of the late 1980s and early 1990s as they played out in courtrooms, and kept readers up-to-date on life and death in and around the mob.

After flirting with the feds, Gaspipe Casso reneged and went away to prison for life. Familiar "Gang Land" names like Sammy Bull, Fat Pete, Wild Bill Cutolo, Sonny Franzese, and Hugh McIntosh were featured as they hit a variety of milestones, mostly bad or sad.

A few new players appeared on the "Gang Land" scene, including Baldy Mike Spinelli, the Toilet Bowl Gangster, and John Pappa, a young wannabe mobster with an eerie tattoo featuring the Italian words for "Death Before Dishonor" emblazoned across his back.

The feds kept on trucking, nailing Spinelli and Pappa for racketeering and murder. They also got Chin Gigante to trial, convicting him of labor racketeering charges, and put together a strong enough case to convince Junior Gotti to plead guilty to racketeering charges that will keep him behind bars until 2004.

JANUARY 20, 1997

Gaspipe's Follies

It was December 31, 1996, and Anthony "Gaspipe" Casso was agitated.

Once one of the richest and most feared gangsters in New York, the former underboss of the Luchese crime family was spending his fourth consecutive New Year's Eve in a federal prison. The future didn't look so good for the 56-year-old mobster.

He began cooperating with the feds in 1994, but hasn't been used yet as a trial witness. Casso, who admitted taking part in 36 "gangland-style slayings" is awaiting sentence. And if the feds don't find any use for him soon, he'll be hard-pressed to get less than the life sentence he faces.

So as Casso strolled along an elevated walkway in the special cellblock for cooperating witnesses, he rolled a magazine into a billy club and attacked Salvatore "Big Sal" Miciotta, another jailed mob informer.

The magazine didn't prove to be much of a weapon, and the guards had to rush in and save Casso—5 foot 8, 165 pounds—before his angry 350-pound adversary canceled his subscription.

Miciotta, who has admitted involvement in four homicides, began cooperating in 1993, has testified against his former associates several times, and is serving a 14-year sentence. He and Casso have been feuding for months.

The fight broke out after dinner, sources said, as Miciotta, 50, was playing cards with other inmates. Casso "came up behind Big Sal," leaned through a railing and started beating Miciotta on his head with the magazine, said one source. "Since this was not a very efficient weapon, and (since) Big Sal is a very large man, this did not render Big Sal help-less."

Miciotta grabbed him by the shirt, pulled him though the railing, and "beat the daylights out of Gaspipe until the (guards) got him off Gaspipe," said the source.

After the fracas, both men were placed in solitary confinement to await transfers to other federal prisons with special units for cooperating witnesses.

The feds would not comment about the altercation.

"I'm not surprised about the outcome but I am surprised that Gaspipe started up with Sal," said one law enforcement source. "Without his gun, Gaspipe was not a tough guy. Sal could handle himself and towers over him."

At least Casso ended the year with a little excitement.

Capo Busted for Bugging Sammy Bull

Gambino capo Danny Marino, a former New York City detective, and a third man were charged with illegally wiretapping the home phone of Salvatore "Sammy Bull" Gravano after he agreed to testify against John Gotti.

Along with long-time Gotti pal Joseph Watts and mobster Dominic "Fat Dom" Borghese, the men allegedly tapped his Staten Island home phone in a desperate attempt to find out something they could use to undermine his testimony against Gotti.

The men also set up a listening device on cellular phone conversations between Gravano and his wife Debra, according to a federal indictment unsealed Friday.

The wiretapped conversations were monitored with equipment set up in Borghese's Staten Island home, which was not far from Gravano's in 1991, when the tap was installed. Borghese is now cooperating and will be the key witness for the government.

Marino, currently serving seven years for taking part in a mob slaying for Gotti, is due to be released in the year 2000. If convicted, Marino, 56, retired detective John Ryan, 64, and Gary Furio, 52, face up to 10 years on the wiretapping charges.

> "Without his gun, Gaspipe was not a tough guy."

Junior Wants His Civil Rights

John A. "Junior" Gotti is really serious that the $350,000 state investigators found in an Ozone Park social club are not proceeds from any rackets, but proceeds from his wedding seven years ago.

The reputed Gambino acting boss and son of John Gotti, the imprisoned real boss, is so serious that he's thinking about going to court to get it back.

"This largely was the residue of the moneys he received at his wedding," said lawyer Richard Rehbock, young Gotti's mouthpiece. "Remember, he had a wedding in 1990 (attended by lots of wiseguys) who brought lots of money. There was in excess of $480,000 given to him as gifts—in cash. And many of the more prominent rats in this city contributed very healthy sums. Law enforcement knows this."

Among the turncoat mobsters who attended the bash and reportedly gave $10,000 gifts were Gambino family underboss Salvatore "Sammy Bull" Gravano, Luchese underboss Anthony "Gaspipe" Casso, and Colombo consigliere Carmine Sessa.

Rehbock said state Organized Crime Task Force investigators also seized watches and rings that belonged to Junior's father, and court records and legal notes that are essential for additional planned appeals of his 1992 racketeering and murder conviction.

"They have stolen these papers in an effort to deprive him of the ability to continue this effort," said Rehbock in an interview with WNBC-TV in New York. "We are considering very seriously filing a federal civil rights lawsuit against the attorney general of the state of New York."

The money and other items were seized in raids on five locations in a state probe of possible tax violations and other crimes by two Gotti-connected construction companies that have done more than $17 million in work since 1992.

Since the state attorney general is not a made guy, a lawsuit would not violate Mafia protocol eloquently stated by Colombo family capo Salvatore Profaci about a year after Gotti's lavish wedding reception at the Helmsley Palace Hotel.

"Good fellows don't sue good fellows," Profaci said. "Good fellows kill good fellows."

But when one considers that Joe Colombo, the Mafia boss who went public and picketed the FBI, was gunned down at a midtown Manhattan rally, wouldn't filing a lawsuit—playing by the rules—be a little unusual, let alone dangerous?

"Quite frankly, that's probably part of the thing that backs up our statement that he isn't the boss that everybody in the newspapers and media says he is," said Rehbock.

"Gang Land" could not reach Sal Profaci for his learned assessment of the situation.

While Junior Gotti, via his lawyer, was threatening to file a lawsuit, his mother, Victoria, was publicly expressing her grief over the tragic death of her son Frank, who was hit by a car and killed 17 years ago while riding a motorbike.

Victoria Gotti, as she has done each year on the anniversary of his death, placed memorial notices in the *Daily News* to Frank, who was 12 when he died.

"Happy Anniversary in Heaven. Words could never describe the feeling of your loss. Your memory is with us every day of our lives," read the notice, placed in the name of her son John and his family.

"We love & miss you always," said the notice from her and her husband. "Love Mom and Dad."

> "Good fellows don't sue good fellows," Profaci said. "Good fellows kill good fellows."

The Dumb Wannabe Wiseguy Award of the week goes to Joseph Gambino Jr. of Howard Beach, Queens.

A Gambino In Name Only

Nabbed for gun possession during a routine traffic stop in Massapequa, Long Island, Gambino, 24, told the cops that he was a relative of imprisoned Gambino crime family capo Thomas Gambino, as if that information would somehow work in his favor.

Well, it did get him some unwanted publicity.

The state police, fully aware that a routine gun arrest would never get much attention from the media, reported Gambino's purported relationship in a press release.

Thomas Gambino's attorney quickly informed reporters that someone as dumb as Joseph Gambino Jr. could hardly be related to the mobster.

Whoops, said the state police, reporting that Gambino had tried to impress the state troopers who busted him but in reality he was merely a "lightweight crime figure."

"Gang Land" seems to recall seeing all this in a movie starring Jim Carrey, *Dumb and Dumber*.

Fat Pete Sits One Out

Prosecutors were looking for a big finish last week at the federal murder and racketeering trial of the Little Guy— Genovese consigliere James Ida. So they scheduled a BIG witness. It was not to be, however.

We're talking about a REALLY big witness here, former Luchese capo Peter "Fat Pete" Chiodo.

Chiodo, whose 400-pound girth saved his life six years ago when mob hit men pumped 12 shots into him, has ballooned to about 500 pounds since he last appeared as a witness three years ago, sources say.

> Chiodo's 400-pound girth saved his life six years ago when mob hit men pumped 12 shots into him.

To complicate matters, Chiodo, who has a new identity through the auspices of the federal Witness Protection Program, had surgery not too long ago to correct a hernia—a problem that often afflicts the grossly overweight.

His recovery was hampered by one postoperative infection after another, however, and federal prosecutors Nelson Boxer and Maria Barton asked Manhattan Federal Judge Lewis Kaplan to allow Chiodo to testify under a high-tech videoconference setup never used before in a federal criminal trial.

They proposed that Chiodo testify from a remote location while all other trial participants, including the jury, would move to a specially equipped courtroom across the street that is used by the Second Circuit Court of Appeals. Through the videoconferencing setup, out-of-town lawyers are permitted to argue appeals via a remote feed.

Ida's lawyer, Jeffrey Hoffman, and co-counsel, Alan Polak, cited numerous legal challenges to the unprecedented procedure, and Kaplan, who rarely hears a government motion he doesn't like, said he wanted to investigate the issue thoroughly before making his decision.

Kaplan excused the jurors, and accompanied the other trial participants to the 17th-floor courtroom to scope out the logistics, including things like the size of the TV screen. (It was big enough to capture the BIG witness, said one source.)

Before reaching the big issue, however, Kaplan needed to conduct a hearing to determine whether Chiodo's condition would, in fact, make a trip to Manhattan dangerous for him, medically speaking.

That opened up another can of worms, since Chiodo's doctor thinks his patient is just John Q. Fatso and not Fat Pete Chiodo. The doctor couldn't testify anonymously, since the defense has the right to challenge his qualifications and couldn't if the lawyers didn't know who he was. And if the doctor testified using his name, his bona fides, and where he practices, Chiodo's location would be disclosed. And then the witness program would have to move him to a new location. And it's hard enough finding one area to hide a 500-pound reformed gangster.

Even if Kaplan were to allow the videoconference testimony, he mused that the appeals judges, whose courtroom they would be using for the historic testimony, might not look too favorably on the proceeding and reverse him. If there were convictions in the case, they could be overturned and they would all have to do it again, said Kaplan on Friday, telling prosecutors to rethink the matter and appear this afternoon for final arguments on all the issues.

On Saturday, however, prosecutors gave it up and notified defense lawyers that they would rest their case without calling their quarter-of-a-ton heavyweight witness.

The jury, which has been kept in the dark about the heavy legal issues that have delayed trial testimony for the better part of last week, is likely to begin its deliberations early next week.

Among other things, Ida is charged with ordering two gangland–style killings—one in 1988 and another in 1991—and with conspiring to murder a third man whose execution was never carried out.

Chiodo's mob superior, former acting boss Alfonse "Little Al" D'Arco, had no physical ailments to speak of and testified for the first time in two years earlier in the case. From the witness stand he implicated Ida in the two slayings he is accused of ordering.

D'Arco admitted taking part in 10 murders and said he deserved to spend the rest of his life in prison, but insisted he had absolutely nothing to do with drugs after 1986, when he got out of prison after serving three years for a heroin rap.

When confronted with allegations contained in court affidavits that he had been seen opening the car trunk of a known drug dealer and tasting something that cops thought was drugs, D'Arco insisted he was tasting sausage and peppers, not heroin or cocaine.

Gaspipe's Worst Enemy — Gaspipe

If nothing else, former Luchese under-boss Anthony "Gaspipe" Casso knows how to make a bad situation worse.

Ever since he signed a cooperation agreement with the feds three-and-a-half years ago, Casso has consistently shown a knack for making things worse for himself. His latest gaff is likely to earn him a life sentence, or something very close to it.

The last straw for the feds came shortly after they convicted Genovese boss Vincent "Chin" Gigante of racketeering—without calling Casso as a witness. Once viewed as a key witness against Gigante, other top gangsters, and corrupt NYPD detectives he dealt with, Casso had fallen out of favor for lying, bribing prison guards, and assaulting rival mobsters—all while he was cooperating with the feds and housed in special prison units for turncoat mobsters. As a result, despite his firsthand criminal dealings with Gigante, the feds felt Casso would have been more of a liability than an asset on the witness stand.

A few days after Gigante was sent off to prison, Casso wrote a letter accusing two key prosecution witnesses, superstar mob turncoat Salvatore "Sammy Bull" Gravano and onetime acting Luchese boss Alfonse "Little Al" D'Arco, of lying at the trial.

After receiving Casso's allegations, prosecutors Valerie Caproni and Andrew Weissmann quickly labeled them as "untrue" and "spurious," declared that Casso had breached his cooperation agreement, and asked Judge Eugene Nickerson to sentence him. The feds felt pretty sure about their characterizations because one of the things Casso said Gravano did—'fess up to ordering the January 1991 stabbing of activist minister and current New York City mayoral candidate Rev. Al Sharpton on the day after the attack while the two underbosses were standing around chatting in a Brooklyn schoolyard—was hard for them to swallow. Casso was on the lam and Gravano was in prison at the time.

Among other things, prosecutors also charged Casso with bribing prison guards, and with beating a handcuffed inmate as he got out of the shower because the inmate had told authorities that Casso was smuggling contraband into his prison cell.

Brought to court, Casso's lawyer charged federal prosecutors with not playing fair with Casso by deciding not to recommend leniency for him despite his more than three years of cooperation.

Lawyer Matthew Brief accused the government of "bad faith" in its dealings with Casso, and asked for the opportunity to back up his claim at an evidentiary hearing.

Nickerson scheduled one for early November, but last week, after prosecutors reminded the judge that Casso had once plotted to kill him, Nickerson

decided he had seen enough of Casso and removed himself from the case. Details of the plot are sketchy, but sources said mobsters planned to execute Nickerson as he walked through Cadman Plaza Park on his way to the U.S. Courthouse in downtown Brooklyn.

Tomorrow, Judge Frederic Block gets his first crack at the somewhat bizarre feud between Casso and the feds.

In his last court appearance, Casso, who reportedly has admitted taking part in 36 murders, let his lawyer do the talking to Nickerson. But on his way out of the courtroom, he turned toward me and said, "They're railroading me, Jerry."

> **Prosecutors also charged Casso with bribing prison guards, and with beating a handcuffed inmate as he got out of the shower.**

NOVEMBER 10, 1997

Death by Reputation

When you're Hugh McIntosh, it's hard to outlive your reputation—even when you're a sick old man.

Last Thursday, at 11:25 P.M., his reputation as a onetime-feared mob enforcer helped kill McIntosh who, at age 70, was many years past his prime.

A longtime cohort of imprisoned Colombo boss Carmine "Junior" Persico, McIntosh died at a Springfield, Missouri, hospital after a whirlwind trip through two federal prisons and two hospitals in less than two months.

The official cause of death hasn't been reported yet, but daughter Elizabeth Sanad knows why her father is dead.

"They killed him," said Sanad, with "they" being federal parole officials who sent him back to prison last September 12 even though they knew he left his criminal ways behind when he was paroled in 1992, and federal prison officials who failed to care for the sick old man when he got to the Metropolitan Detention Center in Brooklyn.

"When they arrested him, he was sick," said Sanad. "He suffered from dementia, he couldn't use his hands to write, or shave. He used to read the newspaper all day and could never tell you what he read. But he was alive."

"Five days later, they finally gave me permission to see him. They took him out of the hole (isolation), they hadn't given him a shower, a shave, or even a cleanser for his false teeth. It was pathetic and disgusting. They killed him."

And after examining court papers submitted by Sanad and federal prosecutors in a lawsuit—filed three weeks before he died—that contested McIntosh's parole violation arrest, it's hard for "Gang Land" to disagree with Sanad.

There's no question that in his heyday, McIntosh, whose criminal career went back at least 40 years, was one tough dude.

Along with Persico, he was a stalwart on the side of mobsters loyal to boss Joe Profaci against those in a rebel faction headed by Crazy Joe Gallo in the first Colombo family war in the early 1960s.

He was involved in an attempt by Persico to garrote Larry Gallo, he was shot in the groin and drove himself to the hospital, and he had a couple of notches on his gun in his long career as a criminal, although he was never convicted of a homicide.

His first heavy prison stretch was in 1969, for hijacking. After his release in 1975, he ran a social club, was a loan shark, was a master of the shakedown—he once wore a size 52 suit and carried an ice pick—and reportedly committed a host of other crimes for which he was never charged, including a mob hit in 1980.

Finally, in 1982, after being stung by an IRS agent posing as a rogue, McIntosh pleaded guilty to offering the agent several bribes, including a $250,000 payoff to win Persico an early release from a 14-year prison term.

While jailed, the same bribery charges were included in a racketeering indictment, and McIntosh was convicted again, and sentenced to consecutive time. He was paroled on December 31, 1992, after serving 11 years.

From 1993 to 1996, he underwent surgery nine times, including an angioplasty, and several bypass operations; suffered a stroke; and had a thrombectomy, in which virtually all the blood vessels in his left leg were removed, according to court records.

Last year, after advising McIntosh that he could have no more vascular operations, Dr. Jonathan Tiefenbrun said, "Mac, you will do very nicely with one leg," according to court records.

By all accounts, he got along nicely, without returning to his criminal ways.

> "Mac, you will do very nicely with one leg."

Even his parole officer grudgingly admitted as much. "During the course of supervising this offender, with long-term ties to the Colombo family, his (parole) officer made numerous law enforcement contacts, which failed to indicate that the parolee was actively engaged in organized criminal activities," said Senior U.S. Probation Officer Madeline Hart, in an official report filed in Brooklyn Federal Court.

For whatever reason—perhaps illness, perhaps old age, perhaps senility—McIntosh had been rehabilitated.

But on May 23, McIntosh was spotted a few blocks from his Brooklyn home sitting at an outdoor table talking to Daniel Persico—nephew of Carmine and son of Teddy, a convicted Colombo capo—by detectives who were looking into alleged drug dealing at the bar.

While he sat with Persico, detectives asked McIntosh who he was. He showed them his driver's license, and watched them write down his name. But weeks later, when his parole officer asked him about his meeting with Persico—a no-no under the special conditions of his parole—McIntosh said he couldn't remember meeting with him.

Hart said it was "not credible" that he could have forgotten the meeting, deciding that McIntosh "paid only lip service to the restrictions placed upon him by the

Parole Commission and has remained, in spite of numerous imprisonments and periods of supervision, a recalcitrant and incorrigible individual.

"There exists sufficient probable cause that the parolee presented a falsified supervision report to his U.S. Probation officer for May, 1997 …. To deny that he recalls these events foists upon the Probation Officer and the Parole Commission the daunting task of judging the present capacity of a frail, elderly man's memory. The history of this offender's supervision, however, containing as it does an account of marginal adherence to the standards of supervision, suggests that the offender may be acting out of self-preservation, rather than dementia," concluded Hart.

"Gang Land" concludes that for McIntosh to own up to who he was last May 23, he must have been suffering from dementia. There is no way that the old, incorrigible McIntosh, the one interested in "self-preservation," would have ever showed those detectives his driver's license if he knew it would send him back to prison. No way!

DECEMBER 15, 1997

Sammy Wants the Home Court Advantage

Salvatore "Sammy Bull" Gravano is trying to make a federal case out of four wrongful death lawsuits filed against him in various New York state courts.

And Gravano, who became a superstar prosecution witness in Brooklyn Federal Court, just may get to defend himself on his home turf before the judge who sentenced him to five years in prison for a life of crime that included 19 killings.

Citing statutes that permit civil suits to be tried in federal court when opposing parties live in different states, Gravano's lawyers have filed papers seeking to move four pending cases to Brooklyn Federal Court. The mother of one murder victim and the children of three others are seeking hundreds of millions of dollars in damages. Since the suits are filed under a New York law that seeks to stop criminals from earning money from book and movie deals, perhaps $1.5 million is at stake.

In an affidavit accompanying the removal papers, Gravano said he is a U.S citizen living outside New York, and has no intention of ever moving back. He says his life is "in serious danger" because

he has testified against "leading organized crime figures like John Gotti and Vincent Gigante" and asks that his address be allowed to remain secret.

Coincidentally, according to Gravano lawyer Larry Krantz and court officials, the first removal motion was assigned randomly to Judge I. Leo Glasser. Two other cases were later assigned to him as related. For technical reasons, one case is currently in Manhattan Federal Court, but that one is expected to end up in Brooklyn as a related case as well.

So far, the plaintiffs in the suits—children of Robert "DeeBee" DiBernardo, Edward Garafalo, and Liborio "Louie" Milito, and the mother of Alan Kaiser—have not responded to the removal motions. "Gang Land" expects them to oppose the motion by Krantz and co-counsel Marjorie Berman, who also seek to merge the suits into one case.

Among other things, consolidation would result in an incredible irony for two of the plaintiffs, Deena Milito and Shirley Shifrin, the mother of Kaiser, who was killed at age 16 in 1977. According to

Gravano, it was Deena Milito's father who fired the shots that killed Shifrin's son some 11 years before Milito himself was dispatched by Gravano.

"Gang Land" also expects the plaintiffs to ask Glasser, who praised Gravano for his transformation from a murderous gangster to a cooperating witness, to disqualify himself from the case. Stay tuned.

Mob Docks Boss Off to Prison

Gambino capo Anthony "Sonny" Ciccone was sentenced recently to three months in jail for his contempt of court conviction earlier this year. It was the first conviction for Ciccone, whom Gotti appointed as the crime family's man on the Brooklyn waterfront soon after Gotti took over as crime boss in 1986.

Ciccone, 63, was found guilty after state and federal investigators photographed Ciccone meeting several mobsters in 1994, including Gambino wiseguy Jerome "Jerry" Brancato, at a Brooklyn restaurant in violation of a court order that forbade the onetime International Longshoremen's Association official from meeting with other mobsters.

Bum's Rush for Mob Capo

Reputed Bonanno capo Vincent Asaro may have gotten respect from a few court officers last week, but a jury gave him the bum's rush.

The dozen Queens residents took just three hours to find Asaro guilty of felony forgery charges and other fraud-related counts for lying on an application for a New York State driver's license in 1994.

Asaro's license had been suspended since 1983 when he was busted for driving under the influence. He was convicted for giving a phony birthday and address when he applied for a new driver's license four years ago.

"It's a bullshit case," Asaro, 62, told *Daily News* reporter Pete Donohue at jury selection. Asaro, in a dapper dark blue suit, dark glasses, and the prerequisite big gold pinky ring, said Queens D.A. Richard Brown was a heartless cad who "would bring charges against his mother."

His lawyer, Stephen Mahler, said Asaro simply made a mistake about his age, and listed his business address because he was separated from his wife and having his mail delivered to work. Asaro listed his correct name and Social Security number, noted Mahler. "In football, this is called piling on."

> "It's a bullshit case," Asaro, 62, told (the) *Daily News*

"The jury found he was not worthy of belief and they revoked his license to commit crimes," said Assistant District Attorney Gerard Brave. "He's been committing crimes for a number of years and he didn't get away with this one."

Earlier, court officers did Asaro a favor and escorted him out the courtroom through a rear door used by the judge and court staff.

Asaro faces up to seven years in prison when he is sentenced by Supreme Court Justice Arthur Cooperman.

Rudy a Frustrated Actor, or Godfather?

It's one thing for New York Mayor Rudolph Giuliani to entertain his loyal staffers with a raspy-voiced imitation of Marlon Brando portraying the fictional Don Corleone in *The Godfather*. But "Gang Land" thinks it was a little tacky for him to kick off his second term with a screening of the mob epic for hundreds of advisers, friends, and fund-raisers.

And for Giuliani to describe his "favorite movie" as an educational film that "probably" helped him and others put together plans on "how to dismantle the five families in New York" was an insult to the intelligence of law enforcement officials, mobsters, and the public.

But that's just what the former Manhattan U.S. Attorney did and said, according to a New Year's Day article by Norimitsu Onishi in *The New York Times*.

For 25 years, law enforcement officials have criticized the film for many reasons, especially its romantic portrayal of mob killers. For nearly as long, gangsters from Salvatore "Bill" Bonanno to Salvatore "Sammy Bull" Gravano have said they enjoyed the movie and its portrayal of guys like them.

Despite the murder and mayhem around Don Corleone in the film, Brando portrays him as a loving grandfather and so-called Man of Honor who kills only to protect what rightfully belongs to him and his family.

According to the *Times*, Giuliani "brushed off such suggestions," stating: "I think movies are movies, and the fact is, that when you consider the major reductions that have been made in organized crime, it should not be something that people are offended by."

It's true that movies are movies and that major reductions have been made in organized crime. But even when you factor in Giuliani's anti-Mafia resolve as a prosecutor and mayor, it doesn't seem particularly appropriate for an Italian-American mayor to kick off his second term of office with a movie that glorifies mobsters.

In "Gang Land's" view, Giuliani should satisfy his love of *The Godfather* the way he did in November, when, according to the *Times*, he entertained staffers during a City Hall sit-down with a throaty: "It's nice of all youse to be here. Some of you come from the Upper West Side. Some from the East Side. We even got some people here from the Bronx."

Junior Pays for Dad's Deeds

The son also rises—and falls.

John A. "Junior" Gotti is taking a lot of heat from the law—and from some "Gang Land" mob buddies—over a few very innocent-looking lists seized by mob busters.

Dubbed the "Holy Grail" by state Attorney General Dennis Vacco, the lists of mobsters in three rival families were on seven sheets of paper that were confiscated in a raid at a building owned by a close pal of young Gotti, Mike McLaughlin.

Like his meteoric rise to acting crime boss of the Gambino family, Junior's current problems with the feds—and now the Genoveses, Bonannos, and Lucheses—are not because of his own actions or decisions, but those made by his father, the onetime Dapper Don and official boss of the Gambino crime family.

Last week, as revealed by Greg Smith and me in the *Daily News*, the lists, found in a jewelry box during a raid last year, contain the names of 45 men whom the Bonannos, Genoveses, and Lucheses had proposed to replace 45 mobsters who died between 1983 and 1991. The mob limits its numbers by only replacing members who have died. To weed out informers, drug users, and other undesirables, they circulate the names of wannabes to determine whether there are any reasons not to induct them. It's sort of like the blackball system used by fraternities.

> When's the last time you ever heard of a bride and groom filling several tables with dead people?

"There's no reason to keep these lists," said Bruce Mouw, recently retired head of the FBI's Gambino squad. "The other families will be irate. Once the proposed members pass muster, the lists are supposed to be destroyed, for obvious reasons. It is supposed to be a secret society."

Most lists were typed with names of the dead mobsters and their replacements preceded by a "Mr. & Mrs." in a lame effort to disguise them as wedding guests. When's the last time you ever heard of a bride and groom filling several tables with dead people?

In the handwritten Luchese family list above, no efforts are made to disguise what the side-by-side lists are about. The "new" wiseguys at the left were proposed to replace "old" mobsters who died in the years noted next to their names. As in the typed lists, many of the names are misspelled.

The lists were all received by the Gambino family during the heyday of John J. Gotti, the still-official boss who now calls home the federal penitentiary in Marion, Illinois. It's likely that some men were proposed even before Junior was inducted into the mob, while he was still bouncing to the beat of his Walkman as he walked along Mulberry Street to and from the Ravenite Social Club—his father's Little Italy base of operations. Almost all of them "were made" before Junior was elevated to capo in the summer of 1990—six months before his father was nabbed on racketeering and murder charges. The decision to keep the lists of rival mobsters had to be made by the father, not the son, meaning the son could wind up paying for the sins of his father.

Junior's got no choice but to take the good with the bad. His wife and kids have at least three homes worth about $2 million at their disposal, but he's spending his days and nights at the Westchester County jail, a reputed danger to society, at least until tomorrow, when his bail status will be reviewed by White Plains Federal Judge Barrington Parker.

Unlike his father, young John hasn't been overheard saying many incriminating things in tape-recorded conversations, but he has on occasion exhibited a certain flair—perhaps stemming from his Walkman days.

Take the September 17, 1996, discussion he had with reputed mobster Craig DePalma, for example. The conversation took place soon after Gotti heard that DePalma's father Greg had been caught on a bug.

> Junior: How's Papa Bear?
> Craig: All right.
> Junior: I just figured out what we can do for your father.
> Craig: What?
> Junior: I think if we all chip in and we raise some money, we get him his own radio station …. Grow his hair one side longer than the other. Like he's going to flip it over like a madman. Yelling up and down, be shouting and screaming, "I want to send a shout out to Brooklyn."

After DePalma laughed and promised he would tell his father, Junior pressed his point.

> Junior: Make sure you tell him I said that.
> Craig: Tonight I'll tell him.
> Junior: Tell him John said, "We'll all chip in and for Christmas we're buying you a radio station."

Prosecutors say Gotti meant to threaten the elder DePalma with those words. But Gotti's lawyer, Gerald Shargel, said the men are friends and

Gotti was not threatening anyone in that or any other conversation.

Ravenite Social Club for Sale

With little fanfare and even less imagination, a Manhattan realtor has begun the job of selling the Little Italy building that for decades housed the Ravenite Social Club—the Manhattan headquarters of the Gambino crime family.

The nineteenth-century building that contained the best-known mob hangout in U.S. history was featured as a 16-apartment building with a vacant store that was "ideal for bar/restaurant." Asking price: $1 million.

Last week, the realtor held an hour-long open house at the club, which still has a light blue loveseat, a brown end table, and some folding chairs in the two small rooms where John Gotti and his mentor, the late Aniello "Neil" Dellacroce, once held court.

The pictures of Gotti and Dellacroce are gone, but the place still has a wet bar—where Gene Gotti once toiled—and a small unisex bathroom with a toilet and a small sink.

"It's a little small for a bar/restaurant, maybe a small cafe or espresso house," said Juliet Papa, a WINS radio reporter who covered all Gotti's trials and co-authored *The Mafia Handbook*, a light-hearted look at the mob. "It was like going back into Mafia history, where the deals were made, the plots were hatched, and where the bugs were planted."

Sonny's Home Again—for Now

John "Sonny" Franzese has been out to lunch—for two extremely long years.

The legendary capo got home a few weeks ago after enjoying a bowl of spinach soup with some friends, the wrong friends.

The feds said his companions at the Great Neck, Long Island, restaurant were a couple of Colombo hoods, guys a parolee like him are not supposed to hang out with.

The meal cost Sonny 24 months, or 730 days, or 17,520 hours or so, in jail. That's a lot of time for low-calorie eats. Hope it was good.

At one time, Franzese, Italian born and tough, was a contender for Colombo family boss. He was released a week after he celebrated his 79th birthday at a halfway house in New York City.

He had been locked up in the federal prison in Milan, Michigan. Sonny always seems to be going to prison or getting out of prison. The halfway house was to prepare him for one more—maybe his last—try at parole.

> **The meal cost Sonny 24 months, or 730 days, or 17,520 hours or so, in jail.**

Franzese's rise in the mob was derailed in 1967 when he was convicted of heading up a gang of bank robbers in Queens. He's been around and is going to have to check his long list of off-limits wiseguys before going out for an ice cream cone.

He was sentenced to 50 years and will be under federal supervision until 2017, when he will be 98.

Meanwhile, Franzese's son Michael, a scam artist who's led a charmed life, is reportedly up to his old tricks on the West Coast. We're cross-checking a few angles, so we're going to hold off a week.

Wiseguy In Name Only

Being a wiseguy doesn't necessarily mean having a lot of smarts. Often it means having a lot of nerve.

Take Luchese capo Anthony "Bowat" Baratta.

Baratta, who had already been serving 15 years for a couple of racketeering convictions, is facing a lot more time for heroin trafficking while he was in jail.

He was supposedly set up by a wily mobster from New Jersey who was looking to buy his way out of jail.

In September 1996, while Baratta was at the federal prison in Otisville, New York, he ran into a hoodlum associated with the DeCavalcantes who said he was looking to earn some cash dealing heroin in the outside world. He said that if Baratta had a source, he had a partner on the outside who would pay $45,000 for 350 grams (about 10.3 ounces) of dope.

So, for a year or so, according to the feds, Baratta's outside guy and the DeCavalcante hood's outside guy—really a federal narcotics agent—exchanged heroin for cash at a Manhattan restaurant until the feds decided Baratta had made enough money and busted everybody for heroin trafficking.

Culter Returns to the Gotti Camp

Seven years after being barred from participating in the federal racketeering trial that put John Gotti in prison for life, Bruce Cutler is doing what he likes doing best: Defending guys named Gotti.

As defense lawyer, Cutler won three cases—including a racketeering trial—for the now-jailed Gambino boss. He also won an acquittal for Gotti's brother Peter, a reputed Gambino capo, in a racketeering trial.

Cutler returned to action last week as an attorney for John A. "Junior" Gotti, who's been caught up in a cruel, like-father-like-son federal racketeering scenario. Cutler's bald pate was glistening and his timing perfect as he rushed into a packed court in White Plains just as a pretrial conference for Junior and more than 20 co-defendants was about to begin. Cutler beamed and shook hands all around, kissed his handcuffed client on the cheek, and let co-counsel Gerald Shargel do all the talking.

Outside, Cutler, who slam-dunked a copy of an indictment into a trash can during his opening remarks at the Dapper Don's first racketeering trial, said he was thrilled to be in it again.

"I came today to announce to the court and the world that Jerry and I would be representing John Gotti's son at trial. We helped his father together, and we have a wonderful relationship. It's nice to be back," he said.

Luchese Class of '91

Beaming with pride and looking as dapper as John Gotti, 13 mobsters joined hands in October 1991 and celebrated the induction of five new members into the Luchese crime family.

There had been a formal Mafia blood oath, administered by consigliere Frank Lastorino, then these words spoken in unison: "We are brothers now, one family, one borghata."

Their boss was in federal prison, their underboss was on the run, but the five Class of 1991 grads were all smiles as they entered a life they thought was full of promise, glory, and ill-gotten riches.

Within six years, however, each would wind up behind bars—where one would die and another would become a prosecution witness.

The fall of the Class of '91 is symbolic of the mob's malaise today, its ranks infiltrated by mob turncoats and wiretaps, and its numbers shrunk by aggressive prosecutions.

Since 1990, the top three mobsters in four crime families have been convicted and sent to prison—including Gotti, the boss of the Gambino family, and his Disheveled Don counterpart, Genovese boss Vincent "Chin" Gigante.

But the mob's downfall is about more than high-profile cases; it is about the scores of capos, soldiers, and associates from all five clans who have been put behind bars, many for life.

Here's the lowdown on the rise and fall of the Class of '91 and their Luchese comrades—according to a review of court documents and interviews with numerous sources on both sides of the law.

Coronation night began with the soon-to-be mobsters—Frank Gioia Jr., 24; Thomas "Fat Tommy" D'Ambrosia, 47; Joseph "Torty Jr." Tortorello, 32; Gregory "Whitey" Cappello, 33, and Jody Calabrese, 36—waiting in a living room of a large home in Howard Beach, Queens.

In a finished basement, eight Luchese mobsters sat around a table, where a knife and a picture of a saint rested.

Lastorino headed the table, seconded by capos Salvatore Avellino, Anthony "Bowat" Baratta and George "Georgie Goggles" Conte. Acting capos Richard "the Toupe" Pagliarulo and Anthony "Torty" Tortorello, and mobsters Frank "Bones" Papagni and Thomas "Tommy Red" Anzellotto filled the other seats.

For the record, Baratta was D'Ambrosia's sponsor; Anthony Tortorello had recommended his son Joseph; Pagliarulo had proposed Cappello and Calabrese, and Conte was filling in for Gioia's sponsor, George "Georgie Neck" Zapolla, a fugitive at the time.

Joseph Tortorello was the first to be summoned downstairs. Replying to questions from Lastorino, he promised to love and honor the Luchese family above his own.

One by one, the others followed, repeating the ritual.

Their trigger fingers pricked, all promised loyalty to the family and watched Lastorino burn tissue paper in their hands and say: "May you burn in hell like this if you betray us."

They didn't know their fates were already sealed.

A month earlier, Luchese acting boss Alfonse "Little Al" D'Arco began cooperating with the FBI, telling mob secrets about murders and racketeering schemes. The feds in Manhattan and Brooklyn had already empanelled grand juries, preparing for wide-ranging indictments. Finally, wired-up operatives for the Manhattan District Attorney's office were taping them in drug deals.

Inducted as a group, the Class of '91 celebrated at different restaurants with their sponsors later that night, and went their separate ways.

Tortorello ran a drug operation in lower Manhattan. D'Ambrosia ran a heroin ring in East Harlem and the Bronx. Cappello became a street thug. Calabrese did strong-arm work in the private carting industry. Gioia did double duty as a hitman and drug dealer.

As a whole, they earned hundreds of thousands of dollars for the Luchese family, bringing riches on borrowed time.

By 1993, three had been arrested and ultimately sentenced to prison. By 1997, all had been arrested—with one dying behind bars.

The pitfalls varied; Tortorello and D'Ambrosia went down together after a four-year undercover drug probe by the Manhattan District Attorney.

Calabrese was nabbed for trying to kill a cohort in a dispute over garbage stops. He is awaiting trial.

Gioia, a hefty martial arts enthusiast, was arrested twice—first in June, 1992, on a gun charge in Brooklyn, and then in 1993 on federal drug charges in Boston in a joint investigation with the Manhattan District Attorney for running a heroin pipeline from Manhattan to Boston.

But the strangest arrest arose from a quirk of circumstances that brought down Cappello on the Fourth of July in 1994.

Cappello, who was being sought by an FBI-NYPD task force on an extortion charge, came out of hiding to celebrate. He would later tell authorities that he assumed that any lawmen who knew him would be off for the holiday.

But because of crowd-control concerns near Coney Island, NYPD Detective John Kenna, a task force member, was pressed into uniform. He happened to spot a dead ringer for Cappello, then noticed the man had a crack pipe protruding from his back pocket.

Kenna collared the man, who turned out to be Cappello's younger brother, said FBI spokesman Jim Margolin.

Suddenly, Gregory Cappello, eyes wild with anger, ran up.

"What the hell are you doing with my brother?" he screamed at Kenna—and was arrested himself.

As FBI agents took him into custody, Cappello moaned, "I lay low for months and come out for a few laughs on the Fourth of July 'cause I know you federal guys are off, and I get popped by a cop doing crowd control."

Cappello died last December in prison.

Today, the only living member of the Class of '91 not behind bars is D'Ambrosia, who was released in October after three years in prison.

Gioia became the informer. In late 1994, he called the feds and offered his services. Sources said he learned from a jailhouse visitor that the Luchese mobster who had driven him to his induction, Frank Papagni, was plotting to kill Gioia's father in a money dispute.

The feds moved quickly. On January 3, 1995, FBI agents nabbed Zapolla, Gioia's fugitive sponsor, at a public phone in Manhattan after a series of monitored calls and beeper messages from Gioia's father.

As for the rest of the attendees at the induction ceremony, all of them—including the eight mobsters who welcomed the class into the family—are in prison.

DECEMBER 21, 1998

The Prosecutor

Good music has always drawn New Yorkers from every corner of their city up to Harlem, where harmony, melody, and rhythm fuse into some of the best jazz in the world.

And a young federal prosecutor and his best friend were no different than countless others before and after them who wanted to hear some good sounds. It was saxophonist Lonnie Youngblood, perhaps best known nowadays for his groundbreaking experience with Jimi Hendrix, who beckoned these two to the western reaches of Harlem.

"Man, is he something," Charles Rose would say enthusiastically, again and again, each time more sincerely than the last. "That man is playing at my funeral."

And last week, a panorama of law enforcement—400 cops, federal agents, prosecutors, lawyers, judges, relatives, and others—squeezed into St. Joseph's Church on the Upper East Side to be mesmerized as Youngblood performed the most haunting rendition of "Amazing Grace" I've heard in my life. We all left the church knowing just a little bit more about this amazing guy.

Charlie Rose grew up in the Bronx and got a bachelor's degree from Cornell University. He earned his law degree from Brooklyn Law School in 1979, when he was 32. That same year he became an assistant U.S. attorney for the Eastern District of New York.

He had a slew of titles during 15 years there, and prosecuted the entire catalog of bad guys—bank robbers, drug dealers, terrorist bombers, murderers, and mobsters. He formed friendships and alliances with police and agents from New York City to Washington, D.C., to Hong Kong and Palermo, Sicily.

His long list of convicted criminals includes Luchese boss Vittorio "Vic" Amuso, members of the Puerto Rican terrorist group FALN, Genovese underboss Venero "Benny Eggs" Mangano, Colombo consigliere Benedetto "Benny" Aloi, mad terrorist bombers from the anarchist United Freedom Front, and enough drug dealers to start a small city.

His success as a prosecutor continued after he hung up his hat in Brooklyn. "Is he crazy or is he sane" Mafia boss Vincent "Chin" Gigante was finally convicted last year, three years after Rose left the office, on racketeering charges Rose filed in 1990.

The son of a cop, Rose had a special bond with cops and federal agents with whom he worked, often accompanying them on dangerous raids, about which most prosecutors would have waited in the office to hear the details after everyone had been locked up.

When NYPD detective Anthony Venditti was gunned down in Queens in 1986, Rose raced to the scene. After several state murder cases ended in mistrials, Rose pushed for federal prosecutions of the suspects, and got them.

And when things didn't go the way he'd hoped, he had an uncanny ability to focus on the positive. After a long racketeering trial ended in acquittals for five of eight defendants, including Gambino capo Peter Gotti, a reporter caught him on a stairwell in Brooklyn Federal Court and asked him what went wrong.

"Wrong? Peter Gotti's a nobody," said Rose. "We just nailed the underboss of the Genovese family and the consigliere of the Colombo family and they'll be away a long time. Go ask Mangano and Aloi if we won or lost."

During that trial, Rose played a tape-recorded conversation—he often said it was his all-time favorite—in which Mangano was overheard berating an associate, Peter Savino, for hanging around with untrustworthy gangsters.

When Savino protested he was different than the thugs in question, Mangano said, "Show me your friends, and I'll tell you who you are."

Mangano is still locked up. If the mobster lives, he will get out of prison in 2006, at age 85.

Rose is dead of cancer at age 51. More than 400 of the prosecutor's friends showed up last Tuesday at a tiny church on Manhattan's Upper East Side to tell the world who Charlie Rose was.

The Deadbeat Dad

The feds hid a lot more than the late mob informer Peter Savino—whose testimony helped put away Vincent "Chin" Gigante—during his eight years in the federal Witness Protection Program, according to his ex-wife.

The government hid and is still hiding his assets, preventing his twin 12-year-old sons from obtaining money that is rightfully theirs, Suzanne Savino charges in a federal lawsuit.

She claims that when Savino entered the program in 1989 he began ignoring the terms of their 1986 divorce, which required him to make weekly child support payments; to pay the boys' medical, dental, and private school expenses; and to buy life insurance that would provide $133,333 for them in case of his death. The couple was divorced seven months after the boys were born.

When Savino died of cancer on September 30, 1997, Suzanne Savino tried to locate and freeze his assets, but was stymied by federal officials, according to the suit, which names Attorney General

Janet Reno and Frank Skroski, the deputy U.S. marshal who runs the supersecret witness program, as defendants. Savino wanted the feds to furnish the information she needs to sue her ex-hubby's estate.

The court records in the case have been redacted (legalese for blacked out) to eliminate Savino's alias and where he lived. Several members of his family were also relocated and still live in that area.

A pretrial conference scheduled last week was adjourned. No new date has been set. The case is assigned to the same judge who handled the Gigante trial, Brooklyn Federal Judge Jack Weinstein.

During the trial, Savino was too ill to travel and his testimony—the most damning and dramatic in the case—was taken in a faraway courtroom and viewed in Weinstein's courtroom by closed-circuit television.

With tape-recordings that backed him up, Savino said he made millions for the Genovese family through bid-rigging, extortion, and kickback schemes involving contracts to replace windows at New York City housing projects.

During his day and a half of testimony, Savino, gaunt and in obvious pain, sweated profusely, constantly mopping his forehead with paper towels. Weinstein had to call frequent recesses.

> Savino said he made millions for the Genovese family through bid-rigging, extortion, and kickback schemes.

"I got to take a break please," Savino said near the end of his testimony, groaning and clutching the armrests of his chair.

Weinstein urged the lawyers to wrap up their questions. "I'm just hoping he survives," he said.

Gigante was found guilty of more than 30 labor racketeering counts and with conspiring to kill Savino after he began cooperating with federal authorities. He was sentenced to 12 years in prison.

The Crybaby Capo

Bonanno capo Vincent Asaro looked quite dapper in his well-tailored and freshly pressed gray suit, which didn't go too well with his incredible five-minute whining, ranting, and raving crybaby performance in Queens Supreme Court the other day.

About the only thing he didn't do at his sentencing on state racketeering charges for heading a lucrative stolen car ring was get on the floor and kick his legs up in the air or bang his well-coifed head on the table.

Glaring at prosecutor Gerard Brave, he complained that he had been framed by a cocaine addict and thief who lied in return for a get-out-of-jail-free card.

"If I have to die in prison I will, but this was not a fair trial," said Asaro, 63.

"I've been in trouble (with the law) a few times in my life, but I was framed here."

Acting Supreme Court Justice Robert McGann let Asaro tire himself out, which took about five minutes, then hit him with a 4-to-12-year bit for enterprise corruption.

Asaro's lawyer, Stephen Mahler, said his client was "railroaded" and that he would appeal his conviction.

As the Mob Turns

As Brooklyn federal prosecutor Daniel Dorsky promised in his opening statement, the jury-tampering trial of Colombo boss Andrew Russo looked and sounded like a soap opera.

Dorothy Fiorenza, a willowy, raven-haired lawyer—she had been a blonde but dyed her hair at the suggestion of an FBI agent for security reasons, she said—told how she and Russo became lovers after they met at a 1994 Christmas party. She said Russo sent her a message that he thought "I was the best thing since baked bread or sliced bread."

A beauty school graduate—before law school—Fiorenza, 32, testified at length about her relationships with various gangsters, their wives, and their mistresses.

She had worked at a Queens barbershop frequented by gangsters and said she was unhappily married at the time. Russo had been back on the streets for five months after an eight-year federal prison stretch and soon became her lover.

They dined at fancy restaurants in Manhattan and Long Island; frequented Elaine's, a celebrity watering hole on the Upper East Side; did Broadway, including *Phantom of the Opera;* and had love trysts in the country during a whirlwind affair that ended in July 1995.

Russo, 33 years her senior, referred to them as "the gangster and the lawyer," she said.

In videotapes played for the Brooklyn Federal Court jury, Russo and Fiorenza are dancing the cha cha, Russo is shooting pool as a blonde Fiorenza looks on lovingly, and in a third, singer Laine Kazan is seen sitting on a couch and actor James Caan, an old Russo friend and frequent attendee at his 1986 racketeering trial, is playing the piano.

Russo is charged with trying to tamper with an alternate juror who sat on the racketeering case of his son, Joseph "JoJo" Russo, who was convicted in April 1994. The elder Russo, along with co-defendant Dennis Hickey, is also charged with obstructing an FBI jury-tampering investigation by getting his son's girlfriend, Teresa Castronova, to dodge a federal grand jury subpoena from May 1994 through July 1995.

The FBI began looking for Castronova after the juror told the trial judge that she recognized Castronova, a schoolmate from her high school days, as a daily spectator, and reported that a private investigator had tried to contact her about the case after the verdict.

Fiorenza testified that Russo and Hickey hid Castronova at Hickey's Long Island farm, where she and Russo had often spent the weekend. She said she also carried messages between him and his son, who at the time was confined at the Manhattan Correctional Center (MCC), as well as love letters from Castronova.

She said she witnessed a screaming match between Joseph Russo's wife and his girlfriend, and after she fell out with Castronova, withheld a love letter to Joseph Russo that was introduced as evidence at trial.

Gradually, her relationship with Andrew Russo soured and she fell in love with Lawrence Fiorenza, a co-defendant of Russo's son, whom she met at MCC. With the help of a friendly prison guard—she said she didn't bribe him—they had sex at the jail and were married there in April 1996.

A year later, claiming she was afraid of Russo after her marriage to his underling, she and her new husband began cooperating with federal prosecutors.

"Her convoluted story is nothing but a last ditch effort to get her husband out of prison," said Russo's lawyer, George Santangelo, noting that Russo was in jail when the juror's family was contacted in May 1994.

Santangelo and Hickey's lawyer, James LaRossa, said their clients violated no laws and argued that Castronova had ducked the FBI because she believed that the FBI had framed Joseph Russo.

The trial is expected to conclude this week.

As the Mob Turns, II

White Plains Federal Judge Barrington Parker is due to set a firm trial date tomorrow for the pared-down racketeering trial of John A. "Junior" Gotti currently scheduled for next month.

Gotti and capo Salvatore "Tore" Locascio—whose fathers were convicted together and jailed for life in 1992—are the only mobsters remaining in the case that had dozens of defendants when filed a year ago.

Ailing and aging Gambino soldier Gregory DePalma pleaded guilty to racketeering charges while lying in a Westchester County prison hospital bed breathing through an oxygen tank.

In a makeshift courtroom, DePalma, 66, admitted conspiring "with a group of individuals" to shake down the upscale Manhattan strip joint, Scores; evading taxes; and engaging in loan-sharking and illegal gambling.

Suffering from diabetes and lung and prostrate cancer, DePalma agreed to plead out and face 10 years in jail in the hopes of lightening punishment for his son and co-defendant, Craig, said defense attorney John Mitchell.

Craig, 32, also a reputed soldier, pleaded guilty in White Plains Federal Court an hour later, admitting to extortion and other charges that could net him seven years in jail.

In exchange for the pleas, federal prosecutors agreed to drop charges that the DePalmas hatched a murder plot to avenge the 1996 shooting of a Scores bouncer and waiter.

Gregory DePalma, who appeared in an infamous backstage photo with Frank Sinatra, will not be testifying against Gotti, but prosecutors plan to use his tape-recorded words against the reputed acting boss.

During the investigation, investigators with the state Organized Crime Task Force planted a bug inside the bedroom of DePalma's Scarsdale home. He was caught boasting of his links to the Gambino family's jailed boss and the son who serves as his father's acting boss.

DePalma implicates Junior in numerous crimes, including loan-sharking and the shakedown of Scores.

In a June 8, 1995, discussion with son Craig, DePalma quoted Junior, who has denied any involvement with Scores, as saying he was "going to throw out" the manager of the club.

On March 13, 1995, DePalma instructed others to leave a parcel in his mailbox, not on his stoop, because "I don't like to leave them outside for the mailman, John Gotti shit."

Two days before the DePalma pleas, as "Gang Land" predicted last week, capos John "Jackie Nose" D'Amico and Louis Ricco, and soldier Mario Antonicelli, resolved their cases with plea bargains.

MAY 3, 1999

Colombo Boys Win the War

In the last battle of the bloody three-year internal Colombo family war that had already claimed 11 lives, the Carmine Persico faction was so depleted that junior wannabe gangsters were sent to whack a rival capo, traditionally a task for made men.

The youngsters appeared to have done everything right—killing big, tough Joseph Scopo, wounding a nephew and his future son-in-law, and escaping into the cool night of October 20, 1993, without a scratch. But boys will be boys, and they were soon waving around their big guns and shooting off their bigger mouths and on a path to the grave or a life behind bars, according to recent testimony in Brooklyn Federal Court.

The day after the hit, Eric Curcio was bubbling with joy when he visited Dino Basciano (a Red Hook, Brooklyn, buddy), who testified at the murder and racketeering trial of John Pappa.

"He was hugging me, kissing me, telling me, 'The war is over. I got the guy,'" said Basciano, who said that Curcio, Pappa, and John Sparacino all bragged to him how they had gunned down Scopo.

Pappa, 24, the only one still living, is charged with murdering Scopo as well as his pals, Curcio and Sparacino, and a fourth young hoodlum, in 1993 and 1994. Calvin Hennigar, 26, is also charged in the Sparacino murder. Both are charged with dealing marijuana and cocaine in Brooklyn and Staten Island.

The braggadocio and boasting was the young hoodlums' attempt to obtain credit and respect from their cohorts and Colombo family leaders, according to Assistant U.S. Attorneys Stephen Kelly and Amy Walsh.

About eight months after Scopo was killed, Sparacino told Basciano about his role in the murder one night as Pappa and Curcio were leaving Basciano's social club. Sparacino threw a disgusted look at them and sneered: "They think they're a bunch of tough guys. They ain't shit. They're a bunch of punks. Remember the Scopo murder. I'm the one, I did the shooting and those two punks left me there."

After the club emptied out, Basciano found Pappa and Curcio and told them what Sparacino had said. Their version was that Sparacino had driven off, and that after killing Scopo they had to run three long blocks from the crime scene in front of Scopo's Ozone Park home to a backup getaway car—the same scenario painted by prosecutors.

"Eric looked shocked. Pappa's face turned beet red. He turned around … and said, 'That motherf-----, I'm going to rip his heart out.' Pappa was going nuts, and I just got in the truck and left," said Basciano.

Curcio and Pappa got Hennigar to lure Sparacino to his house on August 13, 1994, and killed him before Curcio and Pappa could get there, according to testimony from another former cohort, Joseph Iborti.

This is a case where nobody could keep their mouths shut; Iborti's testimony was based on what Hennigar and Pappa told him.

"He (Hennigar) pulled out the gun and shot him in the back of the head," Iborti said, extending his hands in front of his face and squeezing his trigger finger, the way Hennigar described the murder to him. Pappa then "told me how they cut his face and tried to pull it off," Iborti testified, moving his hand back and forth in a sawing motion around his own face.

Sparacino's mother Rose, who has been in the courtroom the entire trial, began weeping during Iborti's gruesome descriptions. Judge Raymond Dearie called a recess. As the jury and Sparacino's sobbing mother left the courtroom, tears streamed down Iborti's face. Before resuming trial, Dearie advised Sparacino

to spare herself the agony of more testimony, but allowed her to stay after she agreed to sit in the back and leave if things got too rough for her.

"I think we have to give her one chance, we owe that to her," Dearie told defense lawyers Michael Bachner and Michael Hurwitz, who complained that further outbursts would prejudice the jury.

"I have to stay," Sparacino said during a recess. "My son is dead and I need to hear about it. These were friends of his that ate at my table."

Her son's body was found shot, mutilated, and burned two days after he was executed. That same year, Iborti testified, he was driving Pappa on his drug route when Pappa told him that he was going to kill Curcio because he was trying to take all the credit.

"I killed Joe Scopo, I did all the work," Pappa complained, Iborti testified. Pappa told him he was going to walk into Curcio's auto body shop in Red Hook and kill him.

On October 5, 1994, a laughing and giggling Pappa telephoned Iborti and asked why Iborti hadn't called and told him that their friend had been killed the day before, before describing how he had made good on his vow to kill Curcio.

"He started making the sounds of gunshots on the phone," said Iborti, placing his right hand next to his ear in the shape of a telephone and imitating the sound of machine-gun fire. "'Boom boom boom

boom boom boom boom boom,' then he'd stop for a second, start laughing, and do it all over again, 'boom boom boom boom boom boom.'"

Asked to describe what was going through his mind at the time, Iborti said: "This guy's nuts."

If convicted, Pappa and Hennigar face life. Early on, prosecutors were considering seeking the death penalty for Pappa.

Gaspipe Loses Again

The Second Circuit Court of Appeals last week rejected arguments by former Luchese underboss Anthony "Gaspipe" Casso that federal prosecutors had reneged on their agreement to recommend leniency for him for information he gave the FBI from 1994 through 1997.

Casso gave up details about an NYPD detective who tipped Casso off to numerous investigations and was involved in two gangland slayings, told about a plan by Colombo mobsters to kill a federal judge, and related how he and Genovese boss Vincent "Chin" Gigante used a munitions expert to blow up Gambino underboss Frank DeCicco as part of a plot to retaliate against him and John Gotti for the unsanctioned killing of Mafia boss Paul Castellano.

Casso, however, committed crimes while housed in a unit for cooperating witnesses, allegedly lied about other crimes, and refused to admit his role in others, and prosecutors charged him with breaking his agreement to refrain from criminal activity and cooperate fully.

The appeals court took three pages to put its stamp of approval on the prosecution's decision and 15 consecutive life sentences Casso received for a lifetime of crime that included 37 murders.

Casso, 58, is at Supermax, the Florence, Colorado, ultra-modern maximum security prison said to be even more restrictive than the 23-hours-a-day lockdown situation of John Gotti and other inmates at the federal penitentiary in Marion, Illinois.

Andy Russo Wins a Little One

Imprisoned Colombo boss Andrew Russo, who faces about 10 years on two federal convictions—one for jury tampering and another for labor racketeering—for which he is awaiting sentencing, won an appeal last month that will save him about 14 months in prison.

Russo, who had been identified by the feds as both a boss and a capo in two different cases, won the prison reduction in a ruling by the same appeals court that slammed Casso.

Through the testimony of a former lover, Russo, 65, was convicted at trial earlier this year of tampering with a federal jury that convicted his son Joseph of murder and racketeering stemming from the Colombo war.

He subsequently pleaded guilty to three-year-old labor racketeering charges involving several private sanitation companies in Islip, Long Island, in a deal that calls for him to receive five years in prison.

In each case, there was conflicting testimony about whether and when Russo was elevated from capo to boss, succeeding his cousin, the jailed-for-life former boss, Carmine Persico.

Essentially, the Second Circuit Court of Appeals ruled that Russo, who had received 22 months for a parole violation because the FBI said he was a boss, should have been classified as a capo and gotten eight months.

Life Without Honor

John Pappa grew up idolizing his dad, telling his young hoodlum buddies he wanted to be just like his father, Gerard, a bloodthirsty mobster who killed for fun and profit and eventually was whacked for breaking mob rules, reputedly by that denizen of mob protocol, Genovese boss Vincent "Chin" Gigante.

On his dresser, Pappa had a picture of his dad, who was blown away in 1980. On his arm was a simple tattoo tribute, "Pappa Bear." On his back was a macabre tattoo that includes, in Italian, a credo young Pappa believed applied to him and his father, "Morte prima di disonore"— Death before dishonor.

Last week, the baby-faced hoodlum with a hair-trigger temper was convicted of racketeering, drug dealing, and four murders, including the 12th and final killing of the bloody Colombo family war.

Pappa was found guilty in Brooklyn Federal Court of the October 20, 1993, rubout of rival capo Joseph Scopo and three other murders in a 12-month period. Pappa, 24, faces a mandatory life sentence. Co-defendant Calvin Hennigar, 26, convicted of drug dealing and one murder, also faces life.

"This prosecution brings the terrible legacy of the Colombo war to a close with the conviction of one of the most dangerous young hit men in the Colombo family," said Assistant U.S. Attorney Stephen Kelly.

During the four-week trial, Kelly and co-prosecutor Amy Walsh put together an overwhelming case against Pappa and Hennigar without the luxury of two staples of most modern-day Mafia trials: They had no tape-recorded admissions from either defendant, and none of their witnesses were turncoat accomplices with firsthand information.

They built their case around circumstantial evidence, such as telephone records showing that Pappa called two of his victims several times right before their deaths. They also had a witness who testified that she saw a slender teenager running away from the Scopo murder scene. They introduced a photo of Pappa's back into evidence, and called an FBI agent who testified that Pappa failed to tell the feds about the tattoo (as required of arrestees) at first and was reluctant to remove his shirt. They argued that under the entire circumstances of the case, it showed Pappa's guilt.

But their best evidence came from Pappa himself, who often shot his mouth off about his murderous achievements. Three former mob associates testified about repeated admissions he made about murder, drug dealing, and assorted mayhem in the early 1990s.

Seven months after the Scopo hit, Pappa boasted how he used a .380 automatic to kill the unarmed Colombo capo, according to Ronald "Messy Marvin" Moran, who followed Dino Basciano and Joseph Iborti to the witness stand.

"He said John Sparacino threw open the door and sprayed Scopo's car with a machine gun," said Moran, a bespectacled, chubby-cheeked killer whose nickname stems from a likeness to a cherubic adolescent in a television commercial.

"He said that the retard Sparacino had missed him with every shot … (and) left him at the scene. The next part of the conversation, John was out of the car. He didn't explain how. Just he was in another location, this time he was hiding behind a tree because he thought Scopo had a gun. He seen Scopo in a crouched position outside the automobile. He said he waited to see if he had a gun.

"He said Scopo was yelling at him, 'You got balls, come on. Come on, you need to kill me, kill me, you little punk.'

> "John said he walked from behind the tree, walked over to Scopo and shot him, I believe eight times."

John said Scopo threw what he believed to be a cellular phone at him. John said he walked from behind the tree, walked over to Scopo, and shot him, I believe eight times."

Lawyers for both defendants said they would appeal. "There are significant appellate issues and we expect our appeal to be successful," said Pappa's attorney, Michael Bachner.

The Messy Mutt

The testimony by Ronald "Messy Marvin" Moran helped sink trigger-happy mob wannabe John Pappa, but the feds aren't too happy with the stoolie they saved for last.

Since owning up to a murderous, drug-dealing life of crime that began when he was 13, Moran's given up loads of wiseguys and drug dealers—and his mother too, for getting him a gun for protection—but he can't stay out of trouble.

Moran has been in the hole "a few times" for various infractions since he was placed into a special unit for cooperating witnesses nearly two years ago, he admitted under questioning by Pappa's lawyer, Michael Bachner.

In addition, Moran admitted ripping off nearly $10,000 in Social Security funds since he began cooperating by collecting monthly $550 disability payments that began five years ago when he faked suicidal tendencies and was judged to be disabled and unable to work after an arrest on gun charges.

At a sidebar conference, as the lawyers discussed whether Moran had attempted to rape a woman in a hotel room or an apartment, Judge Raymond Dearie summed it all up: "This guy is a mutt, period, plain and simple."

B. F. Guerra

Frank "B. F." Guerra, a Colombo wiseguy implicated in a drug sale for which mob associate Frank Smith has been jailed for 11 years, was on the hit team that killed Joseph Scopo, according to testimony at Pappa's trial.

Luchese associate Dino Basciano said Pappa told him that Guerra, a close associate of Colombo capo Alphonse Persico, was in one of at least two cars that contained at least five shooters and backup gunmen.

Messy Marvin Moran testified that Pappa excitedly told him that Guerra had passed along congratulations from Persico for his killings of Scopo and associate Eric Curcio.

Guerra, who owned a bagel shop where an 18-year-old worker was killed by gangsters looking for Guerra in 1991, admitted that he sold cocaine for which Smith was convicted in 1989, according to FBI documents. Guerra made the admission to Smith's mother in 1992, soon after Smith's father was killed in a construction accident, the documents state.

Guerra, 33, is not charged with any Colombo war–related crimes. Persico, who was acquitted of war crimes in 1994, was arrested three months ago on federal gun charges for allegedly possessing loaded firearms while piloting his 50-foot speedboat on the Florida Keys last Labor Day weekend.

One from the Weasel's Book

William "Wild Bill" Cutolo was always a legitimate tough guy. And the handsome and charismatic capo's elevation to underboss of the Colombo crime family and subsequent disappearance seem like one right out of the books.

Cutolo's rapid rise in gangland bears striking similarities to the tale told by Aladena "Jimmy the Weasel" Fratianno about Frank "Bomp" Bompensiero, a soldier in the Los Angeles family who fell out of favor for "bad-mouthing" his Administration. So the bosses made him their consigliere to lower his guard. Not too long afterward, on February 10, 1977, Bomp was lured to his favorite phone booth and bumped off.

Even before Cutolo's crew fired the first shots of the bloody Colombo war that resulted in 12 dead and assorted mayhem and violence from 1991 to 1993, Cutolo was an outspoken critic of longtime boss Carmine "Junior" Persico. After Cutolo's crew began the violence by blowing away two Persico loyalists, Wild Bill got a hold of official court papers from the feds' historic Commission case (in which leaders of five families were hit with racketeering charges.) Waving them around, he blasted Persico, who

represented himself at trial, as a rat for admitting the existence of the Mafia.

Cutolo survived numerous attempts on his life, and after the war, fended off the feds who had gotten indictments against him and his crew on murder and racketeering charges stemming from the bloodshed.

In late 1993, Cutolo, head of Local 400 of the Production Workers Union, and six members of his crew were hit with war crimes charges and held without bail in the dormitory-style Metropolitan Detention Center in Brooklyn. They quickly took over their wing, and until the following September, terrorized the inmates as well as the guards. They stole and hoarded food and turned the television room into their private club, hanging up a sign that read "Italians Only."

"The MDC officials were losing control of the prison, and the people who were running the prison (block) were the inmates," Assistant U.S. Attorney Pam Davis said at a 1994 court hearing.

Cutolo and his crew were acquitted that December.

But Wild Bill's promotion to underboss may have been another gangland subterfuge. Cutolo, who would have been 50 yesterday, disappeared more than a week ago, and is feared dead.

"It's starting to look more and more like he's gone," said one investigator.

Colombo bosses have a habit of going on the lam when they find out they're facing charges—like former bosses Persico and Andrew Russo—but sources on both sides of the law fear Cutolo has been killed.

Relatives, business associates, and law enforcement types who keep tabs on people like Wild Bill haven't seen him. He missed a sit-down with another gangster and didn't show up three hours later for his crew's regular Wednesday night meeting at his social club in Brooklyn.

The heat has been on for a while. The club was raided last year, and he and his crew are the focus of a federal grand jury in Brooklyn probing extortion allegations. Manhattan federal prosecutors have also targeted Cutolo, and his name has come up in a state probe of financial irregularities at a city municipal workers union.

Cutolo and his crew had sided with insurgents led by acting boss Victor Orena. When he was released from prison in 1994, Cutolo was knocked down to soldier as part of a peace compromise between factions of the weakened crime family. But he never lost his swagger, and eventually regained his captain's rank.

After Russo went down for jury tampering and racketeering this spring, Persico's son Alphonse was named boss, Joel "Joe Waverly" Cacace consigliere, and Cutolo was named underboss.

Wild Bill, hailed by union officials as caring and by charity organizations as generous, played Santa at a gala Christmas party he threw six months ago for the National Leukemia Research Association, for which he was a major fundraiser.

"It's all about the children. You'll pardon me if I don't say any more than that," Cutolo told reporter Tom Robbins when he asked about the charity's alleged mob ties and probes linking Cutolo to corrupt union activities.

A secretary at Cutolo's union, which represents about 250 blue collar workers, said she hadn't seen Cutolo. "He is usually here on Wednesdays. He didn't show up."

Allen Weinberg, the Leukemia Association's director, said Cutolo hadn't replied to a memo he had faxed him last week. "He usually gets right back to me. He is in his office on Tuesdays and Wednesdays. He was a beautiful guy. I am

> "He usually gets right back to me .... I am shocked, just shocked. Could this mean the worst?"
>
> In gangland, it sure does.

shocked, just shocked. Could this mean the worst?"

In gangland, it sure does.

Raised Hands Means Death

Paul Gulino was only a low-level drug dealer, but he had to know better than to raise his hands to any made man, let alone a neighborhood legend who happened to be the consigliere of the Bonanno family.

But that's what Gulino reportedly did, and why federal prosecutors in Brooklyn will seek to detain Anthony Spero, 70, as a danger to the community while he awaits trial for allegedly ordering Gulino's murder.

Gulino, whose nickname was Paulie Brass, made his living dealing drugs in Bath Beach, Brooklyn, where guys like him learn mob protocol before they smoke their first joint, let alone sell their first ounce of pot or first gram of coke.

Gulino was schooled enough to know that when two buddies—Joseph Calco and Thomas Reynolds—whacked a "connected" drug dealer in late 1992, they were in big trouble. He approached the dealer's Luchese family protector and tried to smooth things out, explaining that the killers didn't know their victim was with the Lucheses.

Whether Gulino's intercession helped, or if his requests to Bonanno boss Joe Massino on their behalf made a difference, things were cool on Bath Avenue

the following summer. Paulie Brass was dealing marijuana and cocaine for the Lucheses off the corner of Bay 23d Street, and Calco and Reynolds were hanging tough with the Bonannos.

In early July 1993, however, Gulino made a fatal mistake. He shoved Bonanno consigliere Anthony Spero during a heated dispute in Spero's Bath Avenue social club, according to FBI debriefings of mob turncoat Frank Gioia Jr.

On July 25, 1993, Gulino was murdered on Spero's orders, according to a six-count indictment charging Spero and 13 others with racketeering, dealing drugs on the wholesale and retail level, and four murders:

- Spero and Bonanno soldier Joseph Benanti are charged with taking part in Gulino's murder.

- Calco and Reynolds are charged with killing Neil Mastro, the Luchese-protected drug dealer who they didn't know was connected, and Mastro's uncle, on October 18, 1992.

- Calco is also charged with the murder of a suspected informer, Jack Cherin, on January 18, 1995.

And while only Spero and Benanti are charged with Gulino's slaying, his murder has a morbid touch of irony, according to the account Gioia gave the FBI. "Calco and Reynolds shot and killed Gulino in his kitchen while his parents were away for the weekend," said Gioia.

Calco, 31, and Reynolds, 29, are jailed on other charges and have not yet been arraigned in the federal case.

Spero appeared briefly in court last week, long enough to wave hello to his daughter and hear lawyer Scott Leemon adjourn his hearing, and say he hoped to work out a house-arrest bail package with the feds for his client.

Federal prosecutor Jim Walden, who along with colleague Christopher Blank wouldn't discuss any specifics of Gulino's murder, didn't seem interested. He said he believed Spero was a danger to the community and should be detained without bail.

Gangster Goes Down the Sewer

Fittingly, Michael "Baldy Mike" Spinelli, a made-in-the-bathroom mobster, was flushed down the drain the other day for a rock-bottom misdeed. And he took one of the noble myths of organized crime into the sewers with him.

Spinelli was sentenced to 19 years and seven months for trying to whack Patricia Capozzalo, a mother of three who had the misfortune of being the sister of a mob turn-coat. The attempted hit was the low point of the excessive mob violence of the last two decades and belied the supposed axiom that innocent, uninvolved women, children, and family members are off-limits to the treachery of revenge, retribution, and mayhem which still make organized crime the subjects of R-rated movies, best-sellers, and tabloid headlines.

Capozzalo was marked for death by Luchese crime boss Vittorio "Vic" Amuso in an ill-conceived attempt to convince her brother, Peter "Fat Pete" Chiodo, to change his mind about testifying at Amuso's then-upcoming racketeering and murder trial. Amuso is one of those hot-headed gangsters who doesn't always think things through. Capozzalo was shot in the neck and back in front of her home in 1992 after dropping two of her children off at school. Spinelli drove the van that carried the shooter. Had his sister died, it's hard not to imagine Chiodo being even more eager to testify against his old friends.

Baldy Mike's participation in the shooting earned him a place in the crime family. He was officially inducted at a makeshift ritual in a bathroom at the Metropolitan Correctional Center, where he was being held on murder and racketeering charges. Spinelli's inductors had to do without the gun and knife, props in the traditional ceremony, and instead of a picture of a Catholic saint, they set toilet paper afire in his hands as he swore undying allegiance to the family.

> Instead of a picture of a Catholic saint, they set toilet paper afire in his hands as he swore undying allegiance to the family.

Spinelli, 45, isn't likely to resurface until 2027, if he lives that long. The new sentence was tacked on to 13 years he still has to serve for other violent crimes.

In a prepared statement, Spinelli with a straight face and no sign of remorse said he hoped his sentencing would bring closure to his and the Capozzalo families. "They've both suffered enough," he said.

Not surprising, the sentencing judge's sentiments were similar to the pervasive view of the shooting in many corners of gangland.

"This is not just another criminal living and dying by the sword or a gun," said Brooklyn Federal Judge Raymond Dearie. "This is really an unthinkable act of cowardice" that broke one of the "rules that just aren't broken," and is a "black indelible mark (on the Luchese crime family) that will never be washed away."

Three days later in a federal courthouse 60 miles away, a Luchese mobster who once did much of the dirty work for a mob-linked carting company got a shorter stretch for the same crime.

Jody Calabrese, 37, who pleaded guilty, got 10 years for his role in the attempted hit on Capozzalo, as well as the attempted murder of a salesman for a rival garbage hauler Calabrese shot five times in 1997. He's due out of prison in 2006.

In a plea bargain, Calabrese admitted his roles in both shootings, and in two extortion attempts. Prosecutors expected his sentence to be between 135 and 168 months under federal sentencing guidelines. But Calabrese's lawyer, Joel Winograd, convinced Hauppauge Federal Judge Denis Hurley that because both shooting victims did not suffer permanent injuries and because Calabrese had no prior criminal convictions, the guidelines called for less, somewhere between 108 and 135 months.

Spinelli drove the van that carried gunman Dino Basciano to the Gravesend, Brooklyn, street where Capozzalo was ambushed. Calabrese and another mobster, Gregory Cappello—who died in prison two years ago while serving time for unrelated crimes—were in a "crash car" that tailed the van and was ready to block police or other pursuers.

Spinelli's brother Robert drove a "switch car" that took the hit team to safety after they ditched the van. He was also convicted and is to be sentenced next month.

DePalma & Son Sentenced

Gregory DePalma flourished in those halcyon mobster days before federal racketeering cases.

In 1976, a smiling DePalma stood between Frank Sinatra and Mafia boss Paul Castellano for the now-infamous backstage photo with Carlo Gambino and other mobsters that would later be used to bolster tape-recorded evidence against DePalma and 10 others in a bankruptcy fraud case.

Hooked to intravenous tubes and breathing through an oxygen mask, the aging Gambino gangster, who unwittingly helped the feds make a racketeering case against John A. "Junior" Gotti, lay helpless in a sparse hospital room as he was sentenced to six years in prison.

White Plains Federal Judge Barrington Parker had traveled to the Westchester Medical Center in Valhalla to put a cap on DePalma's criminal career.

DePalma, 67, who suffers from cancer, diabetes, and a host of other ailments, could have received up to 13 years, but Parker cited DePalma's failing health and departed from the normal sentencing guidelines.

But a few hours later, back at the White Plains Courthouse, Parker showed no mercy for DePalma's mobster son Craig, meting out the harshest sentence he could for the 33-year-old mobster—87 months.

"You saw what your father's life was like and you saw what that life brought upon your family, particularly the women, (and yet) you cast your lot with Gotti and associates," said Parker.

The DePalmas implicated themselves and Junior Gotti in numerous crimes in hundreds of tape-recorded conversations from 1995 to 1997. In one memorable one, Junior and Craig made fun of the elder DePalma's propensity to be caught on tape.

All three pleaded guilty to racketeering charges that included loan-sharking and the extortion of workers and owners of Scores, a trendy Manhattan strip joint popular with celebrities, sports figures, and tourists.

Junior gets his turn before Parker next month. Like Craig DePalma, he faces up to 87 months. Like DePalma, Gotti saw what his father's life was like and opted to follow in his footsteps, even to the point of getting caught on tape.

"Gang Land" Likes Murray

No matter what the feds say about Murray Kufeld, a longtime buddy of Bonanno family consigliere Anthony Spero, "Gang Land" thinks you gotta like the guy.

Kufeld, who shares Spero's love of racing pigeons, was called as a witness at Spero's recent detention hearing in an effort by prosecutor Jim Walden to buttress his assertion that Kufeld carried messages from Spero to underlings at a Bath Beach, Brooklyn, social club a block from Spero's pigeon coops.

Kufeld denied any improprieties, but admitted under grilling by Walden that he knew many people the prosecutor identified as mobsters—including Bonanno boss Joseph Massino—insisting, however, that he never knew any of them to commit any crimes.

"Where have you seen Mr. Massino," demanded Walden.

"In the newspapers and on 'Gang Land'," said Kufeld.

PART 5

The New Millennium

On June 10, 2002, John Gotti died in a federal prison hospital in Springfield, Missouri, less than four years after doctors diagnosed him with head and neck cancer. As his brother Gene, his son Junior, and former son-in-law Carmine Agnello continued their prison terms, the feds convicted two brothers of the late Mafia boss—Peter, who had taken over as Gambino family boss, and Richard, a capo—and a nephew, Richard G. Gotti, a family soldier, of racketeering charges.

As it had done from its beginning, "Gang Land" chronicled those events and milestones involving turncoat underboss Sammy Bull Gravano, legendary Mafia boss Vincent "Chin" Gigante, and New Jersey wiseguys who fancied themselves as the real-life models for *The Sopranos*, the fictional gangsters on HBO's award-winning television series.

Meanwhile, on the Internet and in print, "Gang Land" reached a few milestones of its own as the column moved into its 15th consecutive year of reporting on "life and death, loyalty and betrayal, greed and honor" in the "world of organized crime in New York."

The New York Press Club gave "Gang Land" its Best Web News Story Award for "Bosko's Back," an exclusive account of the January 1, 2000, arrest of fugitive Westies leader Bosko Radonjich, who left New York to become a Serbian freedom fighter after his 1992 indictment for helping to fix the case for John Gotti back in 1987.

The New York Times and *People* magazine wrote feature stories about "Gang Land" and its author, and on August 8, 2002, the column again became a favorite of New York City newspaper readers as a regular weekly feature in *The New York Sun*.

Respect — Real or Imagined

Some 35 years after the FBI tape-recorded the head of New Jersey's Mafia family talking about murder and assorted mayhem, the feds have done an encore act, capturing the current leader of the crime family in a similar performance.

And just like the 1960s rendition that starred Simone "Sam the Plumber" DeCavalcante, the tapes contain wiseguy banter and bluster about respect, the right and wrong ways to whack people, and the perennial need to dispose of bodies without arousing suspicion.

This time, the electronic surveillance is legal, and the tapes will be admissible in court as evidence.

Vincent "Vinny Ocean" Palermo and members of the DeCavalcante family have been hit with federal racketeering and a murder charge that is potentially punishable by death. In all, 21 associates and made men were charged last month with 42 counts of murder, extortion, loan-sharking, bookmaking, robbery, mail fraud, and trafficking in stolen property, counterfeit goods, and stolen U.S. savings bonds.

Among other things, said Manhattan U.S. Attorney Mary Jo White, the gang dealt in stolen loads of wine, designer clothing, vitamins, Minolta digital copiers, toner, and a refrigerated truck brimming with Kraft food goods. They attempted payroll robberies and tried to unload a truck full of counterfeit Tommy Hilfiger and Jordache designer-label clothes.

No crime was too small or too big for these consummate hoodlums. You name it, they did it, or gave it their best shot.

They also had a pretty high opinion of their criminal acumen and mob prowess. And, they felt they had finally earned the hard-won respect from New York gangsters (who get all the attention, publicity, and high-profile prosecutions) and that the New Jersey gangsters portrayed in HBO's hit television series, *The Sopranos*, starring James Gandolfini, were based on them. In the show, which begins its second season this month, stress-laden capo Tony Soprano sees a shrink to combat panic attacks brought on by the pressures of his work and juggling his mob life with his family life and his *comare*.

On March 3, 1999, as a DeCavalcante crew drove to a mob sit-down, they talked about the respect they felt they had achieved across the Hudson River, triggering a lively discussion about the award-winning show.

At one time, said soldier Joseph "Tin Ear" Sclafani, 62, wiseguys in the Big Apple looked down their noses at them, but in recent months, he told capo Anthony Rotondo, 42, they had begun getting the respect they deserved.

"They make rumors about the Jersey guys, 'They're farmers … but they don't know. They know now," said Sclafani, who wears a hearing aid.

"They know now," echoed Rotondo.

"Hey, what's this f------ thing, *Sopranos*? What the f--- are they …. Is that supposed to be us?" asked Sclafani.

A.R.: "You are in there, they mentioned your name in there."

J.S.: "Yeah? What did they say?"

"Watch out for that guy, they said. Watch that guy," interjected a third gangster, identified on an FBI transcript only as Billy, while a fourth man in the car, a wired-up witness identified only as Ralphie, laughs out loud.

A.R.: "Every show you watch, more and more you pick up somebody. Every show."

J.S.: "Yeah, but it's not me," said Sclafani modestly. "I'm not even existing over there."

A.R.: "Corky."

J.S.: "Yeah."

A.R.: "One week it was Corky. One week it was …" comparing the television mobsters to real ones.

J.S.: "Yeah."

A.R.: "The guy that died, and had stomach cancer."

The gangsters even claimed they had spotted landmarks from their home turf on the show.

- "There's the bookstore."
- "Right across from the church."
- "That's the block."
- "They always sit outside the …. Yeah, they do."

Before the mobsters began focusing on the business ahead of them, Rotondo capped off the discussion: "What characters. Great acting."

Corky

Gangsters love to talk about Corky, and have been doing it for 35 years.

Last spring, it was DeCavalcante capo Anthony Rotondo who saw a similarity between a character in *The Sopranos* and Corky, a 71-year-old mobster whose given name is Gaetano Vastola.

Vastola was a longtime mover and shaker in the record business, promoting concerts for Ray Charles and Aretha Franklin. He played golf with Sammy Davis Jr., was a part owner of Roulette Records, and was the listed songwriter of many top 1950s and 1960s tunes—including the doo-wop classic by the Valentines, "Lily Maebelle," the Cleftones' "You Baby You," and the Wrens' "Hey Girl."

Ten years ago, John Gotti, who had done time with Vastola in the 1970s, was convinced that Vastola would "be a rat someday" and was taped plotting his death in a bugged apartment above his Little Italy social club. Gotti was convicted of conspiring to kill Vastola in 1992.

A quarter century earlier, DeCavalcante and top aide Robert "Bobby Basile" Occhipinti voiced suspicions about Vastola's abilities to avoid serious arrests while making loads of money.

"He made half a million dollars," said Occhipinti. "All of a sudden it died. He paid a $215 fine and walked away. How do you do things like this?"

Good fortune—and a smart decision to stay home—helped Vastola avoid Gotti's wrath and efforts to kill him in early 1990 by the Gambino family's No. 1 hit man, Salvatore "Sammy Bull" Gravano.

Soon after, however, Vastola's luck with the feds ran out. He was convicted of extortion and racketeering conspiracies in 1988, but after spending some time in jail, was freed pending an appeal. In late 1990, he lost the appeal, and was sent back to prison. He was released in May 1998.

JANUARY 13, 2000

Bosko's Back

Bosko Radonjich wasn't too concerned that he had to stop over in Miami International Airport on New Year's Day for a connecting flight to the Bahamas. In fact, the Serbian freedom fighter, former CIA operative, and former head of the Westies wanted for allegedly fixing the jury in John Gotti's first federal racketeering case, was apparently so oblivious to his surroundings he left the safety of a waiting area reserved for in-transit international passengers and had to pass through a U.S. Customs checkpoint.

This misstep caused a giant 180-degree detour in Radonjich's itinerary. Instead of warm beaches and tropical breezes, Radonjich can now look forward to wintering in New York. An alert and persistent Customs inspector located a 1992 arrest warrant, and Radonjich spent the first night of the new year in federal custody, ending eight eventful years on the lam.

Gotti's sensational acquittal in the 1987 racketeering and murder case turned the Dapper Don into the Teflon Don. Former U.S. Attorney Andrew Maloney, whose office lost the tainted Gotti trial but convicted him in a second go-round five years later, was ecstatic about the

arrest, and is looking forward to Radonjich spending a few years in prison. He faces five years if convicted.

"As imperfect as it is, we consider the jury system sacred and when someone tampers with it, he deserves the maximum possible penalty under the law," said Maloney. "The irony is that if John hadn't put the fix in, he probably would have gotten 15 years and be out by now instead of serving life without parole."

Radonjich, 56 and a squat bear of a man, appeared twice before Miami U.S. Magistrate Judge Robert Dube and is currently in federal custody en route to Brooklyn. He will have a detention hearing when he arrives. No one seems to know exactly where he is, or when he will arrive. "Gang Land" was unable to contact Radonjich's lawyer about the case last night.

William Shockley, a federal prosecutor in Miami, and Bridget Rohde and Paul Schoeman, assistant U.S. attorneys in Brooklyn, where Radonjich will face trial for jury tampering, refused to discuss the circumstances of the arrest or say much about the case.

"Gang Land" has learned, however, that Radonjich was traveling with a companion who was having trouble clearing Customs because his name appeared on a list of suspected troublemakers. Radonjich, who was traveling under his own name with a valid passport, had already passed through the check stop. But his companion's difficulties did in Radonjich.

The Customs inspector called Radonjich back, eventually dug up a 1992 arrest warrant for jury tampering, and Radonjich was arrested about 10:30 P.M., sources said. Ironically, his companion cleared Customs.

"Bosko did not expect to go through Customs; he did not expect to be stopped in the U.S.," said one source.

During the 1990s, Radonjich was a close adviser to Radovan Karadzic, the fugitive Bosnian Serb leader charged with genocide, whom Radonjich described in a 1997 *Esquire* article as "my angel, my saint."

His recorded odyssey in the United States began in 1970, when he emigrated from the former Yugoslavia and moved to the West Side of Manhattan, where he worked as a parking lot attendant and became an explosives expert for the Serbian underground.

> When Gotti went to trial in 1986, Radonjich told Gotti's underboss Salvatore "Sammy Bull" Gravano that he had a strong-willed "very very good friend" who was on the jury and could fix the case.

In 1975, Radonjich took part in a bombing at the Yugoslav mission to the United Nations in which no one was hurt. In 1978, he pleaded guilty to conspiracy charges in the 1975 bombing of a Yugoslavian consul's home in Chicago and for plotting to bomb a Yugoslav social club in the Windy City.

After getting out of federal prison in 1982, Radonjich moved back to New York and ran with the Westies, eventually becoming the leader of the primarily Irish-American gang of thugs who worked for the Gambino family, first under Paul Castellano and later for Gotti.

"If you're a freedom fighter, you have to love the Irish," Radonjich told *Esquire*.

When Gotti went to trial in 1986, Radonjich told Gotti's underboss Salvatore "Sammy Bull" Gravano that he had a strong-willed "very very good friend" who was on the jury and could fix the case, according to court testimony.

Gravano testified he gave Radonjich $60,000 in three installments, which he funneled to George Pape, who had been an usher at Radonjich's wedding and was a juror at Gotti's trial.

There was no question Radonjich gave the money to Pape, said Gravano, explaining that if he had lied about having a friend on the jury or giving him the cash, "we would have killed him."

In the *Esquire* article, Radonjich basically admitted that he and his friend Pape, who was convicted and sentenced to three years, had conspired to fix Gotti's trial. "There were people in high places who knew that he was my best friend," said Radonjich. In the same article, Radonjich professed his love for America,

said he had worked for the CIA, and said that he hoped to someday return.

Radonjich is probably not overjoyed about the circumstances of his return, but the FBI, which obtained an arrest warrant for him eight years ago, will take him any way they can.

"We're gratified that this person who has been a fugitive for so many years has been apprehended," said New York FBI spokesman Jim Margolin.

Junkyard Dog

One thing about John Gotti, he knows about doing stupid things and getting caught. He basically predicted the fate that befell his mobster son-in-law Carmine Agnello this week.

"He's gonna get indicted any day, this moron. He's built himself a gallows. He's bought the noose," Gotti said two years ago during a jailhouse visit with his daughter (and Carmine's wife) Victoria and his brother Pete.

At the time, the Dapper Don was lamenting the racketeering indictment of his son Junior, which he also characterized as stemming from stupidity. Several times he warned Victoria, a best-selling author, that her hot-tempered hubby, who's had several dustups with cops and traffic enforcement agents, would be the next Gotti family member to get in serious trouble.

"Look. You want a prediction? By June, her husband's gonna be indicted," said Gotti as he pointed to Victoria. "And every two, three cents he's got, gonna be all tied up."

> "He's gonna get indicted any day, this moron. He's built himself a gallows. He's bought the noose," Gotti said.

Gotti's timing was just a little off, but he accurately predicted that when Carmine was nailed authorities would try to seize assets from his $30-million-a-year string of scrap metal businesses. Probably no one, however, could have predicted he would be busted for allegedly trying to strong-arm undercover cops running a sting operation designed to nab car thieves and insurance scam artists.

This week, Agnello was hit with state racketeering, extortion, and numerous other charges related to threatening and attempting to terrorize the cops. If convicted, he faces up to 25 years. Meanwhile, prosecutors froze millions of dollars of his assets.

Last April, cops opened up Stadium Scrap, a scrap metal business in the Shea Stadium area of Queens that is home to 150 salvage yards, auto body shops, auto glass shops, and scrap metal processors. The cops were crushing cars and reselling them to a nearby scrap metal processor for $2.65 a pound. "The officers set up an office in a trailer on the premises in which they installed various audio and video recording devices, including two video cameras inside the trailer and one outside the trailer overlooking the salvage yard," said Queens District Attorney Richard Brown.

Within a month after they opened up shop, on May 20, Carmine strolled brazenly right onto the set.

"We were in direct competition with them and we were giving better prices than they were, and they were losing accounts," said Detective James Halley, one of four cops who ran Stadium Scrap. "He came to us and said, 'Unless you're willing to do business, we're going to bump heads.'"

The cops were probably silently snickering; they certainly hadn't expected such a big fish to get caught in their net so quickly. Naturally, they refused to knuckle under, and sat back and let the cameras do their thing. Agnello and three confederates were taped firebombing Stadium Scrap's trailer office and a flatbed three times in the next month, prosecutors said.

When Gerard Brave and Peri Kadanoff, two assistant Queens district attorneys determined they had enough evidence to nail Agnello and his buddies, the cops pretended they had gotten the message and agreed to do business with Agnello, selling their scrap metal to his New York Shredding Corporation for $2.10 a pound. Then they followed their initial game plan, nailing 48 others for various auto-related crimes, including insurance fraud and possession of stolen cars, parts, and vehicle identification numbers.

Agnello's media-savvy lawyer, Marvyn Kornberg, says his client, who was held on $10 million bail, was targeted by authorities because he was married to Gotti's daughter, but would be exonerated of all charges.

During Gotti's jailhouse visit, which was videotaped by prison officials, Gotti acknowledged that Carmine was a prime target because of his marriage to his daughter, but switched gears and started berating Agnello for his intelligence and his propensity for getting arrested over the years. Gotti said his son-in-law couldn't even visit him at the federal penitentiary in Marion, Illinois, because of his arrest record.

"He's an imbecile. And you gotta see the charges," said Gotti, pretending to read from Agnello's rap sheet. "Malicious mopery. Possession of brains with intent to use. Malicious mopery. Malicious mopery. Stolen bumper. Hubcab."

At another point, he asked Victoria: "So what's the story with Carmine?"

"What do you mean, what's the story with him?" she asked.

"Is he feeling good? Is he not feeling good? Is his medication increased? Decreased? Is it up? Down? Does he get in the backseat of the car and think someone has stolen the steering wheel?"

Family Scandals

Mobsters in the New York area have been taking a beating for several years. Now, it's their relatives' turn.

Gambino soldier Vincent Corrao, who served as acting capo while his dad, Joseph "Joe Butch" Corrao, served time for racketeering, was nabbed for possessing a small quantity of ecstasy (ketamine) in the parking lot of a Staten Island nightclub last Saturday morning.

Two days earlier, Jennifer Graziano, a daughter of Bonanno capo Anthony "T. G." Graziano, was hit with federal drug charges for being a member of a marijuana distribution ring allegedly run by her sister Rene's husband.

The younger Corrao, 34, of Monsey, was spotted handing something to Gambino associate Shelton Willis by narcotics cops and arrested on misdemeanor drug charges when cops found a small quantity of drugs on Willis, said Chief Assistant District Attorney David Lehr.

After spending a night in jail, Corrao and Willis, 28, of Staten Island, pleaded innocent and were released on their own recognizance.

Graziano, 28, and her brother-in-law, Hector Pagan, 34, husband of Rene Graziano, were overheard discussing pickups, work schedules, and paydays of runners who delivered pot to customers around the city, according to an arrest complaint by DEA agent Michael Cline.

Graziano isn't the first female member of the family to run afoul of the law. Her sister Lana was charged with mail fraud in 1989. Those charges, and similar ones prepared against their mother and Lana's mother-in-law, were dropped when the men of the family pleaded guilty to tax charges in a plea bargain that spared the women.

Jennifer Graziano, a graduate student at New York University, is one of two college students among eight defendants in the case. A third was studying to be a court reporter. All were released on bail.

Cheap Talk

Vincent "Vinny Ocean" Palermo, head of New Jersey's DeCavalcante crime family, was furious. He was livid. He was downright pissed off, so angry at wannabe mobster Joseph Massella, that in a frenzy, he grabbed his brand-new, lightweight but powerful digital cell phone and called Massella's brother-in-law, Joseph Abruzzo.

"I told him just don't f------ call me no more," said Palermo, then proceeding to describe Massella as everything from a degenerate gambler to a "f------ a--hole" to a stupid, sick, retarded lowlife. Palermo erupted July 1, 1998, the day after Massella told an informer that Palermo had threatened to kill him, and three months before Massella allegedly carried out the threat.

Massella and Palermo were partners in a couple of extortion scams. But Massella owed his boss lots of money, was losing it faster than he could make it gambling, and, worse, blowing the rest on younger women while depriving his wife and kids, Palermo complained.

"It's the same f------ story all the time," said Palermo. "He's with a young broad, he's feeding her all kinds of money and jewelry and champagne, and everything, uh, that's why she's with him. Figures, look, what a score."

Palermo said when Massella broke up with his *comare*, Palermo took a bag of jewelry from Massella, who'd promised it to her: "I told (him), 'You c---sucker. Why didn't you buy this for your daughter and your wife?'"

Palermo used the phone from June until November 1998, making tons of phone calls. After all, his good buddy Ralph had told him it was all free—from the cell phone itself to all the usual charges, including taxes. Ralph, as "Gang Land" readers learned a few weeks ago, was working undercover for the FBI for two years. And the phone that Palermo received, like others that Ralph provided, were really courtesy of the FBI.

"There are numerous taped conversations where Mr. Palermo is on this cellular telephone setting up meetings with (other gangsters,)" Assistant U.S. Attorney Maria Barton said during Palermo's detention hearing in December.

That's when Palermo learned that he'd been running his big mouth for law enforcement officials on a government-supplied telephone. This atrocious misplay most likely stemmed from "Gang Land's" eternal bane: Greed—the downfall of many a wiseguy.

"Sometimes wiseguys can be just as cheap as anybody else, so if they get a free phone, they use them," Barton said.

"Essentially," Barton explained to Manhattan Federal Magistrate Judge Frank Maas, "what the cooperator did was, he purported to have contacts where he could get free phone service and he volunteered the phones."

"Probably the last time that will work," deadpanned Maas.

Don't bet on it. In 1994, the FBI pulled the same scam and nabbed Salvatore "Sal the Geep" Candela and 37 other mob associates on a slew of drug and gun charges.

Strange Doings

A year after Palermo stopped using his free FBI phone, he "learned that someone was wearing a wire and recording (his and others') conversations," according to Assistant U.S. Attorney John Hillebrecht.

Palermo began to make himself scarce. For the first time in two years, Palermo failed to sleep at home (except, of course, when he was in Florida on business). He

> "Sometimes wiseguys can be just as cheap as anybody else, so if they get a free phone, they use them," Barton said.

was arrested on his way out of a friend's house along with phone pal/soldier/co-defendant James Gallo, carrying a bag filled with clothes.

In his other hand, Palermo had a briefcase filled with a "variety of papers and a body wire with a number of miniature cassette tapes," said Hillebrecht.

"Certainly an odd thing … for somebody in the seafood business to be carrying, but I assume you'll address that when we get to you," Judge Maas told Palermo's lawyer, Gregory O'Connell.

O'Connell ducked the question. Prosecutor Barton speculated that the "circumstantial evidence shows that if he knew there was somebody who was wearing a wire that he, in fact, wanted to get his own evidence in order to have what other associates and members were doing."

Perhaps.

Or maybe Palermo wanted to gather evidence to corroborate the FBI's tapes.

Or perhaps he wanted to obtain backup tapes in case there was a snafu with the FBI's equipment.

Or he had forgotten what a wire looked like.

Or he thought it was a jump rope.

Or ….

Getting In the Last Licks

With mobsters and wannabe gangsters dropping like flies lately, their sentencings, the last stage in the judicial process, have become pretty routine and anticlimactic, especially when they stem from a plea bargain deal between the defendant and the prosecution.

The recent sentencing of Vincent Rizzuto Jr. for killing Joseph Schiro Scarpa, son of Colombo capo and top echelon FBI informer Gregory Scarpa, in a drug dispute, however, was anything but routine. The proceeding turned into one of the more compelling and dramatic court proceedings in recent memory, even though the 24-year prison term Rizzuto received was a foregone conclusion.

Rizzuto, 27, killed the younger Scarpa in 1995, nine months after his father died of AIDS contracted through a tainted blood transfusion from a member of his crew during surgery in 1986.

After three years on the lam, Rizzuto gave up and pleaded guilty, even though the feds reneged on an initial promise of 18 years.

The atmosphere in the courtroom of Brooklyn Federal Judge Edward Korman got thick and tensions became high almost immediately. Sitting directly opposite Rizzuto's family were Scarpa's mother, sister, widow, and eight-year-old daughter, who had asked to address the judge.

They wanted to condemn Rizzuto and express their pain and loss. Over objections by Rizzuto's attorney, Gregory O'Connell, Korman said he would allow all four of them to speak.

Scarpa's mother, Linda Schiro was up first. "My son Joey stands beside me today as he always does," she said as tears streamed down her cheeks. "You can't see him now, Vinny, but you saw him the night he was killed and sitting alone in a car to die by himself."

Rizzuto glowered at her, his relatives muttered derogatory remarks about Schiro, and his angry mother said: "She's such an actress. She should get an Academy Award. Look at those tears."

Schiro continued undeterred. "Because of you, Vinny, his life is over. When Joey was killed, so was my body and mind. My family's lives have changed so dramatically, and we ask you why. (You) took away a father, a brother, a husband, and my son. He was ripped from my life and left to die and I was given no chance to say goodbye."

James DiPietro, who represented Rizzuto's brother in the same case, shushed Rizzuto family members several times as they became increasingly vocal and agitated. "It doesn't help," he said.

Scarpa's widow, Maria, was next and tearfully described how her husband had spent all his free time with their daughter, "loving her, playing, teaching her to talk and walk."

She then recounted his last day with her and their daughter, nervously dabbing her eyes with a wad of tissues, while holding up a poster-size photograph of her late husband with an image of their daughter superimposed over him: "The day before he was murdered, it was St. Joseph's Day and we all spent the day (March 19) together. That would be the last time our daughter would ever sleep in her father's arms."

The next morning, she said, after breakfast, Linda Marie cried, "Daddy, don't leave; daddy, don't go."

Scarpa kissed Linda Marie goodbye, told her he would bring her a doll when he came home, and drove off.

"Those were the last kisses, hugs, promises, and smiles she saw. My daughter is always crying and asking why that bad man killed her daddy. 'Why did he take my daddy? Everybody at school has their daddy, but I don't.' I am here to beg for the maximum sentencing of Vincent Rizzuto for taking my husband and a father who can never be replaced to his little girl."

Scarpa's sister, also named Linda Marie, addressed the court next. Rizzuto, his mother, sister, and other family members were visibly fuming.

Maria Scarpa then got up and insisted that her daughter, who all the while had been clutching a pink diary, wanted to address the court.

"Tell him. Tell him how you feel," she told her daughter. "Tell him what you wanted to tell him. You'll never have this chance again. Tell him. He's a good man. What he does is put bad people in jail. Go ahead. My daddy …" The child, who looked terrified, froze and refused to say a word.

Korman, a father of two who questioned the young girl's presence in the courtroom several times, finally ended her ordeal and the awkward situation by asking if she wanted him to read her diary. He came off the bench and took it from her outstretched hand. He read several passages and passed it back to her.

"Did you want to speak, Mr. Rizzuto?" Korman asked.

"May I address the court without a child in the courtroom? Is that possible?" asked Rizzuto, shifting anxiously on his feet. Korman said he couldn't exclude the girl. Rizzuto explained he didn't want to speak badly about Scarpa in front of his daughter.

On cue, Scarpa's family exploded.

"Did you care about the child when you killed her daddy?" yelled Maria.

"Did you care about your victims' families?" shouted Rizzuto, as his attorney and the courtroom deputy tried to quiet and calm him.

"Why is she saying something to me?" he said, motioning to Linda Schiro. "Her husband killed like thousands of people. Her son killed four people .... The man killed people for $10 bags (of drugs) on the street. Killed someone in the front of a school with a shotgun ..."

Rizzuto stopped his tirade to allow Linda Marie to be led from the courtroom, then picked up without missing a beat.

He ripped the prosecutors for reneging on a promise of an 18-year sentence. He said they coerced him into pleading guilty and taking 24 years by threatening to prosecute his father. He said the government ignored several murders by the Scarpas because the father was a top echelon informer.

"The government gave Joey, the Scarpas, a pass to commit several crimes against innocent people," he said.

Rizzuto may have exaggerated the notches on Greg Scarpa's gun, but he was a stone cold killer through four decades and two mob wars. And there's little doubt that his informant work helped him and son Joseph get away with loads of crimes.

> **The man killed people for $10 bags (of drugs) on the street. Killed someone in the front of a school with a shotgun ..."**

But Rizzuto did kill Scarpa, a former partner in crime. And both Scarpas are dead, and Rizzuto's still alive, as Korman noted as the proceeding came to a close and as Rizzuto's belligerence degenerated into self-pity.

"You think I want to take 24 years," said Rizzuto. "I'm never going to see my parents again. My kids are going to be my age when I get out. What kind of life is that? I wish I would have died. That's it. I wish it would have been me."

In gangland, wiseguys tell lots of lies and say lots of things they don't mean. But since he's still alive, Vincent Rizzuto gets the last word—in this column, anyway.

A Routine Sentencing

Colombo boss Alphonse Persico will be cooling his heels for at least another year as the feds work to revive loan-sharking charges and make a murder case against him in the slaying of family underboss William "Wild Bill" Cutolo.

Persico, 46, was sentenced to 18 months in prison last week for possessing a loaded .380 automatic and a 12-gauge shotgun on his 50-foot speed boat along the Florida Keys in September 1998. The sentence was a plea bargain worked out by Persico and federal prosecutors in Florida.

While the sentence was routine, Persico's situation is pretty complicated. Suffice to say the feds in Brooklyn and Florida are investigating allegations of murder, racketeering, and more against Persico.

The Neck Plans Ahead

Never let it be said that George "Georgie Neck" Zappola isn't up on the latest in medical technology. Or that he doesn't believe in planning for the future. Or know how to get things done while in jail.

Three-and-a-half years ago, the Luchese capo was in a federal lockup in Brooklyn looking at a very long stretch behind bars. Zappola, 40, pleaded guilty to racketeering and murder. He got 22 years, and is due out in 2014. He decided it might be nice to have a fully grown son waiting for him when he got out of prison.

Federal prisons don't allow conjugal visits, so the only way Zappola could father a son while jailed at the Metropolitan Detention Center (MDC) in Brooklyn was to smuggle his sperm out and get it to a fertility clinic.

With help from a mob associate, a Brooklyn clothier, a corrupt prison guard, and the child's intended mother, Zappola accomplished this feat but he couldn't achieve his ultimate goal, according to court records and federal sources.

Zappola and a Bensonhurst, Brooklyn, woman (we'll call her Connie) concocted the plan in the fall of 1996, according to Special Agent Stephen Grogan of the Justice Department's Office of Inspector General.

Connie, a daughter of a Colombo mobster who was killed two decades ago, "agreed to be artificially inseminated with (Zappola's) sperm," Grogan said in an arrest complaint against the clothier in the alleged scheme.

At Zappola's direction, Connie delivered $500 and two empty plastic medical vials she had gotten from a fertility clinic to David Hage, who owns a men's store called Gentlemen's Quarters, Grogan wrote.

Connie instructed Hage to give the vials and $500 worth of clothing to Derryl Strong, an MDC correction officer allegedly on the payroll of jailed

> Federal prisons don't allow conjugal visits, so the only way Zappola could father a son while jailed at the Metropolitan Detention Center (MDC) in Brooklyn was to smuggle his sperm out and get it to a fertility clinic.

mobsters, who managed to enjoy wine and assorted Italian culinary goodies instead of the institutional food served to other inmates, said Grogan.

Anthony Albanese, 32, a Luchese associate, was an alleged player in the sperm caper. He pleaded guilty to bribery charges, harboring Zappola while he was a fugitive from 1990 to 1995, and was sentenced to 20 months.

In October 1996, Strong picked up the vials and brought them to Zappola, earning a blue and white New York Yankee bomber jacket, a green and white "8 Ball" jacket, and expensive alligator shoes for his efforts, said Grogan.

On October 23, Zappola gave two sperm-filled vials to Strong, who smuggled them out of the prison and gave them to a friend of Connie's a block away from the MDC. ("Isn't it great, the more obvious, the less suspicious," Strong said during another corrupt deal, according to court papers.) Connie's friend delivered the sperm to a Manhattan fertility clinic which froze and stored the sperm for future insemination, the complaint said.

After the sperm was safely tucked away at the fertility center, Connie gave Hage another $500 for Strong, said Grogan.

Strong used the credit to purchase a $127.50 blazer, a $247.50 pair of shoes, and a mock-turtleneck sweater for $47.50. Including tax, the bill came to $457.48, according to the complaint. Sources said Strong took the balance of the $500 in cash.

Strong, 42, was 1 of 11 correction officers arrested on bribery charges in May 1997 in an investigation—dubbed Badfellas—into rampant corruption at the MDC, but was not charged in the sperm caper. And the bribery charges were dropped after the feds learned their jailhouse informer had been dealing drugs while working undercover against Strong, who was fired last fall.

In the meantime, Connie changed her mind about artificial insemination and cooperated in the federal investigation for a time. Ultimately, however, she changed her mind about that, too, and the charges against Hage, the only one arrested in the case, were dismissed. "My client never did anything wrong," said his lawyer, Joseph Mure Jr. "They never had a case against him."

The Bull's Loss Is Bosko's Gain

The federal government last week officially gave up all hope of convicting former Westies boss Bosko Radonjich for fixing the jury that acquitted Gambino boss John Gotti of racketeering and murder charges in 1987.

Prosecutors said Radonjich tampered with the jury that began the Dapper Don's five-year reign as the Teflon Don, but that the recent arrest of turncoat underboss Salvatore "Sammy Bull" Gravano had eliminated him as a viable witness against Radonjich.

In a 1992 tampering trial of juror George Pape, a long-time friend of Radonjich, Gravano testified that he gave $60,000 to Radonjich that the Westies boss funneled to a juror who promised to vote for acquittal and try to convince his fellow jurors to do the same.

Pape was convicted and sentenced to three years, but Radonjich, a Yugoslav immigrant, fled to his homeland and became a freedom fighter for the Serbs. He was arrested New Year's Day at Miami International Airport at a Customs check.

Radonjich is still in custody, accused of giving a false address to Customs inspectors, a minor charge that his lawyer, Lawrence Hochheiser, predicts will soon go the same way as the jury tampering indictment.

Win Some, Lose Some

Anthony "Torty" Tortorello died several weeks ago in a federal penitentiary in Lexington, Kentucky, soon after celebrating his 64th birthday.

Biting the dust in the joint, far from home and family, is not "Gang Land's" idea of a good way to go—if there is such a thing. But in his long life of crime, the Luchese mobster beat a few death sentences before pancreatic cancer caught up with him.

Fourteen years ago, in another federal prison, the one in Danbury, Connecticut, Torty was nearing the end of a six-year stretch for transporting loads of stolen cars and other goods across state lines. During a recreation break, Torty got involved in a philosophical discussion about wiseguys dealing in drugs, an activity the mob had supposedly banned decades ago.

"During the conversation, Tortorello mentioned Gigante's name and questioned why Chin would be so upset with guys dealing drugs when Chin himself dealt in drugs," according to an FBI report about the talk.

Torty's remarks were overheard by a Genovese capo doing time in the same joint who dutifully relayed them to consigliere Louis "Bobby" Manna. Needless to say, they didn't sit too well with Gigante, whose paranoid-schizophrenic act was revved up. Members of his family were forbidden to mention his name, and had to refer to him as "Aunt Julia" or by stroking their chins in the classical thinker's pose.

When Tortorello was released in late 1987, Manna told Luchese underboss Anthony "Gaspipe" Casso that "Chin was very upset with Tortorello and wanted him killed," said the report—largely based on an FBI debriefing of Casso. The Genoveses wanted permission to kill him, Manna said. (This occurred at a time when relations between the two families, usually good, were at an all-time high, following their successful assassination of Gambino underboss Frank DeCicco in retaliation for John Gotti & Co.'s unauthorized execution of the Gambino family's previous boss, Paul Castellano.)

At a follow-up high-level sit-down, Manna laid out his case to whack Tortorello to Luchese boss Vittorio "Vic" Amuso, while off to the side, Genovese underboss Venero "Benny Eggs" Mangano was telling Casso that a good old-fashioned beating might suffice. Gigante thought about it and agreed.

Relations between the families were good, but the Lucheses weren't about to let the Genoveses kill one of their own for telling the truth, even if he had been talking out of school.

A week later, over drinks, Amuso, Casso, and Tortorello all agreed "to stage a phony beating … to appease Chin," the report said. "A short time later, Tortorello was observed walking around with a cast on his arm and telling a story of how four guys had beaten him up and broken his arm."

When he "recovered," Torty went about the gangster business, functioning at times as an acting capo, sponsoring his son Joseph into the crime family in November 1991, and managing to dodge another execution.

He headed a mob crew that pretty much did it all. They trafficked in ecstasy, crack, marijuana, morphine, cocaine, Quaaludes, and Valium, and robbed various businesses and private homes around the city, specializing in ripping off drug dealers.

On December 20, 1996, his crew invaded the Upper West Side home of a

At a follow-up high-level sit-down, Manna laid out his case to whack Tortorello to Luchese boss Vittorio "Vic" Amuso, while off to the side, Genovese underboss Venero "Benny Eggs" Mangano was telling Casso that a good old-fashioned beating might suffice.

dress designer who once worked for Jacqueline Kennedy Onassis and killed him during a robbery. The following February, Torty was arrested on federal murder charges and notified that prosecutors were seeking the death penalty.

By July 1997, however, the case began unraveling, with city police and FBI agents accusing each other of botching the investigation, and Tortorello's lawyer, Mathew Mari, was able to negotiate a plea bargain calling for 10 years in prison.

After Torty pleaded guilty, Mari asked that his client be released pending sentencing. Torty wanted to say goodbye to his mother, who was in her 80s, ailing, and would surely be dead when he was released. In addition, he and his son each had pressing medical problems, Mari told Judge Thomas Griesa. Mari argued that Tortorello's situation had changed drastically—for the better—now that he had pleaded guilty. He no longer faced execution, only 10 years, so there was no reason for him to flee. He would return for sentencing.

Surprised prosecutors strongly objected, and quickly appealed when Griesa granted Tortorello a two-month reprieve to settle his affairs and say good-bye to his mother.

"It's the only case I ever won in the U.S. Court of Appeals," Mari said yesterday, adding that when Tortorello had first asked him to request bail, Mari had told him it was a waste of time, that "no judge is ever going to release you."

He Should Have Smoked It All

Luchese capo Eugene "Boopsie" Castelle was arrested on racketeering charges involving arson, extortion, and drug dealing last week. It was pretty routine until cops and federal agents learned what Castelle was carrying: a smelly half-smoked joint.

That's when they realized why Boopsie's eyes were a little bloodshot and why he looked a little weird when they walked into a Bensonhurst, Brooklyn, luncheonette to arrest him and soldier Scott Gervasi.

"I can't say he was high, but he certainly had a buzz on," said one law enforcement source in the joint state and federal caper, in which a total of two capos, two soldiers, and three associates were charged.

"You'd think wiseguys who smoke pot would smoke 'em like the rest of us smoke cigarettes and throw out the roaches," said one incredulous longtime observer of the gangland scene.

"It wasn't a roach; it was half a joint," said one investigator. "Guess he wanted it for the long ride home (to South River, New Jersey.)"

Capo Joseph "Joey Flowers" Tangorra, 51, co-leader of the family's Bensonhurst crew with Castelle, 40, was also arrested in the case, his third in seven months.

A team of FBI agents, DEA agents, and cops led by detectives John Fisher and Thomas Farley of the Brooklyn District Attorney's office also nabbed soldier Joseph "JoJo" Truncale, 69, and associate Lester Ellis, 50, on racketeering charges. Two others are in custody on other charges.

Assistant U.S. Attorney William Gurin and Assistant Brooklyn District Attorney Patricia McNeill moved to detain the five arrested defendants without bail as dangers to the community.

After a hearing, Gervasi, 36, was released on $700,000 bail under strict house arrest conditions. Tangorra's hearing began yesterday and resumes today. The others will follow.

MARCH 22, 2001

Wiseguy Talk Ain't What It Seems

Wiseguys have a weird way of saying what they really don't mean, especially when they're talking to cops.

Take these utterances that Bonanno consigliere Anthony Spero made to federal mob investigator Kenneth McCabe on September 27, 1991, an otherwise typical Friday afternoon in Bath Beach, Brooklyn. McCabe, a former NYPD detective who began stalking wiseguys in 1969, testified about the conversation at Spero's ongoing racketeering and murder trial in Brooklyn.

Spero was standing in front of his social club on Bath Avenue when he spotted McCabe sitting in his car, taking notes. McCabe was making his rounds, recording the goings on at the club. He had noted Spero's presence and the time (4:15 P.M.) and was about to drive to another social club, and then another. It was all in a day's work of taking the pulse of New York's five crime families.

Before McCabe could leave, Spero came up to his car with a gleam in his eye.

"Did you see Capeci's 'Gang Land' column about Frank Lastorino? The one with his picture," said Spero, referring to my weekly *New York Daily News* column published three days earlier.

Lastorino, a Luchese capo who had won a dismissal of weapons charges—he has since pleaded guilty and is jailed for racketeering—was indeed the main focus of the column. And there was a picture of a wiseguy who was identified as Frank Lastorino.

But the picture wasn't of Lastorino. It was Spero. He was mentioned in the column as the main suspect behind the murder of Vincent Bickelman, who had stolen jewelry in a burglary of the home of Spero's daughter, Jill. Bickelman was shot to death a couple of weeks later. His murder is among three slayings that Spero, 72, is charged with in the case.

Spero was poking fun at the *Daily News* for using his photo and identifying it as Lastorino, but what he was really trying to do was goad McCabe into saying something he shouldn't about the investigation into Bickelman's murder.

McCabe played along. "They used your picture because you're better looking than Lastorino," he said.

"I'm getting old," Spero continued. "Gonna retire and get out. You won't see me around here," said Spero.

"I hope you're moving to a warm climate," said McCabe. "I don't want to do surveillance in the cold."

As is most often the case in gangland, wiseguys just can't retire, and the law kept plugging away. Both Spero and McCabe kept at it. That's why "Gang Land" never runs out of stories. McCabe recorded Spero's comings and goings in Bath Beach, on and off, for seven more years.

Little Robert Talks to the Wrong Guy

Some wiseguys just don't know how to enjoy a good thing.

After a federal court session in Manhattan last week, Bonanno capo Robert "Little Robert" Lino was all smiles as he and his wife left the courthouse.

After a passionate argument by his lawyer, and over objections from the feds, Judge William Pauley had relaxed his bail restrictions. It was not a small thing, considering that Lino, the main target in a 120-defendant "Mob on Wall Street"

> "I hope you're moving to a warm climate," said McCabe. "I don't want to do surveillance in the cold."

case, had pleaded guilty to stock fraud, and sentencing guidelines call for upward of six years in prison.

Lino, 34, and his wife headed to Little Italy for lunch before driving home to Brooklyn. After lunch, Lino had a sidewalk meeting on Mulberry Street with Bonanno capo Richard "Shellackhead" Cantarella while his wife waited in their car.

Cantarella, 57, a former *New York Post* truck driver who pleaded guilty to state labor racketeering charges in the early 1990s, is currently the acting consigliere for the Bonanno crime family, while Anthony Spero is indisposed, according to the FBI.

FBI agents developed photographs of the session, which they claim was a middle-management strategy meeting, and passed them on to prosecutors David Esseks and Karen Konigsberg. They, in turn, asked Pauley to reverse himself, revoke Lino's bail, and send him to jail immediately—even before he is sentenced.

"The FBI believes that the purpose of this meeting was likely for Mr. Lino to discuss with Mr. Cantarella the supervision of Mr. Lino's crew ... while Lino is in prison," the prosecutors said in a letter to the judge.

Pauley restored Lino's strict house arrest conditions immediately and set a hearing for today to determine whether to revoke his bail.

"It was a chance meeting," Lino's lawyer Joseph Benfante told "Gang Land." "It was under two minutes in duration and his bail conditions do not prohibit him from meeting alleged organized crime members, only people connected with the stock market."

Garbage King 'Fesses Up—He Never Really Quit the Mob

Luchese capo Salvatore Avellino, who swore last fall that he retired from the mob after he went to jail for racketeering in 1993, pleaded guilty this week to using threats of violence to run his Long Island garbage business from federal prison.

The about-face came as part of a deal in which Avellino, 65, and son Michael, 36, will serve five years in prison, forfeit $6.5 million, and pay $1 million in back taxes.

The Avellinos, who had been charged with waging a 15-year reign of terror against competitors, told Long Island Judge Denis Hurley they mapped out their plans of arson and other violent acts in jailhouse meetings from 1993 to 1997.

Salvatore Avellino will begin his new sentence after he completes a 10½-year term for a 1993 racketeering conviction that also involved the Long Island garbage industry, according to an agreement worked out by defense lawyers and

prosecutors Paul Weinstein, Cynthia Monaco, and Stephen King.

Son-in-law Michael Malena, who began serving his sentence early when he was busted for drunken driving, pleaded guilty to racketeering and faces four years in prison. Five others also pleaded guilty to various extortion and arson charges and expect sentences from six months to seven years.

Frank Gotti Remembered Again

As she has every year since 1980 when her son Frank was killed in a tragic car accident, Victoria Gotti expressed her family's grief and love for her 12-year-old son in paid notices in the *New York Daily News* last week.

"Dear Frank, You are sadly missed, deeply loved, and never forgotten for even one moment," said one that was signed, "MOM AND DAD."

The "In Memoriam," along with others in the names of the four surviving Gotti children and their families, appeared on March 18, the 21st anniversary of the accident in which Frank Gotti was killed as he drove a borrowed minibike near his Howard Beach, Queens, home.

The following day, the *News* adapted our March 8 exclusive report about the murder of John Favara, the Gotti family backyard neighbor who, blinded by a late afternoon sun, did not see the youngster dart out from behind a dumpster until it was too late.

"Gang Land" reported that eight Gotti crew members, including his brother Gene, using a van and two cars, abducted Favara on July 28, 1980, stole his car, and killed him. They disposed of his body and crushed his car so no evidence would ever be found.

Soup, Chickens, Seinfeld & Longhorns

Frank Persico has a slew of relatives who are bona fide gangsters. Acting Colombo boss Alphonse "Allie" Persico, son of legendary Carmine, is his first cousin. Although he has never been "made" himself, he has been known to carry a gun and use it, if only on a computer monitor.

Persico is among a new breed of sophisticated, computer-smart wiseguys. Instead of illicit drugs, prostitutes, labor racketeering, gambling, and loan-sharking, his turf was Wall Street and his crew was a horde of corrupt stockbrokers.

A licensed stockbroker himself since 1988, Persico surrendered to authorities on Monday to begin serving a 65-month prison term for fleecing hundreds of investors out of millions of dollars in various stock scams. His restitution bill, still being computed, will total more than $5 million.

Persico, 38, pleaded guilty to charges stemming from last year's mammoth 120-defendant "Mob on Wall Street" case that charged him with defrauding investors through a litany of scams and "pump and dump" schemes, including one where his crew of brokers simply bought and sold

stocks for clients when it suited the brokers, not the investors.

He has worked at or controlled numerous brokerages that were cited in stock fraud cases by federal and state authorities in the last decade. His crews of brokers in Manhattan, Staten Island, and New Jersey imposed a six-cents-a-share surcharge on themselves for the millions of shares they traded illicitly. The "tax" was split by the Colombo and Bonanno families.

On January 13, 2000, an FBI bug caught Persico, representing the interests of the Colombo family, at a meet with Bonanno capo Robert "Little Robert" Lino and others in the 16th floor conference room at DMN Capital Investments at 5 Hanover Square in Downtown Manhattan.

At the time, Persico was juggling four scams, according to court papers. Two involved stock fraud conspiracies with top officers and shareholders of Manhattan Soup Man, which sold prepared soups to restaurants, and the Ranch1 fast-food chain that features grilled chicken sandwiches.

Company officers sought to raise money through private sales of their stock at inflated prices and were willing to pay exorbitant commissions, often as much as 50 percent, to the mobbed-up brokers. Sooner or later, but mostly sooner, the timeworn Wall Street axiom of "what goes up, must eventually come down" would kick in and the unsuspecting investors would take a bath.

The mob brokers were relentless schemers.

"Hypothetically, if I'm ABC Napkin Company and I wanted Ranch1 Chicken to use my napkins, could you make that happen?" Persico asked James Chickara, vice chairman of Ranch1.

"It's not easy, but it could be done," said Chickara.

The meeting was interrupted several times by calls to Persico's cell phone. Finally, he barked into it: "Do me a favor. Call all your brokers into your office and put the speaker on right now. Call me back on my cell phone."

"I'd like to get started," he apologized to his hosts, "but I got to take this f------ phone call. I got to blast these guys. You know what you do (while I wait) explain to me some background on the soup deal."

"This is a gourmet soup made famous by Al Yeganah, the famous soup Nazi on (the hit TV show) *Seinfeld*," said Chickara as he handed Persico a folder of news clippings about the product.

Seconds later, Persico's cell phone rang, and all ears were tuned to Persico.

"Am I on speaker?" he asked. "Alright. There's something … called the 'Know Your Client Rule.' Now I don't expect you to know everything about your client, but I do expect you to know when your client is f------ alive or dead. Now this guy Rogers died on December 1. There were 11 trades done after December 1. His executor is calling up the company asking for an explanation …."

After digesting the soup and chicken deals, Persico rushed off to meet Colombo underboss John "Jackie" DeRoss to seek permission for a scheme to divert $10 million in pension funds from Local 400 of the Industrial & Production Workers Union. The crime family installed Persico as treasurer of the local in June 1999—days after his cousin Alphonse allegedly ordered the killing of Local 400's former treasurer, then-Colombo underboss William "Wild Bill" Cutolo, according to court papers.

Permission never came, however, and Local 400's pension funds remained intact, much to the chagrin of James Labate, a close Lino associate and partner in DMN Capital, according to conversations recorded on February 25, 2000.

DeRoss declined to approve the pension fund rip-off. He and Persico were feeling "heat" from the "feds" investigating Cutolo's murder, and DeRoss decided against it, Lino told Labate.

During the conversation, Lino said the words "that guy," extended his pinky and index fingers and curled his middle and ring fingers into his palm to indicate Cutolo, said FBI agent Kevin Barrows, who identified the gesture in court papers as "the 'Hook 'Em Horns' signal commonly associated with the University of Texas (Longhorns) and thereby a reference to 'Wild Bill.'"

"I saw Frankie, he's got a lot of heat, a lot of heat. When he said he's sick, that means he's got a lot of heat," said Lino.

Labate spelled out the significance: "In other words, something happens to Frankie then I'm out my money."

Talkin' Trash 'Bout Frank Persico

During the five months his conference room was bugged, Bonanno associate Jimmy Labate left no doubt about his feelings for Colombo associate Frank Persico—when the burly stockbroker wasn't around.

> "His cousins will put him in a butcher's window—he'll be hangin' like a side of beef."

"There's many people looking at Frankie, people who pass Frankie in the street and want to beef him. That is the only f-----' tool right now, that the heat is on full board. Frankie is hot as a pistol, and now he's going to go throw himself into a union! He's out bar hopping and drinking, partying, carrying on, they're watching this kid like he's John Gotti.

He's f-----' nuts. Instead of being low-key right now, he's out there throwing his jets around. They'll deflate him in a second.

"Listen to me. You think Frankie's one thing. I know Frankie's another thing. I know when Frankie has heat and aggravation, Frankie melts. When the FBI goes knockin' on Frankie's door, they're gonna have to stick an apple in his f-----' mouth to shut him up …. I'm not sayin' he's gonna be a rat. He'll have a heart attack on the spot. I don't think he'll ever be a rat 'cause he won't live two minutes. His cousins will put him in a butcher's window—he'll be hangin' like a side of beef."

Mirror, Mirror …

Bonanno capo Robert "Little Robert" Lino Jr. is trying to figure out how to avoid associating with himself and almost everybody he knows.

This eerie situation came about because Lino, 34, the key gangster in a $50 million Wall Street stock scam, was seen last month embracing and chatting briefly with Richard "Shellackhead" Cantarella, the acting consigliere of the Bonanno family, outside Umberto's Clam House.

Lino, who had pleaded guilty to racketeering and stock fraud and was free on bail awaiting sentencing, had spotted Cantarella as he and his wife were driving through Little Italy last month.

The FBI caught the whole thing on film, and prosecutors, who have claimed since his arrest last June that Lino was a menace to society, figured they had him.

As part of his bail package, which had originally included strict house arrest,

> **Lino was seen … embracing and chatting briefly with Richard "Shellackhead" Cantarella, the acting consigliere of the Bonanno family, outside Umberto's Clam House.**

Lino was not supposed to associate with known gangsters. Prosecutors moved quickly to have his bail revoked, not realizing they had already blown it.

They hadn't placed any wiseguys, except for a few of his 120 co-defendants in the massive stock fraud case, on Lino's restricted list.

"You came within a hair's breadth of being remanded," said Manhattan Federal Judge William Pauley, who confined Lino to his home and told the feds to submit a list of persons with whom Lino could not associate.

This time around, Assistant U.S. Attorneys Patrick Smith and David Esseks covered every possible as well as impossible contingency. They filed a list with the names of every member of the Bonanno crime family, all 111 wiseguys in the FBI's database, from Frank Adamo to John "Porky" Zancocchia. The list includes Bonanno boss Joseph Massino, underboss Salvatore Vitale, and Cantarella.

Quite a few Bonannos—like consigliere Anthony Spero and Lino's cousin, Frank Lino, a capo doing time for stock fraud—couldn't associate with Lino unless they broke out of jail.

Little Robert is also prohibited from associating with six Colombo wiseguys, including acting boss Alphonse Persico and underboss John "Jackie" DeRoss, and "ALL MEMBERS AND ASSOCIATES" of the Genovese, Luchese, and Gambino families whose names are not included.

Perhaps the most interesting name on the list is Robert Lino Jr.

"Talk about overkill," said Lino's lawyer, Joseph Benfante. "I called Pat Smith and I told him I called Robert and told him to rip out all the mirrors in the house because the feds don't want him talking to (or associating with) himself," said Benfante.

An Honest Day's Work?

While Little Robert sits at home waiting to go to jail, his partner in white collar crime, mob associate James Labate, has gotten a reprieve from house arrest to do some good, old-fashioned construction work.

"That's what Jimmy did before he got sucked into the stock market by the government's informer in the case (Jeffrey Pokross)," said Labate's lawyer, Mark Wasserman.

Labate, who was Pokross's partner in a Manhattan brokerage that was knee-deep in the $50 million stock scam, pleaded guilty to racketeering and stock fraud charges similar to those that Lino admitted and, like Lino, faces about six years in prison.

Labate, 46, did not plead guilty to extortion or any acts of violence, Wasserman noted, asking Judge Pauley to relax Labate's bail conditions so he could "provide as best he could for his family" before he goes to jail in July.

Over objections from prosecutors Esseks and Smith, who have argued consistently to no avail that Labate is a danger to the community, Pauley said Labate could leave his home from 9 A.M. to 5 P.M. weekdays to work at a construction site in Manhattan.

"Don't make the same mistake that Mr. Lino did," Pauley warned, referring to Lino hugging Shellackhead in Little Italy, a show of gangly affection that almost landed him in jail to await sentencing.

Colombo soldier Anthony Stropoli made a big mistake when he visited Labate's bugged office 16 months ago and spoke to him and Lino about cash they owed him from a previous stock deal.

Stropoli, who had just been arrested on federal gambling charges, was later hit with racketeering charges. And he didn't fare too well during his sit-downs with his Bonnano rivals either—he got $40,000 of $129,000 owed to him.

But he did much better in his negotiations with the feds.

In return for guilty pleas to the gambling rap, to a New Jersey gambling charge, and the federal racketeering indictment, Stropoli, 38, is looking at about three years, according to sentencing guidelines. He's not cooperating; all the cases, even the racketeering indictment, are primarily bookmaking charges.

"The emotional and financial cost of three consecutive trials—even assuming we won—was simply not worth the gamble," said lawyer Gerald McMahon. "He and his family wanted some certainty to their future."

Operation Payback

For years, relatives of gangsters, like Victoria Gotti, have pronounced their undying affection for departed loved ones through the "In Memoriam" notices in the *New York Daily News*.

Last weekend, on the second anniversary of the death of William "Wild Bill" Cutolo, his son William Jr. declared his respect and his love for his dad—along with an unmistakable message to the Colombo family gangsters who killed him.

While praising his father as his "only true friend," young Cutolo announced his intention to obtain vengeance and called on his old man to place a hand on his shoulder from above and guide him as he works to complete his task.

"I'll be sure to say hello to your trustworthy friends!" he proclaimed in what surely is a sarcastic and gleeful reference to a courtroom meeting he hopes to have with his dad's mob superiors and underlings at their upcoming racketeering trial.

He signed it, "Your honorable and only son, Bill."

"The message was crystal clear, and the beautiful thing about it," said one law enforcement source, "is that everyone for whom it was meant, saw it or heard about it."

"I saw it. No f------ comment," said an underworld source who is usually more free, and less ornery, with his remarks.

Sources say young Cutolo's remarks in the paid newspaper notice echo tape-recorded words he uttered before meeting a Colombo wiseguy soon after he started working undercover for the feds.

"Let's call this 'Operation Payback'," said Cutolo after he turned on the FBI-supplied recording device to secretly tape one of his father's "trustworthy friends."

Although no one has been charged with Wild Bill's slaying, young Cutolo seems well on his way to achieving his goal, according to court documents and information "Gang Land" has obtained from law enforcement and underworld sources.

Acting family boss Alphonse Persico, a dozen members of Wild Bill's crew, and John "Jackie" DeRoss, the Colombo capo who took it over and assumed his post as family underboss, all await trial on racketeering charges stemming primarily from young Cutolo's undercover work.

Along with two others, Persico, 46, DeRoss, 63, and the 12 named crew members are scheduled for trial in December on charges of money laundering, extortion, mail fraud, bookmaking, drug dealing, stock fraud, loan-sharking, and ripping off union workers' benefit funds.

Persico hated the elder Cutolo ever since Wild Bill's crew took up with acting boss Victor "Little Vic" Orena and killed several Persico loyalists in a bloody 1991–1993 war for control of the family, FBI agent Margaret Carmichael said in an affidavit that quoted information from five mob informers and two civilian witnesses.

During conversations with several FBI informers, Persico said Wild Bill had been killed because he was "getting too strong" and had begun "acting like the boss," Carmichael said.

> **Persico said Wild Bill had been killed because he was "getting too strong" and had begun "acting like the boss."**

A few weeks after his father's death, young Cutolo contacted the FBI, began working undercover, and did a masterful job of pitting his father's crew and DeRoss against each other by telling his father's old henchmen that DeRoss was cheating them, and DeRoss that they were "bad-mouthing" him.

During one such discussion Cutolo had with DeRoss about a crew member, an exasperated DeRoss stammered that the associate couldn't talk about him like that: "I'm his captain, I'm his captain."

It's unclear whether the investigation into Wild Bill's disappearance—his body has never been found—will lead to murder charges, but court documents allege that Persico flew to New York from Florida and personally supervised Wild Bill's execution.

On May 24, 1999, Persico, who was officially living in the Sunshine State and free on bail on gun charges at the time, notified federal authorities that he was flying to New York the following day "to take care of some business," according to agent Carmichael's affidavit.

The next morning, using a New York-based cell phone—he had given federal authorities the number so they could contact him—Persico beeped Cutolo three times in nine minutes and put off a scheduled meeting between the men to the following day, May 26, the affidavit said.

After being told about the change in plans, Cutolo "complained openly" about it, stating "that the unexpected change would inconvenience him greatly," Carmichael said.

On May 26, as Cutolo did every Wednesday, he went to his Manhattan office at Local 400 of the Production Workers Union, where he was a business agent. After signing payroll checks, he told his secretary he would see her the next Wednesday and departed for a rendezvous with Persico in Bay Ridge, Brooklyn. He hasn't been seen since.

Before his next scheduled visit to the union offices on June 2, "an official of the union informed (an FBI confidential source) that Cutolo would not be returning and that Frank Persico, the cousin of Alphonse, would be assuming Cutolo's position in the union," Carmichael said.

Soon after, Carmichael said, Alphonse Persico told an informer the family would now "get back to normal."

Through his attorney, Persico denied any involvement in the disappearance/murder of Cutolo. "Allie traveled to New York to see me and another attorney to prepare for a suppression hearing that was scheduled for the next week," said lawyer Barry Levin. "And on the day and the time that he was supposedly meeting Cutolo in Brooklyn, he was in a federal building meeting with a pretrial services officer."

A Little Mystery

Young Cutolo's message to his father's "trustworthy friends" ran below an expression of love from Peggy Cutolo, the gangster's widow, who had purchased a similar notice last year.

This year, however, buying the "In Memoriam" notice was more difficult, since mother and son both moved out of their Staten Island home four months ago and relocated under the federal Witness Protection Program.

There are several ways the Cutolos could have placed the notices without violating strict rules that prohibit all contact with the old neighborhood. For now, though, how they did it remains a "Gang Land" mystery. It's not the kind of suspense thriller to lose any sleep over, but a mystery, nonetheless.

The *Daily News* wasn't saying, and federal prosecutors and lawyers for Persico and DeRoss did not return calls for comment yesterday.

JUNE 14, 2001

An Unspeakable Crime

In early 1992, after some high-level discussions, the DeCavalcante family sent out a hit team to whack acting boss John "Johnny Boy" D'Amato for committing an unconscionable and most dishonorable crime: Being gay.

The family had learned from his girlfriend that D'Amato was a "swinger" who was cheating on her and attending "wild parties" where he engaged in homosexual activity with other men, sources said.

Consigliere Stefano Vitabile, former acting boss Vincent "Vinny Ocean" Palermo, soldiers Anthony Capo and Anthony Rotondo, and associate Victor DiChiara took part in a plot to dispatch D'Amato and dispose of his body so it would never be found, according to court records.

D'Amato's homophobic murder has become a heated issue at the upcoming loan-sharking/money laundering trail of Joseph Watts, a Gambino gangster and longtime pal of the family's jailed-for-life boss, John Gotti.

Prosecutors don't want defense lawyers to question Capo, a key government witness, about the underlying reason for the murder for fear it may be so offensive to some jurors that they would ignore or discount Capo's testimony about Watts's loan-sharking.

Assistant U.S. Attorney Andrew Genser said the motive was irrelevant and "so potentially inflammatory to a jury that they would reject all of the government's case because of anger about that particular incident."

Andrew Weinstein, one of three lawyers representing Watts in the legal fight of his life, argued strenuously that the motive was essential to his defense, but tripped himself up by saying that "nothing was worse than murder."

If nothing is worse than murder— Capo will testify he was involved in several mob hits and many failed rubout attempts—argued Genser, then there was no reason to bring up the homosexuality issue.

> Capo will testify he was involved in several mob hits and many failed rubout attempts.

Brooklyn Federal Judge David Trager agreed with the prosecutor and ruled that defense lawyers could not bring it up during the trial.

After D'Amato's girlfriend lodged her complaints, Capo, 42, reported them to his mob superiors, who satisfied themselves they were true and "that he had to go," said one source. "The order came down. It was open and shut. If a New York crime family ever found out, they would have lost all respect."

While Genser won his main battle, he lost a skirmish with the media when he tried to retroactively seal the record of the proceeding that was attended by *Daily News* reporter Mike Claffey, who broke the story last week.

D'Amato, a cohort of Gotti's who often visited his Little Italy headquarters in the late 1980s and 1990, was overheard on an FBI bug plotting to kill a DeCavalcante soldier whom Gotti thought was a potential informer.

When FBI agents assigned to the Gambino family first spotted D'Amato at the Ravenite Social Club, they thought he was then-U.S. Sen. Alfonse D'Amato, to whom he bears a striking resemblance.

Agents quickly discovered that Gotti's visitor was John D'Amato, and that he had no familial connections to the former senator. They also learned that John D'Amato had occasionally passed himself off as Alfonse D'Amato's cousin, including one time when he was stopped for a traffic violation in Scarsdale.

As "Gang Land" revealed last month, Capo—a fellow Staten Islander and one-time loan-shark customer of Watts—was tapped for Watts's trial to bolster the testimony of the prosecution's main witness, Gambino turncoat Dominic Borghese, whose first trial appearance against Watts ended in an acquittal.

Watts, 60, faces 20 years in prison if convicted. He also stands to lose $3.4 million he allegedly made from a huge loan-sharking business and invested in a luxurious beach hideaway on the Gulf of Mexico.

"Gang Land's" a Keeper

Last year's Surprise Summer Contest created so little excitement—and not a single correct answer—that we haven't run another one.

But one "Gang Land" reader found the contest so near and dear to his heart, however, that he was carrying a printout of it several weeks ago. And, who knows, he may still have it in his car.

On April 1—we're going to resist the temptation to make any April Fool's jokes—Staten Island cops stopped Gambino soldier Jerome "Jerry" Brancato and found a copy of a "Gang Land" column that featured an action shot by *Daily News* photographer Keith Torrie of Atlanta first baseman Andres Galarraga blasting a three-run homer in the third inning of a Braves' 6–4 win over the Mets on June 29.

Brancato had just left a breakfast meeting with a bookmaker at the Unicorn Diner at 2944 Victory Boulevard.

Cops did not arrest Brancato, but during a search of his late model Oldsmobile, they saw the "Gang Land" column print-out.

"You know Jerry Capeci?" said one.

"No," said Brancato. "I think he knows me."

Warden Has Time on Her Side

Two years ago, Warden Susan Gerlinski went to the mat with Tommy Gambino when he went to court and tried to get an early release into a halfway house, a move her staff and a federal judge had approved.

She waged a knock-down, drag-out battle for six months and bested the aging and ailing capo by filing court papers until May 10, 2000, when Gambino completed his sentence at the Allenwood Federal Penitentiary, a low-security prison in White Deer, Pennsylvania.

Last week, however, a Colombo associate who has been in "the hole" for 16 months even though he has not been charged with so much as a violation of prison rules, opted for a less orthodox strategy—a hunger strike.

It began unnoticed on Monday, February 4. Frank "Frankie Steel" Pontillo didn't touch his breakfast. Prison food being what it is, it takes a lot more than one rejected food tray to raise an eyebrow.

By Wednesday evening though, when he refused to touch his ninth consecutive meal, Pontillo passed the minimum threshold needed for a bona fide hunger strike—and forced prison officials to take notice.

The next day, when prison officials inquired, Pontillo said he was protesting his lockdown and demanded to be indicted or transferred anywhere else in the country, even a maximum security prison, according to Pontillo, his attorney, and prison sources.

"What's happening here is insane and she thinks it's a big joke," Pontillo told "Gang Land" in a letter from the prison (a facility that sits on a complex near a camp often likened to a country club). Every Friday, he wrote, Gerlinski takes a tour of the solitary confinement block, where conditions are similar to those at Marion Federal Penitentiary, stops at his cell, smiles, and says, "Do you have any questions?"

Pontillo, 32, said Gerlinski has an anti-Italian bias and has abused her power by keeping him and other reputed wiseguys, also uncharged with any infractions, in a "24 hour lockup in the hole since Oct. 5, 2000."

That's when authorities charged correction officers with taking payoffs to help inmates smuggle their sperm to fertility clinics in the hope of starting families before they finished their sentences.

So far, three guards, three current and former inmates, and the wife of one have been convicted of various charges stemming from an investigation into the practice. A prison counselor awaits trial for warning inmates of the probe. (In May 2000, "Gang Land" reported that Luchese mobster George "Georgie Neck" Zappola had used a similar family-planning scheme in 1996.)

Pontillo, who has been jailed since 1992 for conspiring to kill rival wiseguys in the bloody Colombo war, knows most of the players in the case. But he has never been charged in the bribery scheme and claims he has gone legit since landing in prison.

In 1998, he penned *Price of Blood*, a screenplay based on his experiences growing up in Bensonhurst, Brooklyn, hanging around with Colombo capo Greg Scarpa Sr. and other wiseguys at the Wimpy Boys Social Club.

"Since we been in 'the hole,'" Pontillo wrote, "she removed shampoo, vitamins,

> In 1998, he (Pontillo) penned *Price of Blood*, a screenplay based on his experiences growing up in Bensonhurst, Brooklyn, hanging around with Colombo capo Greg Scarpa Sr. and other wiseguys at the Wimpy Boys Social Club.

Q-tips, radios, batteries, lotion, toothpaste, the typewriter from 'the hole' library. She (says she) removes this stuff for security reasons when in reality they're coercive tactics that crossed the line."

When lunch arrived on the fifth day, he ended his hunger strike, prison officials and Pontillo's lawyer Richard Rehbock told "Gang Land" yesterday, with each putting a different spin on Pontillo's reason.

"The warden assured Frankie she would look into the case and would get back to him," said Rehbock.

"We talked to him and explained to him the health risks he faced by continuing," said spokesman William Smith, adding that Pontillo is still a suspect in a continuing investigation into corrupt activity at the prison.

Meanwhile, Frankie Steel, undoubtedly a few pounds lighter, is still looking for a way out of the hole, before he maxes out on January 11, 2004.

And tomorrow, like every other Friday, Susan Gerlinski, who has time on her side, will likely walk over to Pontillo and say, "Do you have any questions?"

Sammy the Jerk

In his heyday, he was the Bull. In his next life as a turncoat, he was often called the Rat. After his sentencing hearing this week, the tabloids called him the Chicken.

These days, Salvatore Gravano, the pint-sized, onetime savvy, street-smart killer from Bensonhurst, Brooklyn, who sweet-talked his way into a million-dollar book deal and a new life in the Grand Canyon State, is a big jerk.

Here's a guy who got a slap on the wrist—five years for a life of crime that included 19 mob hits—who poses for photographs while signing a baseball bat, making like Barry Bonds after breaking Mark McGwire's home run record, with copies of *Underboss* as part of the back-drop. Only a lunatic or a fool would flaunt his old gangster exploits, auto-graphing baseball bats AND allowing someone to take his picture while he's dealing huge amounts of ecstasy with his immediate family in a new town with a government-financed new identity.

Sammy also has been photographed signing a copy of the best-selling book about his life for one of the young punks or established drug dealers who were thrilled to be working for one of the most feared gangsters in the country.

Michael Papa, a former high school football star and honors student from Long Island who moved to Arizona with his family and met Gravano through the Bull's son, Gerard (whom we'll get to later), was an admitted groupie.

"I was kind of star struck," Papa said Monday from the witness stand, a place that Gravano owned for a couple of years when he first sat there and pointed a deadly finger at John Gotti on March 2, 1992.

"I couldn't believe I was in a pool with Sammy the Bull, actually having a con-versation with him. We were going to use his name to monopolize the ecstasy mar-ket in Arizona. People (other drug deal-ers) feared Sammy the Bull's name, and they pretty much did what we wanted."

Gerard "Baby Bull" Gravano had his own unique way of using his father's name to strike fear in the hearts of Phoenix-area hoodlums, according to turncoats.

Gerard, now 25 and facing up to 14 years for his role in the operation, would pull up his shirt, revealing a tattoo of a bull on his belly, and say: "You know who I am? I'm Sammy the Bull's son." (Sentencing guidelines for the Bull are more complicated. At worst, he could get 15½ years under the guidelines—the subject of the hearing. He still faces enhancement at a later hearing that could bring him to 20 years.)

Once, Papa testified, Sammy the Bull warned a drug dealer who threatened to resist: "I own Arizona. It's locked down. You can't sell pills here without going through me."

And to show that Papa was not making up his claims, Assistant U.S. Attorneys Linda Lacewell and Noah Perlman did what prosecutors did 10 years ago to back up Gravano's testimony against Gotti and dozens more— they played tape-recordings that were made before Papa began cooperating.

On February 9, 2000, Papa explained to his buddy Andre Wegner why Gravano was getting a piece of all their drug deals in a discussion in which Wegner theorized that the guy "might bitch a little" but they really weren't in serious danger.

"No? Watch the movies," said Papa. "Watch the movies, you don't even know. You know (he killed) his wife's brother, like shit you don't even know. I said he's a f------ mess, you don't know what will happen with him, family or not, it doesn't

matter to him. You double-cross him and you're f-----."

Or how about this inscription he wrote inside the copy of *Underboss* that he gave Philip Pascucci, a drug dealer who testified about the gangster do's and don'ts that Gravano taught him as he groomed him to be a mob hit man:

- When you dress for a hit, wear different size shoes than you usually do.
- When the hit is done, the clothes are done: Get rid of them.
- Always use a revolver. It won't jam the way semi-automatics might.
- Don't tell the cops anything.
- Stay strong and don't cooperate.

> When you dress for a hit, wear different size shoes than you usually do.

Pascucci told Brooklyn Federal Judge Alynne Ross that Gravano regaled him and their cohorts with tales of past mob hits, explaining that sometimes victims were left on the street as a message and other times they were made to disappear to lessen the chance of arrest.

Papa, 25, said members of the drug gang often hung out with Gravano at Uncle Sal's, a Scottsdale restaurant operated by Gravano's wife, Debra, who was also part of the drug ring and was heard talking to her husband about drug money on another tape that was played by the prosecutors.

On February 11, 2000, two weeks before the entire family was nabbed by Arizona authorities, Gravano called Debra at the restaurant, complaining that a bag of cash she packed was $5,000 short.

"I just counted it in front of your son .... It's sixty-five, not seventy," said Gravano. "I'll have to double-check when I go home," said Debra.

"Double-check, do whatever the f--- you want," said Gravano. "I know I didn't take it. I mean, unless your daughter took it or dropped it. F---, I don't know where ...."

A few minutes later, after Gravano recounted and found 14 packets of $5,000 instead of the 13 he had counted earlier, his daughter Karen called her mom at Uncle Sal's to set the record straight.

"Ma," said a contrite Karen. "It was right. Alright?"

"Alright," said Debra.

During the two-day hearing, prosecutors also played a tape-recording made three months later, when Gravano was in the Maricopa County jail and called his construction company and spoke to Karen and two women workers in his office, Jennifer Roche and Maria Martell, about Papa.

At the time, Papa's lawyer was trying to get his client to turn, and Gravano, who knew firsthand how devastating the testimony of an insider could be to him, a 55-year-old recidivist facing 20 years, was desperate as he gave each of them important words of wisdom to impart to Papa.

"Tell him," he told Karen, "say watch that this lawyer don't have his own agenda ... so instead of talking about ratting, why don't you talk about severing the case ... and they can fight the case."

"You tell him," he told Martell, "when you do that you ruin your whole life. You'll never have a life again. You lose your family, your friends, your girl, he'll lose everything."

"Tell him," he told Roche, who had worked for Gravano in Brooklyn, "'Listen, you're going to lose your whole family and girlfriend, everything. Your whole life, everything is ended for you, you f------ bum.'"

After hours of devastating testimony and tape-recordings, and his lawyer Lynne Stewart doing little if anything to rebut either, Gravano declined to take the witness stand. He let Stewart give a lame excuse that "once the Gravano name is invoked, things really are skewed out of proportion."

What a jerk. After pleading guilty because the feds had turncoats and tapes that were sure to sink him, he forced prosecutors to call the turncoats and play the tapes—sensational testimony that will be hard for Judge Ross to forget—in order to prove written, relatively dry allegations that he headed a drug ring and had used guns and obstruction of justice, allegations that she could have easily ignored.

And then, after that blunder, he sat on his hands like the loser he has become. What a jerk.

Mafia Sperm Wars

On August 29, 1999, mob associate Kevin Granato became the happiest inmate at the Allenwood Federal Penitentiary complex of prisons in White Deer, Pennsylvania.

Granato, now 42, became the proud papa of Gianna, an 8-lb., 5-oz. baby girl.

Soon after she was born, her mother, Regina, now 39, made a four-hour drive from their home in Staten Island to show her to her father.

"That's my little girl," a beaming Granato announced to just about everyone who happened by the new family in the large, open, relaxed visiting room at the low-security facility where Granato, who has resided at one federal prison or another since 1987, has lived for years.

"It was mid-September; she was two weeks old," said Regina, who began living with Granato in 1981 and whom she married in a jailhouse wedding 16 years later after she began to think seriously about having a child.

The serious thinking, she told "Gang Land," began around 1995, after her husband, already doing eight years for dealing drugs with Greg Scarpa Jr., was nailed for extortion, murder conspiracy, and more drug charges.

"My age was getting up there. I said, 'Wow, I'm going to be way too old to have a baby (if I wait until Kevin gets out.)' I said, 'I have to do something. I don't feel like a woman without a child.'"

Since conjugal visits are off-limits at Allenwood, they had to figure out another way. He smuggled his sperm out of the joint and she arranged for a fertility clinic to artificially inseminate her. After a tough pregnancy—gestational diabetes and hemorrhaging kept her bedridden the last two months—she gave birth and knew she had to "drag" herself and Gianna up to Allenwood.

"He was absolutely thrilled," said Regina, whose husband's convictions for drugs, murder conspiracy, and extortion will keep him locked up until 2012. "She's the best thing that ever happened to him," she added.

But in October 2000, mother and daughter, who had been visiting Granato at least once a month, were turned away, and told that Granato was the subject of an investigation and that Warden Susan Gerlinski had decided he would not be allowed visitors until the probe was over.

"Her first birthday was August 29. The last time he saw her was in September. I took her up to see him in her birthday dress. That's the last time they saw each other. She was wearing that dress."

At the time, three correction officers had just been charged with taking bribes to smuggle sperm from another mob associate to a fertility clinic. So far, the three guards, three inmates, including mob associate Antonino Parlevecchio and wife Maria, have been convicted of various charges in the case.

As "Gang Land" reported two months ago, several inmates—one, Colombo associate Frank "Frankie Steel" Pontillo, went on a week-long hunger strike as a protest—have been segregated in 23-hour-a-day lockdowns without any charges being lodged.

Regina and her lawyer, Richard Rehbock, concede Granato's sperm was smuggled out of the prison and used to inseminate Regina, but deny paying any bribes or breaking any laws during the process.

"Since when is semen contraband," said Rehbock, adding that Granato is paying a heavy, unfair price for succeeding without corrupting any guards, where others, namely Parlevecchio and Luchese capo George "Georgie Neck" Zappola, made payoffs, but were unable to father any children.

"It's just spiteful," said Regina. "Their attitude is, if Kevin doesn't want to be an informer, we will show him. They are spitefully keeping me and my baby from seeing Kevin."

"It makes me sick that he's treated like he's guilty. He's not even charged with anything. My lawyer says our situation would be better if he were indicted, then they would have to take him out of the hole."

"I know he will sit there, and can take it. I can take it, too. But it's just mean and unfair for them to do this to my daughter. She's just an innocent child who wants to see her daddy. She didn't hurt anybody. Neither did I."

"I'm afraid he's going to be transferred to California or another faraway place. That's what I hear they can do to people in the hole. Warden Gerlinski can send them so far away, if she could, she would send him to Hong Kong."

Regina, who works with handicapped children as a school bus aide, said she is a private person, and not happy about how her story has been sensationalized, especially for her daughter, but after 18 months, she had to do something.

> Regina and her lawyer, Richard Rehbock, concede Granato's sperm was smuggled out of the prison and used to inseminate Regina, but deny paying any bribes or breaking any laws during the process.

Tomorrow, she makes her case to John Miller, on ABC TV's *20/20*, where "Gang Land" is also slated to appear.

After that? "Whatever it takes. If I have to go to the ends of the earth, I will. I will do all I can to get him out of that hole."

John Gotti: October 27, 1940 — June 10, 2002

"Listen carefully to me. You'll never see another guy like me if you live to be 5000."
—John Gotti, January 29, 1998

Say what you will about John Joseph Gotti Jr., he had a way with words, words that will survive long after he is buried in St. John's Cemetery in Queens beside his son Frank and his father, John Sr.

When the Dapper Don burst on the big scene shortly after orchestrating the execution of Mafia boss Paul Castellano in 1985, reporters asked him whether he had taken over the Gambino crime family.

"I'm the boss of my family. My wife and kids at home," he said, smiling as Gambino gangsters guided him into Brooklyn Federal Court for a pretrial hearing. He arrived at the courtroom door at the same time as radio reporter Mary Gay Taylor, he grasped the door with one hand and graciously ushered her in with the other. "I was brought up to hold the door open for ladies," he said.

When the case went to trial, he had several tabloid reporters scratching their heads and checking their thesauruses and dictionaries as he made the point that a

witness wasn't telling the truth. "Mendacity," he said. "The word for today is mendacity. It's the art of being mendacious."

In 1992, after lawyer Bruce Cutler was disqualified because of a conflict of interest from representing Gotti at the trial that would doom him to die in prison, Gotti said Assistant U.S. Attorney John Gleeson had "the conflict; he's had one the last eight years. You know how they say I'm Bruce's only client the last eight years? Well, I'm (Gleeson's) only case. This guy, you know what he says to his wife when he gets up in the morning? 'Hi ya, John.'"

Prosecutors weren't Gotti's only targets. He often used words like knives when he talked about his relatives, including his wife, son Junior, and former son-in-law Carmine Agnello, the last two in prison for basically following the Teflon Don's bad lead.

In a jailhouse conversation with his daughter Victoria and his brother Peter, Gotti said his wife, Vicky, was a pig, tramp, and a witch. Son Junior, he said, was an idiot, an a--hole, and an imbecile for allowing investigators to find money, guns, and other evidence in a friend's basement. "This is stupidity from down the line," he said.

Gotti exhibited a special flair for biting sarcasm when it came to his son-in-law, whom he consistently described as a moron and much worse. During that same conversation, he pretended to read from an imaginary rap sheet of Carmine's arrests.

"You gotta see the charges," said Gotti. "Malicious mopery. Possession of brains with intent to use. Malicious mopery. Malicious mopery. Stolen bumper. Hubcab."

At another point, he asked Victoria, who has since divorced Agnello, "So what's the story with Carmine? Is he feeling good? Is he not feeling good? Is his medication increased? Decreased? Is it up? Down? Does he get in the backseat of the car and think someone has stolen the steering wheel?"

He saved some of his most descriptive lines for rival hoodlums.

When he learned that a gambling operation headed by Greek organized crime boss Spiros Velentzas was infringing on his turf, he told a cohort to deliver him a message. "You tell him, I, me, John Gotti will sever his motherf------ head!"

Gotti's crack about what he would do to Velentzas was played at his 1992 murder and racketeering trial. The remark did not show Gotti to be an evil butcher, but merely demonstrated that Gotti ran a gambling business and felt strongly about interlopers.

At trial, prosecutors used the words of Gotti's turncoat underboss Salvatore "Sammy Bull" Gravano to make Gotti out to be a murderer. Gravano told how he, Gotti, and other insurgents killed Gambino boss Paul Castellano and took over the crime family.

But when it came to three other murders for which the jury found him guilty—Gambino soldiers Robert "DeeBee" DiBernardo, Louis Milito, and Louis DiBono—prosecutors put Gotti's own words to great use.

"When DeeBee got whacked, they told me a story," Gotti was heard telling then-consigliere Frank Locascio. "I was in jail when I whacked him. I knew why it was being done. I done it anyway. I allowed it to be done."

Milito was killed, said Gotti, because Gravano reported that Milito had bad-mouthed Gotti: "I took Sammy's word that he talked behind my back. I took Sammy's word."

About DiBono, Gotti said: "He didn't rob nothing. Know why he's dying? He's gonna die because he refused to come in when I called."

Because eavesdropping FBI agents failed to grasp Gotti's exact words about DiBono until much later, they failed to prevent his death, which was carried out in a parking lot of the World Trade Center, by the city's own home-grown terror.

JULY 11, 2002

In Death, the Dapper Don Was Dissed

In the end, John Gotti, rest his soul, got no respect from the mob.

None of the leaders of New York's four other crime families—or even capos, for that matter—paid their last respects to the onetime Dapper Don and head of the Gambinos at his wake at the Papavero Funeral Home in Maspeth, Queens.

In fact, only two old soldiers in the Colombo and Genovese families—and a New Jersey wiseguy—were spotted at the two-day wake by teams of local and federal investigators who kept visual and audio tabs on the comings and goings.

And many Gambino members and associates also failed to show up, often sending regrets that bail restrictions, parole, or conditions of supervised release prevented a personal appearance.

"We may have missed a guy or two, but there was a deliberate, conscious decision not to attend," said one law enforcement source.

In other words, the late Gotti was dissed.

"There is no question that the (mob's) message was one of disdain and disapproval," said another.

Despite the pomp and circumstance of Gotti's sendoff—a 75-car motorcade that included 19 flower cars and four news helicopters—Gotti could not have been happy about the lack of respect he got from his peers.

"He put a lot of stock in these kinds of things, so he must have been turning over in his grave," said one underworld source, an attendee of many wiseguy wakes who skipped Gotti's.

The most obvious snub was by Bonanno boss Joseph Massino, an old friend and Howard Beach neighbor who spent many hours with Gotti at the Bergin Hunt and Fish Club, his Ozone Park headquarters where the funeral procession made a solemn stop en route to St. John's Cemetery.

In 1988, during the height of his power, Gotti supported Massino's eventual ascension to the top of the Bonanno family—he was in prison at the time—and pushed the Genovese and Luchese families to restore the Bonannos to good standing with the Mafia Commission.

Today, Massino, the only New York boss not in federal prison for one thing or another, is very secretive and cautious and often travels abroad to avoid surveillance. With no recent indictments or convictions, he has no restrictions over his movements, or persons with whom he can associate.

But Massino, who has become the Commission's most influential member since his release from prison in 1992, avoided the wake and ordered his family members to follow suit, according to law enforcement sources.

"There were no ifs, ands, or buts about it," said one source, adding that numerous informants told of similar directives from the leaders of the Colombo, Luchese, and Genovese families as well.

In one case, a capo told a social club filled with wiseguys and associates, "Nobody goes," quickly interrupting a query about possible exceptions with: "I said, NOBODY GOES."

Underworld sources also told "Gang Land" that the troops, for the most part, were happy about being ordered not to attend.

"I hope they don't tell me I've got to represent the skipper," one wiseguy was heard to say.

For the record, Colombo soldier Joseph "Joe Black" Gorgone, Genovese mobster Frank Monti, and DeCavalcante soldier Frank D'Amato were the only non-Gambino family "made men" who paid their respects, according to law enforcement sources.

Law enforcement sources speculate—along with "Gang Land's" underworld sources, who are not high enough up the food chain to know for sure—that Gotti's assassination of Mafia boss Paul Castellano is the main reason behind the organized boycott.

> In 1988, during the height of his power, Gotti supported Massino's eventual ascension to the top of the Bonanno family.

"He seized power through a renegade act—killing a boss—and it's a repudiation of the tactics he used to take over the family," said one official.

"It probably goes back to Castellano," agreed another, who noted that the Genovese and Luchese families first tried to kill Gotti in 1986, when they blew up his first underboss, Frank DeCicco, then executed two Gotti soldiers in 1990 and 1991.

"I did see a lot of John's friends there," said longtime Gotti attorney Bruce Cutler, insisting that even though legal restrictions, including incarceration, prevented many friends from paying their respects, the wake and funeral were "well attended and dignified."

But Cutler was hard-pressed to explain why Massino, "definitely a friend of John's and a sweetheart of a guy," did not attend, "if he didn't. I didn't see Joe, but I don't know if he was there or not. I know I didn't see him, because I would have hugged him if I did."

Mob Wife Makes a Split Decision

Camille Serpico married into the mob nearly 40 years ago. She buried two husbands, divorced two others, and is looking to part company with her fifth—at least over a Brooklyn chop shop they ran with Genovese family wiseguys.

The savvy 58-year-old mob wife wants to cop a plea to charges she helped her latest, Ernest "Junior" Varacalli, 59, make big bucks by stealing and stripping late-model cars and selling the parts.

She is willing to give up some cash and take five years probation in a plea bargain to cover money laundering and other charges in connection with Varacalli's auto parts business.

Brooklyn prosecutors Chris Blank, Eileen Ayvazian, and Steven Kramer want $325,000, but Camille is balking at the amount, according to lawyer Richard Herman. "There is no deal yet; there is still discussion about that," he said.

> Camille … was married to Colombo associate Joseph Colucci when he was shot to death in 1970 by up-and-coming wiseguy Salvatore "Sammy Bull" Gravano.

Camille, who uses the surname of one of her former husbands, was married to Colombo associate Joseph Colucci when he was shot to death in 1970 by up-and-coming wiseguy Salvatore "Sammy Bull" Gravano.

According to court papers, Camille, who married Varacalli five years ago, often deposited large amounts of cash for her husband, after making sure she looked just right for the task.

On December 12, 2000, Varacalli called her cell phone to find out what was taking her so long to get back to the office. "I'm on my way to go to the bank," she said.

"You didn't go to the bank yet?" he asked.

"No, I had to do my nails first," she said.

"Camille," said an exasperated Varacalli, "don't walk around with all that money today. It's the holidays, they're robbing everyone."

Serpico, who allegedly cheated her second deceased husband's children out of their rightful inheritance when he died, will not testify against Varacalli at either of his two trials for running a chop shop that stole late-model cars and sold their parts to body shops.

The first trial is next week in Manhattan Federal Court, when jurors will have the opportunity to see Camille as well as three allegedly stolen Mercedes Benz engines that Varacalli sold to undercover operatives.

Camille will be in court to give moral support to her husband. He will need it, and more, to win an acquittal. The feds have many tape-recordings of Varacalli selling air bags, dashboards, and other stolen car parts, some made by auto crime cops and investigators for the Brooklyn District Attorney's office.

And if Varacalli does beat the case, he'll have to confront more tapes and chop shop charges, plus extortion and other charges in Brooklyn Supreme Court along with Genovese soldier Federico "Fritzi" Giovanelli, the reputed boss of the operation.

Last year, on the same day Varacalli was overheard complaining about weekly $8,000 payments he was giving "airbag thieves," he told Camille that Giovanelli had praised his chop shop operation: "Fritzi says to me the other day, 'Nobody could do what you do here.'"

The Mercedes Benz engines, including a huge V-12, the largest the German auto manufacturer produces, won't be lugged into the federal courthouse at Foley Square, but the jury will get a chance to view them, according to a pretrial ruling by Judge John Martin.

It's unclear if they will be on a flatbed outside the courthouse or another nearby location, but Martin ordered prosecutors to produce them after Varacalli's lawyer John Jacobs objected to photographs of the engines being shown to the jury.

Feds Okay Freedom for Mob Wife Lana

It's official. Lana Zancocchio won't be joining her husband, Bonanno soldier John "Porky" Zancocchio; her dad, Bonanno capo Anthony "T. G." Graziano; her sister; and her brother-in-law in federal prison.

Federal prosecutors in Brooklyn have decided not to appeal a huge break Zancocchio got in May when she was sentenced to probation on a tax evasion charge that carries strict sentencing guidelines of 10 to 16 months.

Over objections from prosecutor Ruth Nordenbrook, Judge Jack Weinstein sentenced her four levels lower than normal—highly unusual in the era of strict federal guidelines—sending her home to care for her three kids after they told the judge they didn't want to live with their grandmother.

"I thought the sentence was fair," said Lana's lawyer, Jeffrey Rabin. "The government, in hindsight, realized it was fair. The decision not to appeal was a proper exercise of their discretion."

Feds: Yes, We Have Some Bonannos

The Bonanno crime family—the most impenetrable of the fabled five families—was in an extreme state of panic yesterday as news spread that three jailed family members with close ties to boss Joseph Massino have defected and are spilling their guts to the feds.

The wiseguys—acting underboss Richard "Shellackhead" Cantarella, his son Paul, and capo Frank Coppa—have begun talking to the FBI, underworld and law enforcement sources told "Gang Land" yesterday.

The three gangsters are the first known Bonanno mobsters to break the Mafia vow of silence that has been desecrated scores of times by wiseguys from New York's four other crime families since 1962, when Genovese soldier Joe Valachi paved the way.

The unholy Bonanno trio was hit with racketeering charges three months ago in a follow-up to an indictment that snared the family's consigliere last March. Among other things, Richard Cantarella, 59, was charged with a 1992 murder. Paul, 31, was accused of a kidnapping/home invasion robbery. Coppa, 61, was named in three extortion counts.

During the investigation, Richard Cantarella was overheard boasting to an undercover operative that Massino, the only New York Mafia boss unfettered by indictment or prison today, had pushed for his induction into the Bonanno family while Massino was serving six years for labor racketeering that ended in November 1992.

"Word is out that Shellackhead's a rat, his kid's a rat, and his wife's a rat too," said one underworld source.

"The guy who did it was Joe, the guy you met," the elder Cantarella said. "He was in jail and he sent the word (out.)"

News of the turncoats raced through the family's beleaguered ranks yesterday. "Word is out that Shellackhead's a rat, his kid's a rat, and his wife's a rat too," said one underworld source.

Coppa, who began a three-year stretch for securities fraud at a federal prison in Fort Dix last July, was the first to roll over, agreeing to cooperate in early November, sources said.

"I can't say anything, but you're on target," said one law enforcement official.

Brooklyn federal prosecutors Greg Andres and Ruth Nordenbrook declined to comment about the status of Coppa and the Cantarellas. "The last time I heard from Coppa was on November 13," said his lawyer, Larry Bronson. "I haven't heard anything about it," said Paul Cantarella's lawyer, Gerald Shargel. Richard Cantarella's lawyer couldn't be reached.

According to sources on both sides of the law, Coppa was moved into a special Bureau of Prisons witness unit in mid-November. A few weeks ago, Paul Cantarella was transferred without explanation from the Metropolitan Detention Center in Brooklyn to a segregated unit in the Metropolitan Correctional Center in Manhattan.

On Monday, the elder Cantarella was moved into a segregated unit at the Brooklyn federal lockup. That same day, his wife, Lauretta Castelli, a co-defendant charged with money laundering who had been out on bail, as well as Paul's family, disappeared from their Staten Island homes and haven't been seen since.

"It sure as hell looks like an all-inclusive package deal," said one defense lawyer in the case.

According to court papers, Richard Cantarella took part in the 1992 murder of Robert Perrino, a *New York Post* delivery superintendent, in an effort to thwart a state probe into widespread racketeering and fraud at the *Post* stemming from the Bonanno family's control of the Newspaper and Mail Deliverers Union.

"As the state investigation proceeded, Cantarella and others feared that Perrino might cooperate with law enforcement authorities, and consequently, he was murdered," said U.S. Attorney Roslynn Mauskopf in October as she announced the indictment.

"At the time of the murder," said Mauskopf, "Cantarella and other members of the Bonanno family held no-show jobs at the paper."

In recent weeks, eight other Bonanno mobsters, including consigliere Anthony Graziano, whose sentence will fall between 108 and 135 months, and capo Frank Porco, whose sentencing guidelines range from 24 to 30 months, have copped plea deals in the case.

Reunions Galore for Little Joe Defede

After a successful debut in Manhattan, former Luchese acting boss Joseph "Little Joe" Defede is about to hit the big time in Brooklyn.

Primed by an appearance against a Luchese soldier, Defede will soon take the witness stand against Gambino boss

Peter Gotti and six other wiseguys charged with extortion, labor racketeering, and other crimes on the Brooklyn and Staten Island waterfront.

The feds hope Defede's testimony at the Gotti trial will be the first of several successful appearances by the high-level turncoat against Mafia leaders he met while he ran the Luchese family from 1994 to 1998.

Defede's next stint will be against Genovese boss Vincent "Chin" Gigante, his son Andrew, and six others charged with extortion and labor racketeering on the Manhattan and Miami waterfronts. Defede never met either Gigante but had several sessions with co-defendant Liborio "Barney" Bellomo, the family's acting boss, in the mid 1990s, according to FBI reports obtained by "Gang Land."

It wouldn't surprise "Gang Land" if Defede, who "met Massino several times" during the 1990s, according to an FBI report, has a reunion of sorts with the Bonanno boss in the not-too-distant future.

At the Gotti trial, Defede will testify that he met Gotti and other mob leaders six to eight times to decide whom to recognize as leader of the war-torn Colombo family, according to court papers filed by prosecutors Andrew Genser, Katya Jestin, and Rick Whelan.

During high-level sit-downs, three Mafia leaders agreed to recognize jailed-for-life Carmine "Junior" Persico as official Colombo boss, while the Genovese family "stayed neutral," said the FBI report.

His testimony, prosecutors say, will corroborate tape-recordings and other evidence that Gotti, 64, headed the Gambino family and that he was the ultimate recipient of hundreds of thousands of dollars in extortion payoffs derived from the family's control of the docks in Brooklyn and Staten Island.

Gotti's brother, Richard, 60, a capo, and Richard's son, Richard G. Gotti, 35, a soldier, allegedly served as intermediaries in the scheme. They are among seven wiseguys on trial in Brooklyn Federal Court. Testimony begins following jury selection, which began Monday.

Former co-defendant Frank "Red" Scollo, a corrupt Longshoremen's Union official, and tough guy actor Steven Seagal, an alleged extortion victim, are expected to join Defede as prosecution witnesses at trial, which is expected to last three months.

JANUARY 23, 2003

Feds Nail Joe Waverly for 1987 Murders

Nearly 16 years after one of the city's most heinous and baffling mob hits—the execution of a 78-year-old retired civil lawyer working as a hearing officer for the Parking Violations Bureau—the FBI yesterday arrested a top Colombo mobster for the crime.

Acting Colombo boss Joel "Joe Waverly" Cacace was charged with the March 20, 1987, murder of George Aronwald, the father of a onetime mob prosecutor who was shot to death in a Queens laundry in a bizarre mistaken identity gangland–style rubout.

The key witness against Cacace—as "Gang Land" first reported 16 months ago—is Luchese associate Frank Smith, the only surviving member of a sorry hit team that intended to kill Aronwald's son William, a former federal prosecutor who had been marked for death by the jailed-for-life Colombo boss, Carmine Persico.

Smith and two cohorts who were killed a few months later, Vincent Carini and his brother Enrico (Eddie), allegedly executed Aronwald on orders from Cacace.

Federal prosecutors began putting together a racketeering and murder case more than a year ago, sources said, but several events—including the September 11 attack and the indictment of Smith's lawyer, Lynne Stewart, delayed the investigation until yesterday.

Another major hurdle, sources said, was a stubborn, almost silly feud between Smith, 36, and the office of State Special Narcotics Prosecutor Bridget Brennan.

Brennan's office refused to concede what the FBI, federal prosecutors, "Gang Land," and a host of others believe—that Smith was wrongly convicted of being the supplier of $4,500 worth of cocaine that was purchased in 1987 by an undercover cop. Smith, who admitted taking part in several murders in August 2001, refused to follow through and cooperate when FBI agents couldn't convince Brennan's office to admit Smith was innocent of the drug charge, for which he had been sentenced to 15 years to life back in 1989.

Recently, however, both sides gave a little, sources said. Brennan's office agreed to set aside the verdict without conceding it was wrong. Smith agreed to plead guilty to murders in state and federal court and not to seek damages for malicious prosecution.

Following the murder, detectives scoured the elder Aronwald's civil practice, his work as a PVB hearing officer, and his son's work as a prosecutor, looking for a motive. They even looked into whether Aronwald was mistaken for the late Gambino consigliere Joseph N. Gallo, who was of similar age and stature and lived nearby.

"I am grateful that at this late stage, someone is being held accountable for the death of my father," William Aronwald said yesterday. "It is still very disturbing that because someone had a grudge against me, my father's life was cut short. That is something I will never get over."

The first real break in the case came 10 years after the slaying, on July 9, 1997, when turncoat Luchese soldier Frank Gioia Jr. learned that Smith's sister Kim—the mother of Gioia's only son—had tape-recorded telephone conversations with him and sold them for $10,000 to wiseguys Gioia was cooperating against.

"Once Gioia heard this," said FBI agent Stephen Byrne in an affidavit, "he told me in substance to get my pen out and get ready to write. Gioia then provided us with a list of crimes committed by (her) relatives, including several unsolved murders."

Previously, Gioia, whose cooperation has helped convict more than 80 mobsters, drug dealers, and one cop killer, had spared his then-finance's family after his defection in 1995 following an arrest for heroin dealing. He gave Smith up for Aronwald's murder and the rubouts six months later of two mob associates around the corner from Smith's Bath Beach, Brooklyn, home.

Cacace, 61, is also charged with ordering the Bath Beach slayings and the 1987 murder of a corrupt police officer, Carlo Antonino.

Gioia said Smith told him about the hits during jailhouse visits Gioia made to his future brother-in-law in the early 1990s while Smith was doing time for the drug conviction. Gioia told FBI agents in 1995 that Smith was in jail on a bum rap, even providing them with the identity of the cocaine supplier. Prosecutors, however, never acted on the information until they learned that Smith could help nail Cacace.

Smith's drug conviction, which kept him locked up and out of harm's way, coupled with dumb luck, may have saved his life.

As pressure mounted on cops to find Aronwald's killers, Smith and the Carinis began to lay low, fearing that Cacace would have them killed rather than risk them getting arrested and making a deal to save their necks.

On June 11, 1987, the Carini brothers showed up at Smith's house looking for him, but left before he got home when their beepers went off. As they drove away, they told his mother, "Tell Frankie to stay here until we get back. Tell him not to answer the phone; not to talk to nobody."

Smith got home minutes later, but the Carinis never returned. The next morning, Vincent and Enrico were found shot to death in two cars parked on the same Brooklyn street.

A day or two later, sources said, Cacace and two other Colombo capos visited Smith. "They were trying to get a read on how I felt over my friends being killed," Smith told Gioia. "They asked me if I was looking for vengeance. I said no, there was no problem, and they left."

According to court records, Smith reached out to a Luchese soldier he knew, and after two sit-downs between leaders of the Colombo and Luchese families, the Colombos agreed to spare Smith. But Smith feared that Cacace was still going to get him.

"I always figured they would kill me," Smith told Gioia. "They killed Eddie and Vinny. I never figured Joe Waverly would let me live since I'm the only one left who could tie him to the killing."

Gioia, 35, served six years in prison. He now has a new identity. On occasion, sources say, he lectures rookie and veteran FBI agents about organized crime.

Smith should have company in the Witness Protection Program. Kim Smith, who turned on Gioia and refused to leave Brooklyn with him, has done so for her brother and looks to join him in the future.

> "They killed Eddie and Vinny. I never figured Joe Waverly would let me live since I'm the only one left who could tie him to the killing."

JANUARY 30, 2003

Waterfront Wiseguy
Turns on the Mob

Of all the mobsters snared in a celebrated three-year FBI undercover operation by turncoat Michael "Cookie" D'Urso—so far 47 defendants have been convicted—the most important may be an aging, ailing, battle-weary Hell's Kitchen gangster.

George Barone was a powerful waterfront racketeer in the days when the mob ruled supreme on the city's docks. In his prime, in the 1950s, Barone was a character right out of *On the Waterfront*, a "Johnny Friendly" type who used guns, knives, and his own fists to enforce the rules of his then-boss and close pal, Mafia chieftain Vito Genovese.

Barone, now 79, stoops when he walks. He suffers from lung disease, heart disease, diabetes, and cancer. He is so hard of hearing that he needed a teleprompter to read questions from lawyers when he took the stand last week in his debut as a government witness.

But his memory appears to be pretty good, and Barone is poised to be a key witness against another old friend, 74-year-old Genovese boss Vincent "Chin" Gigante—as well as Gigante's son

Andrew and six other wiseguys—when that case begins in March. Barone is the third family member to defect since Genovese soldier Joe Valachi paved the way in 1962.

Most defectors today have little insight about the mob's glory days and a limited historical perspective about the Mafia. Barone, however, was nabbed for extortion in 2001 and has firsthand knowledge about a half century of crime.

A World War II veteran who took part in five Allied invasions, including the assault on Iwo Jima, Barone spent a couple years at Pace College before acquiring an accelerated education about the waterfront while scrubbing down ships at Manhattan piers in the late 1940s.

He joined the International Longshoremen's Association around 1949 as a working foreman for a ship-cleaning company controlled by Albert Anastasia, boss of what is now known as the Gambino family, according to FBI reports obtained by "Gang Land."

After fending off efforts by Anastasia capo Carmine "the Doctor" Lombardozzi to use nonunion workers, Barone got in bed with Genovese—a fierce Anastasia rival—and began taking payoffs to allow Genovese to use non-union labor.

By the mid-1950s, he was an ILA official and "very close" to Genovese, so close that Don Vitone confided that he had learned about a diabolical plot in which his underboss, Frank Costello, and Anastasia planned to kill him, and how Genovese responded.

"Genovese directed Chin Gigante to kill Costello (and) Genovese was also responsible for Anastasia's murder" in October 1957, Barone said, according to a report by FBI agents Michael Campi and Joy Adam.

"He's the real deal, a guy who knows it all and decided to get out rather than die in jail," said one law enforcement official.

Barone was a personal hit man for acting boss Anthony "Fat Tony" Salerno in the 1960s and '70s. He spent most of the 1980s in prison, but he got back into "the life" in the 1990s, flourishing as the Genovese family's man on the Miami docks until his arrest.

In his day, he was involved in so many murders, he can't remember them all.

"I didn't keep a scorecard, but it was probably ten or twelve," Barone said last

week at the waterfront racketeering trial of Gambino boss Peter Gotti, capo Anthony "Sonny" Ciccone, a rival for 30 years, and five others.

Barone said he dispatched most of his victims in the 1950s, when he belonged to a Hell's Kitchen gang of mostly Irish hoodlums whose name, the Jets, was made famous in the 1957 musical about gang violence, *West Side Story*.

"I am a mongrel. I'm partly Italian, Irish, and Hungarian," Barone testified when asked about his own heritage.

His lucrative labor racketeering partnership with Genovese ended in 1958 after the leader of the Jets was killed. Barone aligned himself with Salerno, who later sponsored his induction into the family.

Barone became a favored hit man for his mob masters. In the mid-1960s, he traveled to Covington, Kentucky, and killed a Salerno nemesis who was causing problems for a gambling operation Fat Tony controlled there. In 1967, he again did Salerno's bidding, killing John Biello, a New York wiseguy who had moved to Miami and earned Salerno's wrath.

Before going to prison in 1983, Barone was ordered to meet Chin Gigante in Greenwich Village with several wiseguys and ILA officials and smooth the way for

> "Genovese directed Chin Gigante to kill Costello (and) Genovese was also responsible for Anastasia's murder" in October 1957, Barone said.

Andrew Gigante to take over some of Barone's responsibilities on the docks, according to an FBI report.

As they waited for Gigante to arrive, Barone saw a man entering the apartment who "looked like the Man From LaMancha," the fabled Don Quixote character, and for a brief moment, "thought this person was there to kill them," the report said.

"As the person came closer, he realized it was Chin dressed in a robe with the hood up over his head. Gigante embraced (Barone), told the others how much he loved (him), and described how they were together years ago with Vito Genovese," the report said.

Turning his back on the mob after a 50-year run was a difficult decision, he testified, but one Barone was forced to make after he was cheated by the Gigantes and suspected that they had marked him for death.

"I wanted to get even. I wanted to survive. I didn't want to get killed by them," he said.

Bittersweet Win for Eager Lawyer

Federal prosecutors were upset last week when Brooklyn Judge Frederic Block refused to let D'Urso testify at the Gotti trial, but one member of the defense team also had a surprisingly long face when Block startled the feds with his surprise ruling.

Lawyer Henry Mazurek, an associate of Gerald Shargel, lead attorney for Peter Gotti, had been prepping for months to cross-examine D'Urso because Shargel, who had once represented the turncoat, was precluded from questioning him.

Mazurek, who represented Rocco Graziosa, a diminutive tough guy convicted of assault for sucker punching New York Yankee pitcher David Wells, voiced confidence he would do better against the savvy turncoat than he had against the burly southpaw.

"The judge's decision was the right one, but I was all ready to go, looking to show the jury who D'Urso really is, a guy who has manipulated the system to get a pass for a murder," he said.

Law & Order, Brooklyn Style

The scene could have been the opening of last night's *Law & Order*. And it played out like the hit television drama.

It's the dead of night. A bullet-riddled man, Tino, is slumped on the floor under a card table. His cards are scattered on the floor around his body. His jacket is on the chair, pushed away from the table, and there is one stack of money on the table.

A deck of cards and the hands the other players had held are visible on the table. There are no 8's, 9's, or 10's—an indication they had been playing Scala, an Italian card game—visible on the table. But the men and their cash are gone. Their empty chairs are at the table.

If Det. Lennie Briscoe had arrived, he would surely croak, "Looks like the guys playing cards with this bird knew he was getting it. When it was over, they just picked up their stuff, and walked out."

Briscoe next would have noticed a shadowy figure lying nearby. The figure moans, places his hand to his head, sticks a finger into a hole made by a .38 caliber bullet.

Cookie, the shadowy figure, tells cops he knew three of the men had guns but he never saw the shooter. Before going into surgery, not knowing if he'd survive, he names five men who were at the San Giuseppe Social Cub in Williamsburgh, Brooklyn, less than an hour earlier, at 2 A.M., on November 30, 1994, when he was shot and his cousin Tino Lombardi was killed.

Seven years later, after Michael "Cookie" D'Urso had stung the Genovese family and its boss and scores of other wiseguys were hit with racketeering, murder, and others raps, the feds still had no other evidence than the five names they had a few days after the killing.

All five had told police, and later the FBI, essentially the same story: "I was in the club, the shooting started, and I ran. I didn't see who did it."

Last year, however, the Brooklyn U.S. Attorney's office did what *Law & Order*'s A.D.A. Jack McCoy would. It got indictments against all of them, as the A.D.A.s (like Serena Southerlyn, McCoy's younger, more by-the-book colleague) of the office shook their collective heads in disbelief.

The three men D'Urso had seen with guns were hit with murder and attempted murder charges. The others were charged with engaging in a conspiracy to cover up the killing. And the feds hoped for the best.

If truth be told, Assistant U.S. Attorneys Paul Weinstein, Dan Dorsky, and Paul Schoeman, the main prosecutors in D'Urso's cases, had no real idea how they would prove it.

It didn't take long for them to figure it out.

Anthony Bruno, 31, one of the men D'Urso had seen standing behind him with a gun, was first in the door to make a deal. Anthony "Rookie" Cerasulo, 29, who had been poised at the social club door as a lookout and get-away driver, was next.

On the eve of trial last month, John Imbrieco, 40, who shot and killed Lombardi after Bruno shot D'Urso in the head, pleaded guilty and took 20 years.

Carmelo "Carmine Pizza" Polito, who makes pizza, robs banks, is a degenerate gambler, and owed the cousins $60,000 in 1994, and Mario Fortunato, an owner of a landmark Brooklyn bakery and occasional bank robber, rolled the dice and went to trial.

> **Carmelo "Carmine Pizza" Polito, who makes pizza, robs banks, is a degenerate gambler, and owed the cousins $60,000 in 1994, and Mario Fortunato, an owner of a landmark Brooklyn bakery and occasional bank robber, rolled the dice and went to trial.**

On the witness stand, Cerasulo, a coke abuser, said he was recruited by Polito to do the work, and had gotten a gun from Fortunato at his bakery. He stalked the men, but couldn't do it. "I chickened out," he said. "I didn't have the heart."

To satisfy Polito, though, Cerasulo had the courage to enlist Bruno, a crack user, who testified he also lost his nerve the first time he stalked his prey, with two guns on him.

At 2 A.M. that night, after "freaking out" pacing back and forth behind D'Urso, Bruno fired a single shot into D'Urso's head. "I saw his hair part. I'll never forget it," said Bruno.

Imbrieco quickly followed Bruno's lead, emptying his gun into Lombardi. Bruno fired a few shots at Lombardi as well, and then turned to blast D'Urso one more time. When he pulled the trigger, however, instead of shots, he heard only clicks. He thought of stabbing D'Urso in the back, but that was more than the crackhead could handle. He ran.

A.D.A. Southerlyn might opine, "This is not the way they said we should do it in law school." Whatever, it worked. The jury convicted both men. On April 3, Judge I. Leo Glasser will sentence Polito,

43, and Fortunato, 55, to life without parole, sentences mandated by federal law.

Ashcroft Thinks Like a Mob Boss

George Barone's hearing is shot, but his memory and voice are still pretty sharp as the 79-year-old turncoat gangster continues telling the feds what he knows about a half a century of mob murders and other mayhem while preparing to take on Genovese boss Vincent "Chin" Gigante next month.

But several prosecutors privately noted last week that the recent move by U.S. Attorney General John Ashcroft to impose the death penalty—on cooperators—could jeopardize such future agreements.

As reported by *The New York Times*, Ashcroft overruled a decision by the Brooklyn U.S. Attorney's office to accept a life sentence for a murder suspect in two killings in return for his testimony against cohorts in a deadly drug ring that operated in Queens.

Ashcroft decided life without parole, like Polito and Fortunato will get, isn't enough. The feds, Ashcroft feels, should handle murderers who agree to help the law the same way John Gotti dealt with wiseguys who helped the law—whack them.

Ashcroft—you recall he moved from lawmaking to law enforcement after he lost re-election to the U.S. Senate to a dead man—has the legal right to bigfoot decisions about capital punishment. He has done so in the past, but this was the first time in which the victim had agreed to cooperate.

Many former federal prosecutors voiced outrage that Ashcroft's decision will cause problems for real crime fighters in solving murders and taking violent criminals off the streets, but U.S. Attorney Roslynn Mauskopf ate crow and applauded Ashcroft's decision to overrule her.

"Gang Land" declines to quote any former feds criticizing Ashcroft's decision. We will wait for one of the country's 93 politically appointed U.S. attorneys—maybe Mauskopf or her Manhattan counterpart, James Comey, will find the courage—or forget about it.

Next week, more nuggets from Barone, who'd be gone by now if Ashcroft had his way.

The Bonanno Boat Springs a Big Leak

Mafia boss Joseph Massino—and leaders and members of all five families—have just received the most devastating news possible: His brother-in-law and longtime Bonanno family underboss has defected, "Gang Land" learned yesterday.

Salvatore Vitale, who has been at the pinnacle of New York's underworld for two decades, was quietly moved into a special unit for turncoats last week after he reached a cooperation agreement with federal prosecutors in Brooklyn, sources said.

Vitale's decision greatly strengthens the government's pending case against Massino and his cohorts. Vitale took part in seven mob hits with Massino, according to court papers, and he is also an important potential witness against leaders of other families.

"He fills a big void at the top of the charts," said one law enforcement official, citing a paucity of high-level turncoats since Gambino underboss Salvatore "Sammy Bull" Gravano and Luchese acting boss Alfonse "Little Al" D'Arco turned on the mob in 1991.

"He (Vitale) knows the current crop of top guys," the official said, noting that until January, when the Bonanno leaders were indicted and jailed on murder and racketeering charges, Vitale often served as "Massino's emissary with the other families."

If Vitale had cooperated sooner, for example, prosecutors could have used him to identify Peter Gotti as the current boss of the Gambino family, something one-time Luchese acting boss Joseph "Little Joe" Defede—jailed since 1998—was unable to do at Gotti's trial.

Massino, 60, and Vitale were hit with racketeering and murder charges January 9: Massino for the 1981 murder of Bonanno capo Dominick "Sonny Black" Napolitano and Vitale for the 1992 murder of former *New York Post* delivery superintendent Robert Perrino.

As "Gang Land" first reported, the charges stemmed from the first public defections of Bonanno family "made men"—Frank Coppa, Paul Cantarella, and his father, capo Richard "Shellack-head" Cantarella. Shellackhead was charged with Perrino's murder last year.

The charges were a rude awakening for Massino, who had been unscathed since taking over the family in 1991, while Gambino boss John Gotti and the leaders of the other families were hit with murder and racketeering charges and jailed, some for life.

When Massino was indicted, the feds filed court papers stating that he had suspected that Vitale may have cooperated. Massino feared the worst, the papers said, because Vitale had gotten a "good deal" of 44 months for a 2001 loan-sharking case and because Vitale was not originally charged with Perrino's slaying.

Federal prosecutors in Brooklyn refused yesterday to confirm or deny that Vitale is cooperating, but according to Federal Bureau of Prisons records, Vitale, 55, was released from the Metropolitan Correctional Center in Manhattan last Wednesday.

On Friday evening, his lawyer, John Mitchell, received a hand-delivered letter notifying him that Vitale had retained a new attorney, an unmistakable, albeit not quite official, notice that Vitale had begun cooperating.

"Until then, I had no indication that he has apparently decided to cooperate," said Mitchell, who added that since last Wednesday, he has been unable to reach Vitale or his wife, with whom he previously had maintained frequent contact.

Vitale's wife, Diana, their sons, and other family members were relocated by FBI agents the same day Vitale was transferred out of the MCC, sources said.

In 1987, the brothers-in-law were acquitted of racketeering charges stemming from the undercover work of FBI agent Joe Pistone, a.k.a. Donnie Brasco. Vitale had been charged with hijacking and obstruction of justice, Massino with taking part in three 1980 mob hits that he later admitted to turncoat capo Coppa, according to court papers.

It's unclear if the feds can use information from Vitale to again charge Massino with those killings—capos Philip Giacone, Dominick Trinchera, and Alphonse Indelicato—but "we'll have plenty of options once we debrief Vitale," said one law enforcement source.

"I'm having difficulty understanding his creatures from the id that would make him cooperate against his brother-in-law," said Massino's lawyer, David Breitbart. "The case was ill conceived, poorly drafted, and required someone to cooperate. We only hope that he tells the truth, because that would vindicate Mr. Massino. We know there are many instances, unfortunately, when cooperators are not truthful."

> Shellackhead was charged with Perrino's murder last year.

Chin 'Fesses Up;
His Lawyer Doesn't

Supporting casts were strategically placed on either side of the courtroom and the stage was set for Vincent "Chin" Gigante's grand finale in Brooklyn Federal Court.

FBI agents Tom Krall, Joy Adam, Craig Donlon, Bob Vosler, and Michael Campi—and paralegal Kathryn Cintron—were in the first row on one side waiting for Gigante and Judge I. Leo Glasser to enter.

On the other side sat Gigante's sons Vincent and Salvatore; daughters Carmela and Lucia; and his brother, Father Louis Gigante, who for years had walked arm-in-arm through Greenwich Village with pajama-clad Vincent as the straight man for the crazy-man act of the legendary Mafia boss.

The priest, who wore a white collar for those strolls, and when attending his brother's racketeering and murder trial in 1997, was not wearing one this time—a hint that Father Gigante was there for moral support, not for an appearance before the television cameras stationed right outside the courthouse. There was no indication, however, that a final plot twist in the endless Gigante saga would place someone into the priest's former role.

As the play began on Monday, it looked for a fleeting moment like Chin was going to put on his old mumbling, bumbling, Daffy Don routine, the one he used to fool shrinks for more than three decades.

His hair and prison duds were disheveled, and as courtroom deputy Louise Schaillat began the pro forma reading of the "promise to tell the truth" oath that all defendants take before they plead guilty, Gigante started to raise his left hand.

But after a few seconds—old habits are often hard to break—Chin raised his right hand and followed the new script that prosecutors and defense lawyer Benjamin Brafman had crafted.

Gigante listened attentively as Glasser told him that according to his plea bargain, any relatives who may have aided him obstruct justice would not be prosecuted. Pausing occasionally to confer with Brafman—who assured Glasser that his client understood what was going on—Gigante answered the judge's queries appropriately.

"No, your Honor," said Gigante, shaking his head back and forth for emphasis, when asked if he had taken any prescription drugs that would have clouded his ability to comprehend or if anyone had forced him or threatened him to plead guilty.

"Yes, your Honor," he said, nodding his head, when asked whether he had discussed the plea agreement with his attorney, whether he had obstructed justice by deceiving psychiatrists for seven years, whether he understood that he would receive three more years in prison and have to pay $100 in court costs.

His only ailments, said Brafman, were common for 75-year-old men. He was undergoing treatment for an eye infection and suffered hearing loss, a condition that prompted Glasser, a notorious low talker, to speak loud enough for Gigante and the entire courtroom to hear his words—a rare treat for reporters.

Courtesy of Glasser, who allowed Gigante and his son Andrew to say their good-byes in the well of the courtroom—Andrew would plead guilty later—the proceeding featured a smiling, animated Gigante shaking hands with defense lawyers and blowing kisses to his children and his brother in the spectator section.

Though it played a lot like a 10-minute silent movie, a relaxed Gigante cracked jokes, smiled often, and looked alert. His actions, reinforced by the lucidity he displayed during his plea as well as Brafman's assurances that his client was mentally competent to plead guilty, left no doubt in "Gang Land's" estimation that he was.

Outside the courtroom, however, Brafman stood before the television cameras and sounded a lot like Father Gigante did six years ago, not like the lawyer who had just stood next to Chin Gigante and guided him through a plea deal that he had worked out with prosecutors Paul Weinstein, Dan Dorsky, and Joey Lipton.

While Gigante was competent enough to plead guilty to obstructing justice from 1990 through 1997 by deceiving doctors about his mental state, Brafman said, his client was "clearly suffering from dementia."

He had "become too old and too sick and too tired to fight," said Brafman, implying that if Gigante were younger and in better health, Brafman the hotshot lawyer could have engineered an acquittal despite the multitude of evidence prosecutors had amassed.

Even if true, and "Gang Land" thinks it's not, it seems like poor form to blame a client who paid him a healthy legal fee for negotiating a guilty plea, while arguing that he could have won an acquittal.

More likely, however, as law enforcement and defense sources say, the aging and ailing gangster was doomed to be convicted again, and Brafman engineered a good plea deal for Gigante because he was able to convince his co-defendants, some of whom had cases they could win, to plead guilty, too.

Chin's Last Dom Runs the Show

During his heyday, when Gigante ran his crime family out of the Triangle Social Club on Sullivan Street, he was closely attended by four wiseguys named Dominick—Fat Dom Alongi, Baldy Dom Cantarino, Dom the Sailor DiQuarto, and Quiet Dom Cirillo.

Today, only Quiet Dom, 73, still survives, and sources on both sides of the

> During his heyday, when Gigante ran his crime family out of the Triangle Social Club on Sullivan Street, he was closely attended by four wiseguys named Dominick—Fat Dom Alongi, Baldy Dom Cantarino, Dom the Sailor DiQuarto, and Quiet Dom Cirillo.

law say Cirillo, like Gigante, a former professional boxer who was convicted of drug dealing in the 1950s, is the Genovese crime family's go-to guy or "street boss."

His name came up frequently during the three-year probe that led to racketeering charges against three capos who served as an acting family boss—two who pleaded guilty the same day as Gigante, Liborio "Barney" Bellomo and Ernest Muscarella—and a third who died of cancer following his indictment, Frank "Farby" Serpico.

But Quiet Dom, who never discusses family business on the telephone, preferring "walk talks" on city streets away from FBI bugs, remains an elusive target.

Index

A

Abbatiello, James, 32
Agnello, Carmine, 93, 118, 257
Albanese, Anthony, 267
Allenwood Federal Penitentiary, 288
Alogna, Ignatio, 6
Aloi, Benedetto, Windows case, 68
Aloi, Vincent, Colombo internal conflict, 62
Amato, Gaetano, 74
Amato, Pasquale "Patsy," 106, 123
Ambrosino, Joseph, 123
Amoroso, Anthony, 93
Amuso, Vittorio "Vic," 51, 113, 246, 270
    Christmas furlough, 73
    Colombo internal conflict, 63
    Windows case, 68
Anastasia, Albert, 50
Angelo, Guiseppe, 13
anonymous juries, 132
Anzellotto, Thomas, 225
Arcuri, Guiseppe, 90
Arena, Vito, 25
Armone, Joseph, 84
Arnold, Frank, 146
Aronwald, William, 308
Aronwalk, George, 308
arson, Thomas Masotto, 117
Arthur Avenue social club, 188

Asaro, Vincent, 218, 230
Astuto, Louis, 100
Avellino, Salvatore, 114, 225, 274

B

Bailey, F. Lee, 83
Baratta, Anthony Bowat, 142, 223
Barnes, Leroy "Nicky," 25, 169
Barrone, Anthony, 51
Barone, George, 311-312, 316
Bartels, John (Federal Judge), 15-17
Basciano, Dino, 235-240, 247
basketball fixing (Boston College), 10
Batchelder, Harry, 51, 143
    Windows case, 69
Battistoni, Thomas, 43
Bayrodt, Frank, 6
Bellomo, Liborio "Barney," 192, 321
Benfante, Ernest, 60
Benfante, Joseph, 154
Bergin Hunt and Fish Club, 22, 108
    listening devices (bugs), 59
Bickelman, Vincent, 272
Bilotti, Joseph, 60
Bilotti, Thomas, 60, 155
Bishop, James, 146
Bless Me, Father, 182

Blossner, Robert, 14
Blum, Howard, 139-140
Bologna, Rita, 97, 101
Bompensiero, Frank "Bomp," 242
Bonanno family, 4, 12, 37, 127, 305
    Gotti murder and racketeering trial, 86
Bonavolonta, Jules (FBI agent), 17, 45
Borghese, Dominic, 286
Borriello, Bartholemew "Bobby," 112
Boss of Bosses, 53-56
Boston College (basketball fixing scandal), 10
Bowles, Pete, 199
Brafman, Benjamin, Windows case, 69
Brancato, Jerome, 286
Brave, Gerard (Queens Assistant District Attorney), 218
Breitbart, David, 30, 147
bribery, jury, 81
Broderick, Vincent (Manhattan Federal Judge), 29
Brooklyn Democratic Party, 20
Brooklyn Organized Crime Strike Force, 10, 32
Bruno, Angelo, 51
Bruno, Anthony, 315
Bucknam, Robert, 21
Buffalino, Joseph, 6

bugs (listening devices), 59
   Bergin Hunt and Fish Club,
      59
   Ravenite Social Club, 59
Burke, James "the Gent," 10,
   196
Burke, Kathleen, 144
Burstein, Judd, 30
Butler, Dick, 11

C

Cacace, Joe Waverly, 191, 243,
   308
Cafaro, Vincent "Fish," 21, 114
Café Biondo, 28
Calabrese, Jody, 225-226, 247
Calco, Joseph, 244
Caldwell, Leslie, 28
Cammarano, Joseph Jr., 180
Campanella, Joseph, 134
Campione, Frank "Frankie
   Camp," 43
Candela, Salvatore "Sal the
   Geep," 173
Cantarella, Paul, 305
Cantarella, Richard, 273, 279,
   305-306
Canterino, Dominick "Baldy
   Dom," 68
   Windows case, 69
Capo, Anthony, 285
Capozzalo, Patricia, 246
Cappello, Gregory "Whitey,"
   225-226
Carcappa, Steve, 152
Cardinale, Anthony, 91
Cardinali, James, 25
Carew, Thomas "Tommy Irish,"
   151
Carini, Enrico, 308
Carini, Vincent, 308

Carneglia, John, 9, 17, 24, 201
Carrao, Vincent, 259
Carter, Jimmy, 25
Caserta, Tony, 167
Casso, Anthony "Gaspipe," 31,
   113, 147, 151, 205, 237, 269
   prosecutorial deal, 211-212
   Windows case, 68
Castellano, Paul "Big Paul," 15,
   24, 38, 53, 60, 155, 193
Castelle, Eugene "Boopsie," 271
Castignaro, Frank, 137
Castillo Diner, 144
Cedarbaum, Miriam (Federal
   Judge), 132
cell phones, 260
Celli, Raphael, 57
Centore, Salvatore "Sal the
   Nose," 174
Cerasulo, Anthony, 315
Cestaro, Frank, 137
Chen Fu Xin, 190
Chen Jia Wu, 190
Chickara, James, 277
Chiodo, Peter, 147, 151,
   171-172, 209-210, 246
   Windows case, 68
Christmas furlough (Amuso,
   Vittorio), 73
Ciccone, Anthony, 174, 217
Ciccone, William, 195
Cinquegrana, Louis "Louie the
   Pigeon," 14, 22
Cirelli, Michael, 59, 141
civil lawsuits, Gravano,
   Salvatore, 216
Cobb, Ernie, 11
Coffey, Joseph, 6
Cohn, Roy, 21, 24
Coiro, Michael, 48
Colombo family, 4-5, 43, 106
   Gotti murder and racketeer-
      ing trial, 86

informants, 157
internal conflict. *See*
   Colombo war
Colombo war, 62-63, 74, 94-95,
   122-123, 149, 242
   Cutolo, William, 135
   Gotti, John, 157
   Grancio, Nicholas, 96
   Persico/Orena conflict, 149
   Rosario, Nastasa, 96
   Scopo, Joseph, 235
   Scopo, Ralph Jr., 119
   Sessa, Carmine, 120, 149
   Smurra, Henry, 96
Colombo, Joe, 94, 186, 208
Colucci, Camille, 175
Colucci, Joey, 175
conjugal visits (sperm-smuggling
   case), 294
Considine, Michael (U.S.
   Attorney), 57
Conte, George "Georgie
   Goggles," 225
Conte, Pasquale, 129
Coppa, Frank, 305
Corallo, Tony "Ducks," 6
Corozzo, Nicholas, 200
Corrao, Joseph "Joe Butch," 28,
   47, 100, 108, 193, 259
Costello, Frank, 312
Cotter, Patrick (prosecutor), 32
crack-cocaine, 27
Cuomo, Ralph, 164
Curcio, Eric, 235-236
Cutler, Bruce, 5, 8, 30, 44, 107,
   159, 224, 297
   Windows case, 69
Cutolo, Peggy, 284
Cutolo, William "Wild Bill,"
   106, 134, 185, 242, 282
   Colombo war, 135
Cutolo, William Jr., 283

D

D'Amato, Frank, 300
D'Amato, John, 285
  homophobia murder, 286
D'Ambrosio, Alfonse "Funzi,"
  106
D'Ambrosia, Thomas, 225-226
D'Amico, John "Jackie Nose,"
  118
D'Angelo, Joseph, 83
D'Arco, Alphonse, 66, 113, 151,
  181, 210
D'Urso, Michael "Cookie," 311,
  314
Dapper Don. *See* John Gotti
Davidson, Jeffrey, 90
Davis, Larry, 18
De Niro, Robert, 11
DEA (Drug Enforcement
  Administration), 13
  Reale, Salvatore, 35
deals (prosecutorial), 167
  Gravano, Salvatore, 168
Dearie, Raymond (Judge), 6
  Windows case, 69
DeCavalcante family, 260
DeCavalcante, Simone "Sam the
  Plumber," 251
DeChristopher, Fred, 23
DeCicco, Frank, 15, 60
DeCicco, Joseph "Butter," 69
  Windows case, 69
Defede, Joseph, 306
DeFendis, Angelo, 182
Del Cioppo, Peter, 181
Dellacroce, Aniello, 222
DeMartino, Vincent, 96
Demeo, Roy, 65
Dempsey, William (prosecutor),
  8
DePalma, Greg, 221, 233, 247
DeRoss, John, 277, 282

DeSantis, Michael, 147
DeVecchio, Lindley (FBI), 120
DiBello, George "Fat Georgie,"
  93
DiBernardo, Robert "DeeBee,"
  78
DiBono, Louis, 78
DiChiara, Victor, 285
DiCostanza, Nicholas, 182
DiMaria, Leonard, 199
DiPiertro, James, 18
Ditre, Angelo, 173-174
Doyle, Michael, 35
Driscoll, Peter, Windows case,
  69
Dugan, Patrick (attorney), 45
DuLucia, Dennis, Windows
  case, 68
Dupont, Norman, 94

E–F

Edmonson, Samuel "Baby Sam,"
  20
Edwards, Delroy "Uzi," 7, 20, 43
Egitto, Frank (Brooklyn
  Supreme Court Justice), 40
Eppolito, Lou, 152
Esposito, Meade, 4, 20
Express Mail stamps, 136

Failla, James, 100, 108, 112, 137
families
  Bonanno. *See* Bonanno
    family
  Colombo. *See* Colombo
    family
  Gambino. *See* Gambino
    family
  Genovese. *See* Genovese
    family
  Luchese. *See* Luchese family

Farace, Costabile "Gus," 36, 72
Farenga, Barclay "Bobby," 31
Favara, John, 275
FBI, cell phones, 261
Featherstone, Mickey, 25
Fenza, Louis, 137
Ferrante, Lou, 125
Fiorenza, Lawrence, 149
Fiorito, Joseph, 133, 143
fireworks, 14, 22
Fischetti, Ronald, 12, 17
Fiske, Robert, 25
Foley Square, 29
Foley, Elizabeth (District
  Attorney), 37
Forenza, Dorothy, 232-233
Fourth of July Barbeque (John
  Gotti), 22
Fox, James (New York FBI
  Chief), 54, 83
Fragos, Frances (U.S. Attorney),
  30
Franchesini, Remo (Queens
  District Attorney), 8
Franzese, John, 137, 196, 223
Franzese, Michael, 43, 137, 223
Fratianno, Aladena "Jimmy the
  Weasel," 25, 242
Fugazy, Bill, 125
Fujianese Flying Dragons, 190
Fulton Fish Market, 187
funerals
  Gotti, John, 299
  Rose, Charlie, 228-229
Furnari, Christopher "Christy
  Tick," 146
Fusco, Richard, 149
Futerfas, Alan, Windows case, 69

G

Gabriel, George, 166
Gaggi, Anthony "Nino," 42

Gaggi, Rose, 42
Galante, Carmine, 6
Gallagher, Robert, 185
Gallo, Joe, 17, 50, 153
Gambino family, 14, 28, 38, 42, 44
   See also Gotti, John
   Gangland (book by Blum), 139
   Garment District, 15
   Gotti, John A "Junior," 112
Gambino, Carlo, 117, 146
Gambino, Giovanni, 79
Gambino, Giuseppe "Joe," 29, 79
Gambino, Thomas, 14-15, 193, 288
Gammarano, John "Johnny G.," 177-178
Gangi, Frank, 187
Gangland, 139-140
Garment District, 15
Geller, Kenneth, 75
Genovese family, 14, 22, 31, 38
   Luchese family conflict, 114
   Windows case, 68
Genovese, Vito, 311
Geritano, Preston, 112
Gerlinski, Susan (Warden), 288
Gervasi, Scott, 271
Giacalone, Diane (prosecutor), 8
Gigante, Louis, 19, 197, 319
Gigante, Mario, 21
Gigante, Salvatore, 319
Gigante, Vincent "Chin," 4, 19-21, 182, 192, 197, 229, 239-240, 319
   insanity, 160
   trial, 319-321
   Windows case, 68
Gigante, Yolanda, 197

Gioia, Frank Jr., 225-226, 244, 309
Giordano, Jack, 6
Giovanelli, Federico "Fritzi," 144
Glasser, I. Leo (Brooklyn Federal Judge), 71, 91, 168
   Gotti murder and racketeering trial, 89
Gleeson, John (U.S. Attorney), 12, 44, 91, 166
Godfather (movie), Rudolph Guiliani, 218
Goldberg, Jay, 10, 129
Goldstein, Richard (U.S. Attorney), 42
Gorbone, Joseph "Joe Black," 300
Gotti murder and racketeering trial, 71, 86-93
   Bailey, F. Lee, 83
   Cardinale, Anthony, 91
   Carmine, Agnello, 93
   Colombo family, 86
   D'Angelo, Joseph, 83
   Davidson, Jeffrey, 90
   Fox, James, 83
   Glasser, I. Leo (Federal Judge), 89-91
   Gleeson, John, 91
   Gravano, Salvatore, 77, 85, 162
   Lino, Edward, 81
   Locascio, Frank, 87-88
   Luchese family, 86
   Maloney, Andrew, 91
   McLaughlin, Michael, 93
   Mouw, Bruce, 83
   Ravenite, 87
   Sasso, Bobby, 86
Gotti, Frank, 186, 274
Gotti, Gene, 9, 12, 17, 21, 24

Gotti, John, 3-5, 8, 15-17, 24, 35, 39, 69, 111, 155, 166-171, 179, 190, 257
   Colombo war, 158
   Fourth of July Barbeque, 22
   funeral, 299
   Gravano, Salvatore, 79
   jury tampering, 81, 254-255
   Justice Not Found, 126
   Marion (Federal prison), 95
   murder and racketeering trial, 71, 77, 83-93
   postage stamps, 136
   quotes, 297-298
   racketeering trial, 44
   Ravenite Social Club, 59
   the Gotti tapes, 47
Gotti, John A. "Junior," 40, 90, 118, 179, 207, 233
   Holy Grail (mobster lists), 220
Gotti, Peter, 179
   Windows case, 68
Gotti, Richard G., 307
Gotti, Victoria, 185, 282
Grado, Anthony, 160
Granato, Kevin, 294
Granato, Regina, 294
Grancio, Nicholas "Nicky Black," 96, 105
Grasso, William "Wild Guy," 57
Gravano, Gerard "Baby Bull," 290
Gravano, Salvatore "Sammy the Bull," 3, 59, 111, 121, 155, 162, 166, 175, 267, 290
   Bless Me, Father, 182
   ecstasy, 290
   Ecstasy trial, 292
   Gotti murder and racketeering trial, 77-85

informant deal, 162, 166
omerta, 83
sentencing, 168
Teamsters' Local, 282, 85
wrongful death lawsuits, 216
Graziano, Anthony, 37, 259, 303
Graziano, Jennifer, 259
Graziano, Lana, 259
Graziano, Veronica, 37
Graziosa, Rocco, 313
Greater Blouse, Skirt and
Undergarment Association,
193
Greek mafia, 170
Grubczak, Jeffrey, 130
Gualtiere, Carmine, 144
Guerra, Frank, 241
Guerrero (Mexico) police, 13
Guerrieri, Anthony "Tony Lee,"
36
Guido, Nicholas, 31
Guiliani, Rudolph, 21, 24, 218
Guillen, Pedro, 13
Gulino, Paul, 244
Gurino, Caesar, Windows case,
68
Guterman, Gerald, 57
Guy Lombardo Marina, 116

H

Haftez, Frederick, Windows
case, 69
harness racing, 11
Hatcher, Everett, 40
Hawaiian Moonlighters Social
Club, 100
Hickey, Dennis, 191
Hill, Henry (character from
Wiseguy), 10
Hoffman, Jeffrey, 37
Windows case, 69

Holy Grail (mobster lists), 220
homophobia (D'Amato murder),
285-286
Hynes, Charles (Brooklyn
District Attorney), 40

I–J

Iannaci, Joseph "Joe Notch," 194
Iborti, Joseph, 240
Ida, James, 209-210
Imbrieco, John, 315
Industrial & Production
Workers' Union, 277
informants
Casso, Anthony, 205
Ditre, Angelo, 173
Johns, Jack, 58
Gravano, Salvatore, 162, 166,
168

Jackson, James, 169
Johns, Jack, 58
Johnston, Robert Jr., 22
Joker Poker machines, 177
jurors
anonymous, 132
bribery, 81
questioning, 133
Justice Not Found, 126

K

Kane, William, 29, 79
Kaplan, Lewis, 209
Kaplan, Steven, 93
Karadzic, Radovan, 255
Keenan, John (Federal Judge),
23
Kellman, Susan, 13
Kerns, Joseph "Joey K," 133

Kistner, Ralph (Federal proba-
tion officer), 36
Knapp, Whitman (Judge), 30
Kolatch, Sari (Brooklyn Assitant
District Attorney), 40
Kourakos, Pete, 171
Kram, Shirley Wohl (Manhattan
Federal Judge), 71
Kraus, Eric (Brooklyn D.A.), 18
Kriegal, Mark, 182
Kufeld, Murray, 248
Kurins, Andris (FBI agent), 53

L

LaBarbara, Michael, 32
Labate, Jimmy, 278-280
labor racketeering, 68
Laborers' International Union
(Local 66), 32
Lanza's restaurant, 54
LaPerla, John, 19
Larry King show, 56
LaRusso, Robert (U.S.
Attorney), 9, 12, 17
Las Vegas, University of Nevada,
11
Lastorino, Frank, 63, 114, 272
Leonetti, Philip "Crazy Phil," 51
Leventhal, Brad, 143
Lieb, Peter (Manhattan prosecu-
tor), 28
Light, Martin, 23
Lino, Edward, 81
Lino, Robert "Little Robert,"
273-280
loan-sharking
Grado, Anthony, 160
Persico, Michael, 75
Romantique Limousine case,
75

Locascio, Frank "Frankie Loc,"
3, 59, 87-88, 111
Gotti murder and racketeer-
ing trial, 78, 89, 93
murder and racketeering, 71
Locascio, Salvatore "Tore," 233
Lombardi, Salvatore "Sally
Dogs," 74, 97
Lombardi, Tino, 314
Lombardozzi, Carmine "the
Doctor," 312
Lopez, Frank, 23
LoPresti, Giuseppe, 81
Loreto, Alfredo, 183
Lucas, Joseph, 116
Luchese family, 38, 63, 66, 181
class of 1991, 225
decline, 226
Genovese family conflict, 114
Gotti murder and racketeer-
ing trial, 86
Spyredon, Velentzas, 171
trials, 151
Windows case, 68
Lufthansa Airlines, 10

M

Mack, Walter (U.S. Attorney),
45, 66
Maffeo, Bruce (prosecutors), 32
Magnuson, Edward, 8
Malangone, Alfonse "Allie
Shades," 187
Maloney, Andrew (U.S.
Attorney), 17, 49, 91
Gotti murder and racketeer-
ing trial, 72
Maltese, Steven, 144
Manes, Donald, 20
Mangano, Rosolino, 165

Mangano, Venero "Benny Eggs,"
112, 270
Window case, 68
Manna, Louis "Bobby," 21, 269
Manning, Kenneth, 7
Mannino, Lorenzo, 30, 174
Manzo, Frank, 179
Mareu, Aaron, 23
Marino, Corrado "Dino," 146,
151
Marino, Danny, 206
Marion (Illinois Federal prison),
95
Marion, Joseph "Joe Cakes," 51
Windows case, 68
Mashor, Michael, Windows case,
69
Mason, Howard "Pappy," 27
Masotto, Thomas, 116
Massaro, Joseph "Joey Bang
Bang," 133, 142
Massella, Joseph, 260
Massino, Joseph, 37, 244, 299,
305, 317-318
May, Levirteen, 42
Mazzara, Philip, 136
McCabe, Kenneth, 272
McCarthy, Andrew (Assistant
U.S. Attorney), 30
McConnach, Angelo, 181
McDonald, Edward, 10, 54
McFadden, Kimberly (prosecu-
tor), 32
McGowan, Thomas, Windows
case, 68
McIntosh, Hugh "Mac," 96,
213-214
McLaughlin, Joseph (Brooklyn
Federal Judge), 9, 36
McLaughlin, Michael, 93
McNally, John, 155

media influence
Gotti murder and racketeer-
ing trial, 72
other trials, 132
Mexico, Guerrero police, 13
Meyer, Stanley, 23
Michael, Persico, loan-sharking,
75
Miciotta, Salvatore, 205
Milito, Louis, 78
Mill Basin, 3
Miraglia, Rocco Jr., 186
Mishler, Jacob, 32
Molini, Robert, 160
money-laundering, Romantique
Limousine, 75
Monteleone, Joseph "Joe
Monte," 121, 149
Monti, Frank, 300
Montiglio, Dominick, 65
Moran, Ronald "Messy Marvin,"
240
Morgenthau, Robert (Manhattan
District Attorney), 162
Morici, Frank, 18
Morissey, John "Sonny Blue," 51
Mouw, Bruce, 83, 166
Mr. Dino Hair Styling Salon,
146
Murder Inc., 50
Muscarella, Ernest, 321
Musillo, Charles "little Charlie,"
12

N

Nalo, Sarecho "Sammy the
Arab," 171-172
Napolitano, Dominick "Sonny
Black," 317
Nastasa, Rosario "Black Sam,"
74, 96

New Jersey mob, 251
New Orleans mob, 177
Newman, Gustave, 24
Noon, William (FBI agent), 9
Nordenbrook, Ruth (U.S. Attorney), 37
Notch, Joe, 194

O

O'Brien, Joseph (FBI agent), 53, 56
O'Connor, John, 44
Obermaier, Otto (U.S. Attorney), 45
omerta, 83
Orena, Paul, 126
Orena, Victor "Little Vic," 62, 76, 95, 105, 125, 135
    conflict with Carmine Persico. *See* Colombo war trial, 106
Organized Crime Control Bureau, 4
Organized Crime Task Force, 6
Original Ray's Pizza, 164
Our Friends Social Club, 108, 118

P

Pagliarulo, Richard "the Toupe," 147, 225
Palermo, Vincent "Vinny Ocean," 251, 260, 285
Papa, Michael, 290
Papavero Funeral Home, 299
Pappa, Gerard, 239-240
Pappa, John, 235-236, 239-240
Pappadio, Michael, 181
Paradiso, Michael, 18
Paradiso, Philip, 18
Pascucci, Philip, 291

Pate, John, 122
Patterson, Wanda, 27
Peist, William, 100
Pellicane, Frank "Frank the Barber," 181
Peng You Zhong, 190
Perrino, Robert, 306, 317
Perry, Richard "the Fixer," 11
Persico, Alphonse, 62, 75, 122, 154, 264, 276, 282
Persico, Carmine "Junior," 5, 23, 50, 62, 75, 94-95, 122, 135, 214
    conflict with Victor Orena. *See* Colombo war
Persico, Frank, 276
Persico, Michael, 75
Persico, Theodore, 122, 149
Pesce, Michael, 27
Pileggi, Nick, 4, 10
Pisapia, Anthony. *See* Waterguns, Tony
Pistone, Joe, 127, 318
Pitera, Thomas "Tommy Karate," 187
point-shaving (Boston College), 11
Pollack, Milton (Judge), 65
Pomerantz, Mark, 54
Pontillo, Frank "Frankie Steel," 288
Price of Blood (screenplay by Pontillo), 289
Profaci, Joe, 153
Profaci, Salvatore, 207

Q–R

Quattrache, Al, 109

racketeering, labor, 68
Radonjich, Bosko, 254-255, 267
Rampino, Anthony, 201

Ravenite Social Club, 3, 5, 36
    bugs (listening devices), 59
    Dupont, Norman, 94
    Gotti murder and racketeering trial, 87
Reagan, Ronald, 25
Reale, Salvatore, 35, 39
replacement-window industry, 68
Reynolds, Thomas, 244
Ricciardo, Vincent "Three Fingers," 68
Rizzuto, Vincent Jr., 262
Roche, Tom, 28
Romano, Benito (U.S. Attorney), 26
Romano, Carmine, 187
Romantique Limousine
    loan-sharking, 75
    money-laundering, 75
Roosevelt Raceways, 11
Rosa's Restaurant, 37
Rose, Charles (Assistant U.S. Attorney), 72
    convictions, 229
    funeral, 228-229
Rose, Charlie (U.S. Attorney), 8
Rosen, Michael, 15
Rossi, Vincent, 38
Rotondo, Anthony, 252, 285
Ruggiero, Angelo, 9, 78
Ruggiero, Benjamin "Lefty Guns," 127
Ruggiero, Matteo "Matty Square," 186
Russo, Andrew, 191, 232-233, 237
Russo, Anthony "Chuckie," 121, 149
Russo, Carmine, 166
Russo, Joseph "JoJo," 121, 134, 149

S

Salerno, "Fat" Tony, 6
San Gennaro Festival, 189-190
San Giuseppe Social Club, 314
Santangelo, George, 24
Santobello, Rudolph, 183, 188
Santoro, Salvatore, 38
Santucci, John (Queens District Attorney), 35
Sasso, Bobby, Gotti murder and racketeering, 86
Savino, Pete (government informer), 31, 50, 68, 229
Savitt, Ephraim (U.S. Attorney), 17
Scarfo, Nicodemo "Little Nicky," 51
Scarpa, Greg, 153, 262
    AIDS battle, 156
    double life, 157
Scarpa, Joseph, 105, 262
Schlanger, Jeffrey, 185
Scianna, Gabriel, 96
Sciascia, Gerlando, 81
Sclafani, Augustus "Little Gus," 40
Sclafani, Joseph "Tin Ear," 36, 40, 252
Scopo, Joseph, 235-236
Scopo, Ralph Jr., 119
Scorsese, Martin, 11
Scurry, Moses, 11
second seat (prosecutor), 12
Semetis, Arthur (prosecutor), 32
Senter, Anthony, 29, 65, 80
Serpico, Camille, 302-303
Serpico, Frank, 183, 321
Sessa, Carmine, 120-122, 135, 149
Shargel, Gerald, 12, 47, 159
Sifton, Charles (Judge), 150

Silvera, Oswald, 43
Smith, Frank, 308
Smurra, Henry "Hank the Bank," 74, 96
Snyder, Leslie (Manhattan Supreme Court Justice), 97
Somma, Dominick, 153
Sopranos, The (television series), 251
Sparacino, John, 235
Sparks steakhouse, 193
sperm-smuggling, 294
Spero, Anthony, 4, 272
Spero, Ralph, 50
Spero, Thomas, 50, 175
Spinelli, Michael "Baldy Mike," 246
Spinelli, Thomas, 137
Spreo, Anthony, 244, 248
St. John's Cemetery, 299
Stair Cargo (Kennedy Airport trucker), 36
stamps (U.S. postage), 136
Stanboulidis, George (Assistant U.S. Attorney), 75
Strong, Derryl, 267

T

Taglianetti, Richard, 174
Tali's Lounge, 80
Tangorra, Joseph "Joey Flowers," 271
Teamsters', Local, 282, 85
Teflon Don. *See* Gotti, John
Testa, Dennis, 66
Testa, Joseph, 29, 65, 80
Thornburgh, Dick (Attorney General), 32
Todaro, Jacqueline, 66
Tolino, Joseph, 74

Tortorello, Anthony "Torty," 225, 269
traffic violations, Lastorino, Frank, 63
trafficking
    cocaine, 29
    crack, 27
    fireworks, 14
    heroin, 17, 26, 29
Traynor, Matt, 8
trials
    jury questioning, 133
    media influence, 132
Truncale, Joseph, 271
Tutt, Ornge T., 43

U–V

U.S. postage, 136
Underboss, 291
Univsersity of Nevada at Las Vegas, 11
Ustica, Ronald, 42
Uva, Rosemarie, 108
Uva, Thomas, 108

Valenti, Anthony, 19
Vallario, Louis, 174
Vanasco, John "Johnny AMC," 43
Varacalli, Ernest, 302
Vario, Paul, 4
Vario, Peter, 32
Vastola, Gaetano "Corky," 252
Velentzas, Spyredon "Spiros," 170-171, 298
Venditti, Anthony, 6, 144
Verrazano Bridge, 113
Veterans and Friends Social Club, 100

Villagrana, Margarito, 13
Vitabile, Stefano, 285
Vitale, Salvatore, 317-318
Viteretti, Robert (Manhattan
   Assistant D.A.), 14

W–X–Y–Z

Ward, Laura (U.S. Attorney), 60
Waterguns, Tony, 189
Watts, Joseph, 155, 195
Weinberg, Allen, 244
Weinstein, Jack (Judge), 35, 39,
   125
Wells, David, 313
Williams, Patricia (Judge), 14
Wimpy Boys Social Club, 289
Windows case (labor-
   racketeering trial), 68
   Aloi, Benedetto, 68
   Amuso, Vittorio, 68
   Casso, Anthony, 68
   Canterino, Dominick, 68
   Chiodo, Peter, 68
   D'Arco, Alphonse, 113
   DeCicco, Frank, 69
   defense lawyesr, 69
   DuLucia, Dennis, 68
   Gigante, Vincente, 68
   Gotti, Peter, 68
   Gurino, Caesar, 68
   Mangano, Venero, 68
   Marion, Joseph, 68
   McGowan, Thomas, 68
   prosecutors, 69
   Ricciardo, Vincent, 68
Wiseguy, 4, 10
wrongful death lawsuits,
   Gravano, Salvatore, 216

Yoswein, Leonard (Brooklyn
   judge), 27

Zambardi, Robert "Bobby Zam,"
   62, 121
Zancocchio, John "Porky," 37,
   303
Zancocchio, Lana, 303
Zancocchio, Rose, 37
Zappola, George "Georgie
   Neck," 113, 266, 295
   conjugal visits, 266
Zarbano, Giovanni, 79

We're Making You an Offer You Can't Refuse!

The Best of the Mafia from Alpha Books/New American Library

ISBN: 0-02-864225-2

Co-authored by Gene Mustain
ISBN: 0-02-864416-6

Coming in May 2004:

Wiseguys Say the Darndest Things: The Quotable Mafia

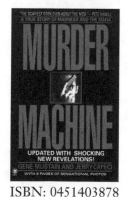

ISBN: 0451403878